SUBJECT INVERSION IN ROMANCE AND THE THEORY OF UNIVERSAL GRAMMAR

OXFORD STUDIES IN COMPARATIVE SYNTAX
Richard Kayne, General Editor

Subject Inversion in Romance and the Theory of Universal Grammar

Edited by
Aafke Hulk
Jean-Yves Pollock

OXFORD
UNIVERSITY PRESS
2001

OXFORD
UNIVERSITY PRESS

Oxford New York

Athens Auckland Bangkok Bogotá Buenos Aires Cape Town
Chennai Dar es Salaam Delhi Florence Hong Kong Istanbul Karachi
Kolkata Kuala Lumpur Madrid Melbourne Mexico City Mumbai
Nairobi Paris São Paulo Shanghai Singapore Taipei Tokyo Toronto Warsaw

and associated companies in
Berlin Ibadan

Copyright © 2001 by Oxford Unversity Press

Published by Oxford Unviersity Press, Inc.
198 Madison Avenue, New York, New York 10016

Oxford is a registered trademark of Oxford University Press

Library of Congress Cataloging-in-Publication Data
Subject inversion in Romance and the theory of universal grammar /
edited by Aafke Hulk and Jean-Yves Pollock.
p. cm. — (Oxford studies in comparative syntax)
Includes bibliographical references.
ISBN 0-19-514269-1; ISBN 0-19-514270-5 (pbk.)
1. Romance languages—Word order. 2. Romance languages—Topic and comment.
3. Grammar, Comparative and general. I. Hulk, A. (Aafke)
II. Pollock, J.-Y. (Jean-Yves) III. Series.
PC213 .S83 2000
440'.045—dc20   00-062386

This thematic volume was developed from a selection of the papers presented at the Inversion in
Romance conference, held at the University of Amsterdam in May 1998. In addition to six chapters that reflect different ways of dealing with subject inversion in Romance and the theory of universal grammar, it contains an extensive introduction to the state of the art in the field in relation
to the topics addressed in the other chapters.

9 8 7 6 5 4 3 2 1

Printed in the United States of America
on acid-free paper

Contents

Contributors

PILAR BARBOSA
Instituto de Letras e Ciências Humanas
Universidade do Minho,
4709 Braga Codex
Portugal
pbarbosa@ilch.uminho.pt

ADRIANA BELLETTI
Facoltà di Lettere
Università di Siena
Via Roma 47
53 100 Siena
Italy
Belletti@unisi.it

JOÃO COSTA
Universidade Nova de Lisboa
Faculdade de Ciências Sociais e
  Humanas
Avenida de Berna 26-C
1069-061 Lisboa
Portugal
jcosta@fcsh.unl.pt

AAFKE HULK
University of Amsterdam
Romance Linguistics
Spuistraat 134
1012 VB Amsterdam
The Netherlands
aafke.hulk@hum.uva.nl

RICHARD S. KAYNE
Department of Linguistics
New York University,
719 Broadway, 5th floor
New York, NY 10003
United States
rsk8@is4.nyu.edu

JEAN-YVES POLLOCK
19, Rue Michel-Ange
75016 Paris
France
JYPollock@compuserve.com

KNUT TARALD TARALDSEN
University of Tromsø
Det humanistike fakultet
N-9037 Tromsø
Norway
Knut.tarald.taraldsen@hum.uit.no

MARIA LUISA ZUBIZARRETA
University of Southern California
Department of Linguistics
University Park
Los Angeles, CA 90089-1693
United States
zubizarr@rcf.usc.edu

SUBJECT INVERSION IN ROMANCE AND THE THEORY OF UNIVERSAL GRAMMAR

1

Subject Positions in Romance and the Theory of Universal Grammar

AAFKE HULK AND JEAN-YVES POLLOCK

1. Some Problems in the Theory of Grammar and Old Ways of Solving Them

There is a consensus among both traditional and generative grammarians that the canonical surface word order of the Romance languages is subject-verb-object (SVO). Granted this, sentences such as (1) in Italian, French, Portuguese, and Catalan, which are all clear cases of noncanonical word order, raise important descriptive and theoretical problems:

(1) a. Che cosa ha detto Maria?
        What has said M?
    b. E' partito Gianni
        is gone G
    c. Qu'a dit Jean?
        What has said J?
    d. Onde foi a Maria?
        Where went the M?
    e. Què farà en Joan?
        what will-do the J?

In all of these, the subject is at the right periphery of the sentence. and it obligatorily follows participles and infinitives when they are present. In this respect the Subject Inversion of (1) contrasts sharply with what Rizzi (1982) has dubbed

3

"Residual V2 constructions," in which the subject is in the same position as in the Germanic V2 languages, immediately to the right of the finite verb before the participle or infinitive, as in French Subject Clitic Inversion constructions like *A-t-il dit cela?* (Has he said that?), and *Où veut-il aller?* [where wants he (to) go?].

Although there were early attempts to unify the account of the "Germanic" and "Romance" subject inversion—that is, of French Stylistic Inversion and Subject clitic Inversion—[1] it is fair to say that largely because of the impact of Kayne (1972), most linguists over the last twenty years have kept the two types of subject inversion distinct. More precisely, there is a consensus that constructions like French *A-t-il dit cela?* and *Où veut-il aller?* are to be analyzed as involving V (+ Infl°)- to-C° movement (cf. Rizzi & Roberts 1989) and that no such head movement could in and of itself yield the word order in (1). Indeed, in the present volume Barbosa (chapter 2)explicitly argues against a V-to-C movement analysis for (free) Subject Inversion in Romance.

With this initial problem thus (temporarily)[2] out of the way, the Subject Inversion constructions in (1) raise at least the following three problems:

A. How is the Extended Projection Principle—taken to require movement or generation of some appropriately case-marked DP to or in the Specifier of Inflection position—satisfied in such sentences?
B. In what structural position is the postverbal subject standing in the different sentence types in (1)?
C. In French, which disallows the "free"[3] inversion of the other Romance languages exemplified in the Italian (1b), what is it that makes the postverbal subject in (1c) licit?

The articles in this volume address these and related problems on the basis of a substantial array of Romance—and to a far lesser extent, Germanic (cf. Taraldsen, chapter 6)—languages and dialects. To set them in proper perspective, it is of interest to see how Kayne and Pollock (1978), one of the early generative studies devoted to the sentence type in (1), tried to solve A, B, and C, although it evidently is an anachronism to ignore the fact that the formulation of these problems has changed considerably over the last twenty years.[4]

Concerning A, the assumption was that subjects were, by definition,[5] obligatorily rewritten in preverbal subject position to the left of Infl/Aux; in more contemporary terms this would mean that subjects are merged with Infl.[6] This takes care of A trivially. In line with all traditional studies, which took it for granted that sentences like (1) involve some displacement of the subject,[7] Kayne and Pollock (1978) suggested further that (optional) rightward NP movement derived the postverbal occurrence of the subject in (1c) and, say, (2):

(2) a. Dimanche est le jour où partira ton ami.
         Sunday is the day when will-go your friend
     b. Avec qui jouaient les enfants?
         With whom played the children?

    c. Où voulaient dîner tes amis?
       Where wanted to dine your friends?

Since free rightward NP movement would also have yielded the sharply ungrammatical (3), they hypothesized that "Stylistic Inversion"—henceforth SI—was a rule that applied to (nonclitic) subject NPs structurally adjacent to (lexical)[8] wh-expressions like *quand, que, où, avec qui,* and so on.

(3) a. *Dimanche partira ton ami.
       Sunday will-go your friend
    b. *Avec Jean jouent tes enfants.
       With Jean play your children.
    c. *Voulaient dîner tes amis?
       wanted (to) dine your friends?

If so, (3) could never be derived, thus solving part of problem C. The surprising fact that (4b), unlike (4a), is well formed and that (4c) is unambiguous—with *quand* only an adjunct on *partirait*, not on *as dit*—becomes understandable if SI applies at a point in the derivation where the wh-phrase is still structurally adjacent to the subject, that is, in the Comp domain of the embedded sentence:

(4) a. *Qui croyait que jouaient tes enfants?
       Who believed that played your children?
    b. Avec qui croyais-tu que jouaient tes enfants?
       With whom did you believe that played your children?
    c. Quand as-tu dit que partirait ton ami?
       when did you say that would-leave your friend?

Paradigms like (4) thus provided a striking argument in favor of the (then highly controversial[9]) idea that wh-movement is successive cyclic. As Kayne and Pollock (chapter 5, this volume) show in their section 17, that conclusion is still valid, despite the fact that their new analysis shows that there is no need for any "trigger" for SI.[10]

    In addition to (1), (2), and (4b, c), French has other licit cases of SI constructions, among them those in (5), in which the verb is in the subjunctive mood:

(5) a. Je veux que parte Paul.
       I want that leave Paul
    b. J'exige que soit éliminée cette solution.
       I require that be eliminated that solution

In part because of such sentences, Kayne and Pollock (1978) argued that the trigger for SI—that is, the context predicate in the structural description of the transformation—could profitably be dissociated from the movement part of the rule. On that view, the latter could be seen as operating freely; in short, SI was analyzed as an instance of the computation later called "move A" (cf. Chomsky 1981) and was formulated as in (6):

(6) NP X => e 2 1
     1 2

However, the trigger took the shape of the filter (cf. Chomsky & Lasnik 1977) in (7):

(7) Mark as ungrammatical any sentence containing an empty subject position not immediately preceded by the trigger {wh/+F}.[11]

Thus, (7) dealt with (1), (2), (4), and (5) in uniform fashion. The disjunction {wh/+F} also accounted for the fact that sentences like (8b), which seem to—exceptionally [cf. (8a)]—lack a lexical subject, can surface in sentences in the subjunctive or in sentences whose left periphery contains the trace of a wh-phrase, as in (8c):

(8) a. *sera procédé à la révision de la loi
         will be proceeded to the revision of the law
     b. J'exige que soit procédé à la révision de la loi.
         I require that be proceeded to the revision of the law.
     c. Quand (penses-tu que) sera procédé à la révision de la loi?
         When (do you think that) will be proceeded to the revision of the law?

This followed on the view that (8b, c) have a null (expletive) subject that requires—just like other empty subjects, among which wh-traces—an appropriate "licenser," an idea that Kayne and Pollock (1978) expressed through filter (7). In short, (6) and (7) and the view that subjects were obligatorily generated in preverbal position had fruitful empirical consequences for the study of French syntax, provided A and C with plausible solutions,[12] and shed unexpected light on some fairly intricate and highly specific aspects of the theory of Universal Grammar (UG).

The studies in this volume show that subject inversion in Romance continues to bear on the modules and principles of UG in quite crucial ways and that our present theory of UG can lead to better, more principled answers to the three problems above.

2. Subject Inversion and Universal Grammar

One need hardly stress that the structure of UG has been considerably refined since the 1970s; in addition, the empirical scope of work on subject inversion has been extraordinarily increased, as shown by the studies in this volume.

Linguists who are broaching the subject today, therefore, have both more theoretical "space" to play with, which is a mixed blessing, and many more (comparative) facts to take into account. This means that their task is much harder than in the 1960s and 1970s but also that any descriptively adequate analysis of the facts will of necessity eliminate many—perhaps most—a priori conceivable theoretical accounts.[13]

The extra leeway arises chiefly because of the following three (conditional) additions to UG, unknown in the 1960s and 1970s:

D. Subject DPs are merged low in the sentential structure—in the V/vP layer (cf. Larson 1988; Sportiche 1988)—and are attracted to various layers of the "split" Infl (cf. Pollock 1989) for feature-checking purposes (EPP).

E. Verbs are attracted to various heads in the IP field (cf., e.g., Chomsky 1995, chap. 1 and passim; Pollock 1989, 1997b), as well as for feature-checking purposes.

F. The "Comp domain," like the Infl domain, has a complex architecture; it is the sum of several functional heads—including Force, focus, topic, and Finiteness—that occur in a fixed hierarchical order and attract phrases bearing the relevant features (Rizzi 1997).

2.1. Subject Inversion, VP Internal Subjects, and the Split Infl

It is easy to see that combining D and E provides a new way of dealing with the postverbal subjects of (1): In such an account the "displaced" subject simply stays low in the clausal architecture—perhaps even in the position in which it is merged, that is, the specifier of "small v" in VPs headed by (in)transitives or the complement of unaccusative verbs (cf. Burzio 1986)—and the verb adjoins to various heads in the split Infl, as sketched in (9a, b):

(9) a. $[\ldots V_i + \text{Infl}° [\ldots t_i \ldots [_{vP} \text{DP} [t_i \text{ (DP)}]]]]$
     b. $[\ldots V_i + \text{Infl}° [\ldots t_i \ldots [_{vP} t_i \text{ DP }]]]$

In this analysis, then, a precise answer to problem B becomes readily available. Concerning A, (9) evidently presupposes either that some other lexical or nonlexical phrase can check the Case and D/N features associated with Infl°—forming a Chain, with the "associate" in the V/vP—and/or that verb movement somehow suffices to check the EPP features (cf., e.g., Alexiadou & Anagnostopoulou 1998; Barbosa chapter 2, this volume; Pollock 1997a, chap. 13); furthermore, the uninterpretable Case features of the associate subject DP must then be assumed to be checkable in situ. In the same vein, the optional object DP of (9a) will have to check its own case feature, which may lead to its crossing over the subject DP to adjoin to some head in the split Infl (see Chomsky 1995; for conflicting views on the availability of this option when a "low" subject is present, see Belletti and Costa (chapters 3 and 4, respectively, this volume).

As pointed out by Belletti (chapter 3, this volume), this line of thought has inspired much work on subject inversion in Romance in the so-called "Government and Binding" framework of Generative Grammar. As far as French

SI is concerned, it was initiated by Déprez (1986), and since then many linguists have adopted the idea that in (1c) the postverbal subject NP is in its base
position inside VP (cf. Friedemann 1997). Deprez also argued that a null expletive, subject to various licensing conditions—which solved problem C in the same
spirit as Kayne and Pollock (1978) did—was merged in the IP field of all types
of SI sentences, thus generalizing Pollock's (1986) analysis of subjunctive-
triggered SI, and satisfied the requirements of the EPP (problem A).

On the theoretical side, analyses of this kind have the immediate advantage of solving a major downgrading problem if, as transparently expressed in
(9), postverbal subjects remain "low" in the sentential architecture.[14] On the
empirical side, one of the chief arguments in its favor rests on the incompatibility of SI and quantifier float from postverbal subjects, illustrated in (10):

(10)   a. *Qu'ont tous fait les enfants?
           what have all done the children?
       b. *L'homme à qui ont tous parlé les linguistes c'est Jean.
           the man to whom have all spoken the linguists is J

In Sportiche's (1988) influential analysis, quantifier float configurations are a
(deceptive) consequence of a DP that is moving to the IP field and stranding
its QP layer; therefore hypothesizing that in (1) the postverbal subject stays
where it is merged neatly accounts for (10).

Many variants of this analysis have been explored over the last ten to fif-
teen years.[15] The chapters in this volume by Barbosa, Belletti, Costa, and
Zubizarreta, despite important differences in other respects, incorporate many
of its essential ingredients and refine it in various ways. They can be read as
attempts to vindicate this general line of thought by showing that it lends itself
to revealing comparative analyses of many Romance languages and dialects.

2.2.   Subject Inversion and the Left Periphery

That the left periphery of the clausal architecture (see F above) might be involved in subject inversion is far from transparent.[16] The idea grew out of the
need to take Kayne's (1994) ban on rightward adjunction and right-hand specifiers seriously; the wish to generalize to Romance some version of the Germanic "Remnant Movement" (cf. Den Besten & Webelhut 1987, 1990); and
an attempt to capture the fact that Subject Inversion interacts in crucial ways
with various discourse factors, in particular with the topic/focus distinction.

Each of these facts and conjectures has been discussed independently in
the literature, and each of them can therefore be vindicated on its own strength.
Concerning the first two, we refer the reader to the work just cited. Concerning the third, it has been known for quite a while that sentences with and without (free) subject inversion are not felicitous in the same discourse contexts
(cf., e.g., Vallduví 1993; Vallduví & Vilkuna 1998; Zubizarreta (1998).

In sharp contrast to the work on subject inversion in the 1970s, which largely
ignored these problems,[17] all the chapters in this volume discuss these discourse

facts and try to integrate them in their respective conceptual frameworks. Using Italian as a representative example of Romance, except French, (11) and (12) show that a subject can express new information and make up the informational focus of the sentence only when it is in postverbal position: (11), but not (12), is a felicitous answer to a question such as 'Who has arrived?':

(11)   e arrivato Gianni
       is arrived G

(12)   # Gianni e arrivato
       G is arrived

Preverbal subjects in Italian—but not in French, in which the counterpart to (12) is a well-formed answer to the question—are topics ("old" information), not foci [see also, e.g., Belletti's example (4) in chapter 3 and Costa's (7), (8), and (9) in chapter 4, this volume].[18]

In the recent generative literature, there are probably two conflicting views on how to take notions like topic and focus into account. For some—most notably Cinque (1993)—foci must surface as the rightmost constituent in a clause in order to receive what defines them, the neuclear sentence stress.[19] In the present volume, Costa (chapter 4) makes crucial use of this theory. For others (cf., e.g., Aboh 1995; Brody 1990, 1995; Rizzi 1997) focus and topic can be construed as functional features of the ordinary variety; if so, they can head distinct functional projections in the clausal architecture to which appropriately marked constituents can move to satisfy the requirements of checking theory. Under the impact of Culicover (1992) and Rizzi (1997), it is currently held that such projections are in the left periphery of the clause, at least in Romance and Germanic.[20] In this view, those functional projections of the Comp domain of a sentence that "look outward" provide information about the type of the sentence and define a space in which discourse and sentence grammar interact.

Adopting this second tack, we may suppose that some discourse feature [+F] is associated with the DP in the (topmost) Spec Infl, to be checked in the specifier of one of the layers of the Comp domain; on the further assumption that Remnant Movement to the specifier of some other higher GP layer can apply to the phrase out of which the subject has moved, configurations like (13c) can be derived as shown:

(13)   a.   Input: $[_{IP}$ DP Infl VP] $\Rightarrow$ merge F and move DP to Spec F $\Rightarrow$
       b. $[_{FP}$ DP$_i$ F $[_{IP}$ t$_i$ Infl VP]] $\Rightarrow$ merge G and Remnant IP movement to Spec G $\Rightarrow$
       c. $[_{GP}$ $[_{IP}$ t$_i$ Infl VP]$_j$ G $[_{FP}$ DP$_i$ F] t$_j$]

Clearly, (13c) provides a possible analysis for all or some subject inversion configurations; it provides A and B with precise solutions; in such derivations the EPP is satisfied exactly as in sentences with canonical SVO order, and so there is no a priori need for (null) expletive or associate chains in such an analysis. Furthermore, the representations and computations in (13) abide by Kayne's

(1994) Linear Correspondence Axiom (LCA) since all the adjunctions are leftward and as desired, (13b) is an extension to Romance of Remnant (IP) Movement.[21] In this volume the work by Kayne and Pollock (chapter 5); Taraldsen (chapter 6); and to a more restricted but significant extent (see her section 1.4), Belletti (chapter 3) all argue that (13) can capture important empirical aspects of the syntactic and discourse properties of (some) subject inversion constructions.

Concerning problem B, one of the most striking differences between (13c) and the structures sketched out in (9) is that in the former the postverbal subject is very "high," as opposed to very "low," in the functional hierarchy of the clause; in fact it is no longer even in IP since it has moved to a topic or focus position in the split CP (cf. Kayne & Pollock, chapter 5, note 21 and section 16; and Belletti, chapter 3, section 1.4, this volume). In addition, because of Remnant IP Movement to a higher layer in the Comp domain, no phrase contained in IP in (13c) can c-command (into) the postverbal subject. This property plays a major role in Kayne and Pollock's analysis of the general ban on extraction from the postverbal subject in French SI (see their part I).

3. Comparing Romance Subject Inversion

There evidently is a tension between the two approaches to subject inversion shown in the previous section, and hence also a tension between some of the chapters in this volume, although as witnessed by Belletti (chapter 3), they are certainly not necessarily incompatible; it may well turn out, as she claims, that some phenomena in Romance require the approach in (9) and others the one in (13). If so, the spectacularly different syntactic structures the derivations sketched in (9) and (13) associate to identical spell-out strings should have major syntactic consequences elsewhere, for example, with respect to extraction from, and binding of, the postverbal subject. No doubt future work will cast light on this still unsolved problem.

Be that as it may, the chief goal of this volume is to give easy access to a substantial array of facts in a representative sample of Romance languages in the hope that comparing the analyses offered here will sharpen the issue and solve—maybe dissolve—the tension between the two theoretical approaches described above.[22]

We conclude this introduction by briefly summarizing the chief descriptive goals of each of the chapters, trying to highlight what we take to be the core of their theoretical proposal.

3.1. Barbosa's "On Inversion in Wh-questions in Romance"

The main empirical goal of Barbosa (chapter 2) is to explain why in many Romance languages (e.g., Romanian, Italian, Catalan, and Iberian Spanish), the subject may not intervene between a non-d-linked wh-phrase and the inflected verb, as the Italian, Romanian, and Catalan examples in (14) show:

(14) a. Che cosa (*Maria) ha detto?
         what (M) has said
      b. Unde (*Ion) s-a dus?
         where (I) has gone?
      c. Què (*en Joan) farà
         what (the J) will-do

One of Barbosa's leading ideas is that as long as the CP layer is not required by lexical properties or other constraints, clausal complements may be
IPs.[23] Moreover she follows the tack taken by Sola (1992), Vallduvi (1993),
and many others, according to which in (many, in fact, all if she is correct)
Romance languages wh-phrases need not move to the CP layer but rather adjoin to the topmost IP head; in her framework, this means that Rizzi's (1982)
"wh-criterion" may be satisfied inside the IP layer. If, as she also claims, in
(many) null subject languages of the Romance variety the verb's rich agreement morphology can check the EPP features by adjoining to Infl, then preverbal
DP subjects are always in a left-dislocated topic position, (necessarily) preceding
the wh-phrase in Spec IP.

To account for minimal differences between Italian and Catalan in the
distribution of wh-phrases and sentence initial foci, Barbosa claims that the
architecture of the left periphery is open to parametric variations; some languages have a single (IP) slot for foci and wh-phrases; others allow for an additional Focus slot in the Comp domain.

To accommodate (Standard) French (wh-triggered) SI, Barbosa claims
further that the EPP features can be checked not only by (expletive) subjects
but also by wh-phrases in Spec-IP; seen in this light, pairs like *est venu Jean
(is come J?) vs. *Quand est venu Jean?* (when is J come) are dealt with in terms
of EPP violation vs. EPP satisfaction (cf. chapter 2, section 2.5).

Finally, to explain other minimal variations in embedded contexts in which
Portuguese and French form a pattern together and are sharply different from,
say, Catalan and Spanish, Barbosa suggests additional parametric variations
having to do with what heads can be +wh, on the one hand, and, on the other
hand, when the CP layer need not or, on the contrary, must be projected.

3.2. Belletti's "'Inversion' as Focalization"

Belletti's chief descriptive goal is to shed light on the discourse import of (free)
"Subject Inversion" in Italian and to account for various restrictions on VSO
and VOS strings. As pointed out in chapter 3, section 2.2, she shows that Subject Inversion is tied to the "old" versus "new" dimension of the clause; in affir-
mative subject inversion, postverbal subjects carry the new information.[24] She
argues further that the FocusP in the left periphery of Rizzi's (1997) system is
contrastive focus, whereas another FocusP inside the IP field immediately above
V/vP is the locus of "new information" and hosts the postverbal subject in, say,
ha parlato Gianni (has spoken G), where *Gianni* adjoins to it for licensing reasons. Taking advantage of this "low" focus position, Belletti deals with the

ungrammaticality of VSO order in Italian as a minimality violation; when the
subject is licensed in the low Focus position intervenes between the (source)
position of the object and its (case) licensing position; usual minimality considerations thus prevent the object from reaching AGRoP—hence no converg-
ing derivation can yield (15):

(15)   a. *Ha spedito Maria la lettera
            has sent M the letter
       b. *Capirà Gianni il problema
            will-understand G the problem

The same account carries over to (16) since in her analysis it will always be
the case that either the subject or the object will fail to have their relevant Case
or Focus features checked:

(16)   a. ??Ha spedito la lettera Maria
            has sent the letter M
       b. ??Capirà il problema Gianni
            will-understand the problem G

To account for the fact that in dialogues like (17), such strings as (16)
become fully acceptable, with *Gianni* interpreted as contrastive focus, Belletti
appeals to the idea that in such examples *Gianni* moves to the "high" contrastive focus position and IP undergoes Remnant Movement to a Topic position
in the left periphery:

(17)   a. Chi ha capito il problema?
            Who has understood the problem?
       b. Ha capito il problema Gianni
            Has understood the problem G

Since Spanish, unlike Italian, allows VSO order, as in (18), she suggests, in
the spirit of Ordonez (1997), that the postverbal subject in (18) and the like is
not in any low FocusP but rather in an extra Case position, higher up in the IP
field and not blocking Case licensing of the object:

(18)   Espero que te devuelva Juan el libro
        I hope that to you lend J the book

3.3.   Costa's "Marked versus Unmarked Inversion and Optimality Theory"

Costa's chief descriptive goal is to compare Subject Inversion in two dialects
of Spanish (Spanish A and B), Portuguese, Italian, and Greek and to shed some
light on the fact that Portuguese and Greek (as well as Spanish A and Spanish B)
have different unmarked word order;[25] whereas SVO qualifies for Portuguese
and Spanish A, only VSO does so for Greek and Spanish B.

Unlike Belletti's work, Costa's makes exclusive use of the type of derivations shown in (9) in section 2.1, but like hers it relates differences in word order to differences in information structure. In the Optimality Theory framework that Costa adopts, this relationship arises as a result of the way in which syntactic constraints and discourse constraints mesh: In OT it is possible for discourse constraints to outrank syntactic constraints.[26] If so, it is possible to claim that in Portuguese the constraint "Align Focus," which states that the focus constituent must be rightmost in the clause, is ranked higher than "Subject Case," the constraint that requires subjects to move to Spec-IP to license nominative Case; moreover, in English (also French, presumably) the ranking of the two very same constraints is reversed, thus indicating why English (and French) do not allow focalized subjects to stay in the rightmost position.

For comparative Romance syntax, Costa shows that within his system Spanish A forms a pattern with Portuguese in having SVO unmarked order because the constraint "Subject Case" outranks the constraint "Stay"—a global economy constraint that states that phrases typically do not move—whereas Spanish B forms a pattern with Greek in having VSO order because "Stay" outranks "Subject Case." In the same spirit, he claims that the Spanish vs. Italian contrast for VSO (also discussed in Belletti, as pointed out above) follows from the respective ranking of Stay, "Object Case" (which requires movement of Objects to Spec-AGRo), and "Topic First" (which requires topics to move to sentence-initial position).

3.4.   Kayne and Pollock's "New Thoughts on Stylistic Inversion"

Kayne and Pollock's work (chapter 5) is primarily concerned with French SI and aims at providing an integrated description of many facts discovered since their 1978 article. Of particular relevance are facts about extraction from and binding of the postverbal subject; weak and strong pronouns in SI; anti-indefiniteness effects (part I); SI in indicative vs. subjunctive contexts (part II); "quirky subjects" [see (8b, c) above]; ordering restrictions on postverbal complements and subjects in wh, subjunctive, and *ne . . . que* varieties of SI; and lack of SI with certain wh-phrases like *pourquoi* ('why'), *en quel sens* ('in what sense'), and topicalizations (part III).

They show that theoretical and empirical considerations converge toward an analysis of French SI in which the lexical subject moves to a high position above IP, leaving behind a phonetically unrealized subject clitic. The (remnant) IP then moves leftward past the landing site of the subject [cf. (13) above].

The analysis deals with SI that involves Wh-movement, as well as cases that involve subjunctives. From their new perspective, the notion of 'trigger for SI' (cf. section 1 above), which seemed necessary, turns out to be superfluous. In their analysis, French, contrary to appearances [cf. discussion of (8) above], has no null expletives in SI sentences, although it has quirky subjects that in part resemble those of Icelandic.

The fact that postverbal SI subjects can sometimes be followed by a complement is due, in their analysis, to the pied-piping of the complement as a side effect of Wh-movement; this provides an account for a major difference between "Wh-" SI and "subjunctive" SI, recently discovered by Kampers-Mahne (1998). When the postverbal SI subject is preceded by a complement, Kayne and Pollock claim that the position of the complement is due to topicalization (across the subject) prior to IP preposing. Such topicalization cannot apply to a direct object, except when the subject is strongly focused, as in *ne . . . que* SI. More generally, they try to show that multiple leftward movements interact in such a way as to provide accounts for various phenomena that resisted explanation in frameworks that countenanced rightward movement, like their 1978 article (see section 1 above).

3.5. Taraldsen's "Subject Extraction, the Distribution of Expletives, and Stylistic Inversion"

Taraldsen (chapter 6) deals mainly with the well-known *que*-to-*qui* alternation of (19):

(19)   a.   Quel livre crois-tu que/*qui les filles vont acheter
             which book think you that/*qui the girls will buy
        b.   Quelles filles crois-tu *que/qui vont acheter ce livre-là
             which girls think you that/qui will buy that book-there

He provides a new analysis of the phenomenon that carries over to similar ones in Norwegian and Danish, on the one hand, and Vallader, a Rheto-Romance dialect, on the other hand. The main proposal is that French *qui* is really *que* + *i*, where *i*, like Vallader *i(d)*, though (idiosyncratically) less transparently so, is a pronoun in the highest Spec-Infl position. This explains (19a) neatly since this sentence could arise only if two DPs had the ability to fill the same Spec-Infl position. That strategy will thus be available only when extraction takes place from a "low" position in the clause, as originally argued in Rizzi (1982). Taraldsen shows further that the limited distribution of *i*, restricted to (19b) and to "conjugaison interrogative" examples like (20) follows entirely from its impoverished morphology, that is, from its lack of any specified gender and number features:

(20)   Vous allez-ti mieux
       You go-ti better = are you feeling better?

This analysis has interesting consequences for the analysis of SI. If, as in Kayne and Pollock (1978), there were a null element in the preverbal subject position of SI sentences, licensed in the same way as the null expletive in impersonal constructions [cf. discussion of (5b) above] we would incorrectly predict that there should be no that-trace effect, hence no *que*-to-*qui* alternation, in (19b) since the wh-trace in the intermediate C would qualify as a licenser for the empty subject position.

To solve that problem, Taraldsen suggests (in his section 3.2), as do Kayne and Pollock (chapter 5, this volume), a Remnant Movement analysis for SI. If he is right, adequate analysis of the *que*-to-*qui* phenomenology across quite a few languages provides independent support for the analysis of Subject Inversion summarized in (13) above.

3.6.   Zubizarretta's "The Constraints on Preverbal Subjects in Romance Interrogatives: A Minimality Effect"

Like Barbosa's, Zubizarreta's work (chapter 7) concerns itself mainly with the fact that many Romance languages disallow the occurrence of (lexical) subjects between wh-phrases and the inflected verb in Root questions; it also discusses some puzzling cross-linguistic variation for the same configuration in embedded sentences.

In the spirit of, though differently from, recent work by Koopman and Sportiche and Iatridou, Zubizarreta argues that in Romance, nominative and accusative arguments may be generated in two different ways: either by merging within the VP, as in English, or by merging with a (lambda Operator) Clitic projection, which externalizes a verb's arguments with respect to its tense. Nonfocalized subjects are "externalized" and merged with this abstract clitic position. This creates an Operator-variable relation with an empty position inside VP; thus minimality-like intervention effects arise, blocking configurations in which both the wh-phrase and the (externalized) subject precede the finite verb.

Zubizarreta suggests further that whereas the abstract Clitic projection is generally mapped in the higher part of the Middle Field between CP and IP, it may also project within the left periphery in certain well-defined cases. When that occurs, minimality violations are avoided and the structures generated show no intervention effects, as in complex inversion sentences such as *A qui Pierre a-t-il parlé?* (to whom Pierre has he spoken) in French.

4.   Conclusion

To conclude this short presentation it is worth noting that, beyond many important disagreements and conflicting proposals, most current analyses of Romance Subject Inversion and cross linguistic variations in VSO and VOS orders share a number of significant assumptions and properties; for example, there is a clear shift from purely syntactic approaches to accounts in which discourse-syntax interface features like topicalization and focalization are taken into account and often put to crucial use. This is reflected, among other things, in the keen interest many authors in this volume show for the structure and activation of the left periphery of the clause, one of the spaces[27] in the sentential architecture in which syntax and discourse interact.

It is also worth pointing out that the idea that there is a sharp distinction between the "free" Subject Inversion of Romance null subject languages and the SI of French is losing ground, at least if Kayne and Pollock's new account of the "trigger" of SI is on the right track. Similarly, Taraldsen's analysis of subject extraction in *que/qui* contexts and Kayne and Pollock's (section 1) analysis of quirky subject extraction both involve moving the relevant phrase from a position in the lower functional layers of the sentence, a property that Rizzi (1982) tied to null subject languages and then to "free" inversion.

In short, we believe that this volume is a faithful testimony to the fact that many fine-grained analyses of Subject Inversion in Romance are being fruitfully investigated. We feel confident that the analyses of the complex (comparative) facts discussed here will play an important role in the development of a truly explanatory theory of Subject Inversion.

NOTES

1. See, for example, Langacker (1972, sect. 3).

2. Ultimately, of course, one will need to account for why languages have these two very different types of constructions. That they share properties, despite many differences in their distribution, is argued in, for example, Deprez (1990) and, in a very different way, in Pollock, Munaro, and Poletto (1999). On why subject clitics cannot occur in the sentence-final position in (1), see Kayne and Pollock (chapter 5, section 5, this volume).

3. This terminology is a bit misleading; it means only that subject inversion in languages like Italian or Portuguese is not contingent on the presence of any obvious syntactic "trigger," contrary to French (1c) (see below). It does *not* mean that Italian and Portuguese inverted and noninverted structures are in "free variation"; among other things, they have clearly distinct discourse correlates (see 2.2 below), a point first made, to the best of our knowledge, in Ambar (1985, 1988) for Romance.

4. The EPP didn't exist as an independent principle in the 1970s. It did, however, have a counterpart in the (Extended) Standard Theory of Generative Grammar; subject NPs were not optional constituents in the base component, although direct and indirect object NPs and PPs were (cf., e.g., Chomsky 1965, p. 102).

5. See Chomsky (1965, sect. 2.2).

6. Kayne's (1994) LCA would then require the subject to be merged to the left of Infl.

7. See, for example, Lebidois (1952). Our own terminology, "Subject Inversion," is merely descriptive and does not presuppose any such computation.

8. See Kayne and Pollock (this volume, chapter 5, note 3).

9. See, for example, Bresnan (1977) and Chomsky (1977).

10. Because Stylistic Inversion is always optional in embedded sentences, that argument was then and is still today only an existence argument.

11. "+F" stood for whatever feature characterized the Comp domain of subjunctive clauses.

12. No attempt was made in Kayne and Pollock (1978) to say anything precise on B beyond what Kayne (1972, pp. 73–74, note 6) said about the problem.

13. Taraldsen's work in this volume (chapter 6) is a good illustration of this: It shows that broadening the data base of the well-known *que*-to-*qui* alternation in French to include similar phenomena in Danish, Norwegian, and Vallader (a Rheto-Romance dialect) forces one to view the phenomenon in a fresh light and leads both to a better analysis of French—if only because it relates *que* to *qui* to other aspects of French syntax, for example, its "conjugaison interrogative" morpheme *-ti* and its proper analysis—and to a better understanding of the way in which French and UG are related.

14. This is a particularly acute problem for analyses such as that in Emonds (1976), which claim that the postverbal subject of SI moves to object position. In the framework sketched in (9), such approaches need only claim that subjects can be merged in object position, as Legendre (1999) does. On some empirical problems for such analyses of SI, see Kayne and Pollock (chapter 5, sections 2, 3, 4, 5, 16).

15. See the references in the previous footnote and, for example, Belletti (1988), Belletti and Rizzi (1981), and essentially all the considerable literature on transitive expletive constructions in Romance and Germanic. In this general perspective, some discussion concerning Romance has been devoted to whether the subject is merged to the left or, contra Kayne (1994), to the right or V. See Friedemann (1997).

16. See the text for the reference in note 4. To our knowledge the idea that French SI might be so analyzed was first publicly speculated on during Marc Ariel Friedemann's thesis defense in Geneva in 1995 and later suggested independently by Pollock (1998, note 37) and—on a much broader cross-linguistic basis—Orndoñez (1997, chap. 4). Independently of subject inversion, Pollock, Munaro, and Poletto (1999) show that the comparative syntax of wh-questions in French, Portuguese, and Bellunese offers striking support for the existence of Remnant IP movement (to the left periphery) in Romance.

17. But see Rochemont (1978).

18. On the discourse role played by postverbal subjects in French SI, see Kayne and Pollock (this volume, chapter 5, note 21 and section 16) and, for contradictory views, Legendre (1999).

19. This approach has to fall back on a different principle to explain the fact that topics in Romance invariably stand at the left edge of the sentence (cf. Costa, this volume, chapter 4, note 3).

20. Belletti (this volume, chapter 3, section 1.4) makes the interesting claim that Italian distinguishes two types of focus structurally; the first type is noncontrastive and is clause internal, contiguous to VP below the (split) Infl field; the second is contrastive and is the focus head of Rizzi's split CP. She argues that Subject Inversion in Italian requires both.

21. Like all other cases of Remnant Movement, (13) presupposes that the c-command constraint on antecedent-trace pairs is satisfied derivationally since, in (13c), DP_i does not c-command t_i.

22. The evidence discussed in part I of Kayne and Pollock (chapter 5) evidently strongly argues in favor of the approach to SI sketched out in (13); in that framework, on the other hand, the ungrammaticality of (10) is hard to explain (cf. Taraldsen, chapter 6, note 25; Kayne & Pollock, note 77) but follows nicely from (9). As usual, only interpreted facts can be brought to bear on theoretical issues, and "naive falsificationism" should be avoided here as elsewhere.

23. In this point, her work sharply diverges from Rizzi (1997).

24. Belletti argues that in interrogative clauses the wh-phrase is moved to the FocusP in the Comp domain and claims that the postverbal subject cannot then fill the "low" FocusP. In such cases the postverbal subject is analyzed as a clause-internal topic, much in the spirit of Kayne and Pollock's (this volume, chapter 5, note 21) analysis of postverbal subjects in French SI.

25. "Unmarked" word order is the order of answers to "What happened?" questions.

26. As Costa notes—see his remark following his (10)—that view of constraint interaction rather sharply diverges from that of other traditions in Generative Grammar.

27. See the short discussion in section 2.2. above.

REFERENCES

Aboh, E. (1995). "Notes sur la focalisation en Gungbe." Ms., University of Geneva.
Alexiadou, A., & H. Anagnostopoulou. (1998). "Parameterizing AGR: Word Order, V-Movement and EPP Checking." *NLLT* 16, 491–539.
Ambar, M. (1985). "Gouvernement et Inversion dans les interrogatives Qu- en portugais." *Recherches Linguistiques de Vincennes* 16, 5–51.
———. (1988). "Para uma sintaxe da inversão sujeito verbo em português." Ph.D. diss., Lisbon University.
Belletti, A. (1988). "The Case of Unaccusatives." *Linguistic Inquiry* 19/1, 1–34.
Belletti, A., & L. Rizzi. (1981). "The Suntax of 'Ne': Some Theoretical Implications." *Linguistic Review* 1, 117–154.
Bresnan, J. (1977). "Variables in the Theory of Transformations." In A. Akmajian, P. Cilicover, & T. Wasow (eds.), *Formal Syntax*. Academic Press, New York, 157–196.
Brody, M. (1990). "Some Remarks on the Focus Field in Hungarian." *UCL Working Papers*, vol. 2. University College, London.
———. (1995). "Focus and Checking Theory." In I. Kenesei (ed.), *Levels and Structures, Vol. 5: Approaches to Hungarian*. Jate, Szeged, Hungary, 30–43.
Burzio, L. (1986). *Italian Syntax: A Government-Binding Approach*. Reidel, Dordrecht.
Chomsky, N. (1965). *Aspects of the Theory of Syntax*. MIT Press, Cambridge, Mass.
———. (1977). "On Wh-movement." In A. Akmajian, P. Cilicover, & T. Wasow (eds), *Formal Syntax*. Academic Press, New York, 71–132.
———. (1981). *Lectures on Goverment and Binding*. Foris Publications, Dordrecht.
———. (1995). *The Minimalist Program*. MIT Press, Cambridge, Mass.
Chomsky, N., & H. Lasnik. (1977). "Filters and Control." *Linguistic Inquiry* 8, 425–504.
Cinque, G. (1993). "A Null Theory of Phrase and Compound Stress." *Linguistic Inquiry* 24, 239–298
Culicover P. (1992). "Topicalisation, Inversion and Complementizers in English." In *OTS Working Papers*, D. Delfito et al. (eds.), *Going Romance and Beyond*. University of Utrecht.
Den Besten, H., & G. Webelhut. (1987) "Remnant Topicalization and the Constituent Structure of VP in the Germanic SOV Languages." *GLOW Newsletter* 18, 15–16.
———. (1990). "Stranding." In G. Grewendorf & W. Sternefeld (eds.), *Scrambling & Barriers*. Academic Press, Amsterdam, 77–92.
Déprez, V. (1986). "Verb Movement and Stylistic Inversion." Ms, MIT, Cambridge, Mass.
———. (1990). "Two Ways of Moving the Verb in French." *MIT Working Papers in Linguistics* 13, 47–85.
Emonds, J. (1976). *A Transformational Approach to English Syntax, Root, Structure-Preserving and local Transformations*. Academic Press, New York.
Friedemann, M.-A. (1997). *Sujets syntaxiques, positions, inversion et pro*. Peter Lang, Berlin.
Kampers-Mahne, B. (1998). "'Je veux que parte Jean,' a neglected construction." In A. Schegler, B. Tranel, & M. Uribe-Extebarria (eds.), *Romance Linguistics, Theoretical Perspectives*. John Benjamins, Amsterdam, 129–141.
Kayne, R. (1972). "Subject Inversion in French Interrogatives." In J. Casagrande & B. Saciuk (eds.), *Generative Studies in Romance Languages*. Newbury House, Rowley, Mass., 70–126.

————. (1994). *The Antisymmetry of Syntax*. MIT Press, Cambridge, Mass.

Kayne, R., & J.-Y. Pollock. (1978). "Stylistic Inversion, Successive Cyclicity and Move NP in French." *Linguistic Inquiry* 9, 595–621.

Langacker, R. W (1972). "French Interrogatives Revisited." In J. Casagrande & B. Saciuk (eds.), *Generative Studies in Romance Languages*. Newbury House, Rowley, Mass., 36–70.

Larson, R. (1988). "On the Double Object Construction." *Linguistic Inquiry* 19, 335–391.

Lebidois, R. (1952). *L'inversion du sujet dans la prose contemporaine*. Editions d'Artrey, Paris.

Legendre, G. (1999). "Focalization in French Stylistic Inversion." Ms, Johns Hopkins University, Baltimore.

Ordoñez, F. (1997). "Word Order and Clause Structure in Spanish and Other Romance Languages." Ph.D. diss., Graduate Center, City University of New York.

Pollock, J.-Y. (1986). "Sur la syntaxe de *en* et le paramètre du sujet nul." In M. Ronat & D. Couquaux (eds.), *La Grammaire Modulaire*. Editions de Minuit, Paris, 211–246.

————. (1989). "Verb Movement, Universal Grammar, and the Structure of IP." *Linguistic Inquiry* 20, 365–424.

————. (1997a). *Langage et Cognition*. PUF, Paris.

————. (1997b). "Notes on Clause Structure." In L. Haegeman (ed.), *Elements of Grammar*. Kluwer, Dordecht, 237–279.

————. (1998). "On the Syntax of Subnominal Clitics; Cliticisation and Ellipsis." *Syntax* 1/3, 300–330.

Pollock, J.-Y., N. Munaro, & C. Poletto. (1999). "Eppur si Muove, Comparing wh-movement in French Portuguese and Bellunese." Ms., UPR 90-75, Lyon and University of Padua.

Rizzi, L. (1982). *Issues in Italian Syntax*. Foris Publications, Dordrecht.

————. (1997). "The Fine Structure of the Left Periphery." In L. Haegeman (ed.), *Elements of Grammar*. Kluwer, Dordrecht, 281–337.

Rizzi, L., & I. Roberts. (1989). "Complex Inversion in French." *Probus* 1, 1–30.

Rochemont, M. (1978). "A Theory of Stylistic Rules in English." Ph.D. diss., University of Massachusetts, Amherst.

Sola, J. (1992). "Agreement and Subjects." Ph.D. diss., Universitat de Barcelona, Bellaterra.

Sportiche, D. (1988). "A Theory of Floating Quantifiers and Its Corollaries for Constituent Structure." *Linguistic Inquiry* 19, 425–449.

Vallduvì, E. (1993). "Catalan as VOS: Evidence from Information Packaging." In A. Ashby et al. (eds.), *Linguistic Perspective on the Romance Languages*. John Benjamins, Amsterdam, 335–350.

Vallduvì, E., & M. Vilkuna. (1998). "On Rheme and Kontrast." In P. Culicover & L. McNally (eds.), *The Limits of Syntax*. Academic Press, San Diego, 79–108.

Zubizarreta, M.-L. (1998). *Prosody, Focus and Word Order*. MIT Press, Cambridge, Mass.

2

On Inversion in Wh-questions in Romance

PILAR BARBOSA

In most Romance languages, a subject may not intervene between a non-d-linked wh-argument and the inflected verb in main questions, as illustrated below for standard Italian (Iberian Spanish, Romanian, European Portuguese, and Catalan behave essentially in the same way):

(1) *Standard Italian* (Rizzi 1991):
     a. *Che cosa Maria ha detto?
        what   Maria has said
     b. Che cosa ha detto Maria?
        what   has said Maria

Several researchers (Ambar 1988; Raposo 1994; Rizzi 1991, 1997; Rizzi & Roberts 1989; Torrego 1984; Uriagereka 1995; among many others) have proposed that obligatory adjacency between fronted wh-arguments and inflection in Romance is due to overt Infl that is raising to the C-system. In this approach, Romance inversion in questions is analyzed on a par with English subject-Aux inversion:

(2) What (*Mary) has Mary said?

Romance and English would share the same strategy in questions: I-to-C movement applies, creating the required Spec-head configuration, involving the wh-element and the inflected verb.

Even though it is tempting to give a unified account of English subject-Aux inversion and Romance inversion, a straightforward extension of Germanic-type inversion to Romance faces problems (see Bonet 1990; De Wind 1995; Drijkoningen 1997; Hulk 1993; Uribe-Etxebarria 1991; among others). A well-known characteristic of V-second effects is the asymmetry between root and embedded environments. Thus in English, subject-Aux inversion does not apply in embedded questions. In Romance, by contrast, there is a great deal of variation. In Catalan, Romanian, and Iberian Spanish, there is no root or embedded asymmetry: Inflection must be strictly adjacent to the fronted wh-argument in matrix, as well as in embedded, questions. In Italian, judgments are shakier and appear to vary according to mood. In Portuguese and French, on the other hand, the order wh-Subject-V is fine in embedded questions and alternates with inversion.

Studies on Catalan (Bonet 1990; Sola 1992; Vallduví 1992), Romanian (Dobrovie-Sorin 1994), and Iberian Spanish (Contreras 1991; Uribe-Etxebarria 1991; Zubizarreta 1997) have claimed that the lack of root or embedded asymmetry observed in the phenomenon of obligatory adjacency between question operators and inflection in these languages should be analyzed in terms of the raising of the wh-operator to Spec-IP rather than in terms of Infl that is raising to the C-system. We thus have two different approaches to Romance wh-triggered inversion, and the question arises of whether a unified analysis of this phenomenon can be given.

My goal in this chapter is to provide a unified account of the dissimilarities between Germanic and Romance wh-triggered inversion while also capturing the different word order patterns found in Romance.

For English, I essentially assume Rizzi's (1991) analysis. In root questions, the locus of the [+wh] specification must be the head that contains the independent Tense specification of the whole sentence; I-to-C movement raises [+wh] Infl high enough to establish the required checking configuration. The occurrence of [+wh] in an embedded Comp is determined by lexical selection, so I-to-C doesn't need to take place.

The crucial property that distinguishes Romance from English is that [+wh] Infl does not raise up to C. I claim that the Wh-criterion *can* be checked against the highest Infl head in *all* of Romance in root, as well as in embedded, clauses. I adopt Pesetsky's (1982, 1992) proposal that categorical selection can be eliminated as an independent syntactic mechanism. This proposal is developed in Boskovic (1996; see also Grimshaw 1993), who suggests that, as long as the CP status is not required by lexical properties or other constraints independent of c-selection, clausal complements may be IPs. I present evidence in support of Boskovic's proposal, and I defend the view that clausal projections may be bare IPs unless further structure is independently required.

Since the wh-criterion can be satisfied at the IP level in Romance, root questions may be bare IPs. Obligatory adjacency between Infl and the wh-constituent follows. The subject may stay in situ, yielding the order wh-(Aux)-V-Subject:

(3) $[_{IP}$ wh-operator $[_{I'} [_{I [+wh]} V] \ldots [_{VP}$ subject $]]$

I follow recent proposals (Alexiadou & Anagnostopoulou 1998; Barbosa 1995; Pollock 1997) according to which the Null Subject Languages are languages in which rich agreement checks the EPP and the N-features of Infl. In these languages, Spec-IP is not an A-position. The real A-position occupied by subjects is postverbal. Whenever lexical subjects appear to the left of inflection, they are either left-dislocated topics doubled by subject *pro*, or if they belong to a restricted class of QPs that cannot be topics, they are A'-moved to Spec-IP. In the absence of A'-movement to Spec-IP, Infl doesn't project a specifier. This property will account for certain differences between French and the other Romance languages. In the latter, Spec-IP doesn't necessarily need to be filled in overt syntax. In French, the EPP can only be satisfied by overt raising to Spec-IP.

One important difference distinguishes French from English, however. In French, the EPP feature doesn't necessarily need to be checked by a subject: A wh-phrase in Spec-IP may satisfy *both* the wh-criterion and the EPP. Hence, both root and embedded questions may be bare IPs in French as long as the subject is allowed to stay in situ. When the subject raises in overt syntax, however, CP must project.

In the Null Subject Romance languages, embedded questions can also in principle be bare IPs (wh-checking can be done against the highest T-head), but they can involve additional layers, depending on whether the Topic or Focus layer is activated. The cross-linguistic variation detected for the adjacency requirement between the wh-constituent and inflection is due to variation in the structure of the 'left periphery', combined with the featural makeup of complementizers in the inventory of each language.

1.   The Structure of the "Left Periphery"

Based on a study of the interactions among the elements that typically involve the left periphery of the clause, Rizzi (1997) argues for an articulated CP layer, minimally consisting of two independent heads: The higher head is a specification of *Force*, basically encoding clause type, and the lower one encodes *Finiteness* (in the spirit of Holmberg & Platzack 1988). Evidence for the need to distinguish between the two comes from the distribution of Clitic Left-Dislocated (CLLD) topics with respect to the complementizer *che* and the prepositional element that introduces infinitives, *di*. *Che* always precedes, but *di* always follows, a CLLDed phrase, as illustrated below:

(4)   a.   Credo che il tuo libro, loro lo apprezzerebbero molto.
            'I believe that your book, they would appreciate a lot.'
        b.   *Credo, il tuo libro, che loro lo apprezzerebbero molto.
            'I believe, your book, that they would appreciate a lot.'

(5) a. Credo, il tuo libro, di apprezzarlo molto.
         'I believe DI your book to appreciate it a lot.'
     b. *Credo di, il tuo libro, apprezzarlo molto.

This distribution is unexpected if both *che* and *di* occupy a unique C-position but is readily accounted for under a split-C-system, where *che* occupies a position higher than *di*. The Clitic Left-Dislocated topic appears between the two positions. According to Rizzi (1997), the impossibility of the occurrence of a topic between the Force head and the matrix verb is due to selection. Force bounds CP up and represents its interface with the superordinate structure. Fin bounds the clause downward and represents the interface with the inflectional system. Topics, fronted *foci*, and question operators occupy the space between ForP and FinP.

Before I turn to an investigation of the interactions among Topic, Focus, and wh-movement, I must first clarify what is meant by 'topic' and 'fronted focus'. The topic-comment articulation is commonly expressed in Romance by the construction that Cinque (1990) has labeled Clitic Left Dislocation. In this construction, the topic constituent is placed in the front of the clause and is resumed by a clitic coreferential with it:

(6) Il tuo libro, lo ho letto.
     'Your book, I read it.'

In all of the Romance varieties under discussion, with the exception of Portuguese, the clitic is obligatory when the topic is a direct object. In English, the topic-comment relation is expressed by the construction traditionally referred to as *Topicalization*. In this construction, the topic is associated with a gap:

(7) Your book, you should give ec to Paul.

Among the Romance languages, Portuguese is the only one that has English-type Topicalization, as illustrated below (see Duarte 1987 and Raposo 1994, 1996). This option coexists with CLLD:

(8) O teu livro, comprei de certeza.
     'Your book, I bought, for sure.'

The focus-presupposition articulation can be expressed in many Romance languages by preposing the focal element and assigning it special stress (see Cinque 1990 and Rizzi 1997 for discussion of the properties of this construction in Italian):

(9) IL TUO LIBRO ho letto (, non il suo)
     'Your book (focus) I have read (not his).'   [Rizzi 1997]

Sentence (9) is restricted to contrastive focus. Other Romance languages that have equivalents to (9) are Romanian (Dobrovie-Sorin 1994), Spanish

(Torrego 1984; Contreras 1991; Laka 1990; Raposo 1994, 1996; Uriagereka 1995; Uribe-Etxebarria 1991; Zubizarreta 1997), and Catalan (Bonet 1990; Sola 1992; Vallduví 1992).

Several properties distinguish CLLD from Focus. The main superficial difference is that a 'resumptive' clitic is impossible with a focalized object but is obligatory with a CLLD object. As discussed in Cinque (1990), Iatridou (1991), Raposo (1996), Rizzi (1997), and Tsimpli (1994), the differences detected between CLLD and Focus point to the conclusion that Focus is akin to wh-movement whereas CLLD involves some different form of construal. Focus fronting passes all of the diagnostics for wh-movement: it reconstructs, it proceeds successive-cyclically, and it displays Weak Crossover effects. On the other hand, CLLD, doesn't display any of these properties. Therefore, I assume that Focus is a genuine case of movement, whereas CLLDed topics are merged directly in their surface position. One important property that distinguishes CLLD from Focus is that there can be multiple topics per clause but only one focus:

(10)   Il libro, a Gianni, domani, glielo darò senz'altro.
        'The book, to John, tomorrow, to him-it will give for sure'

(11)   *A GIANNI IL LIBRO darò (non a Pero, l' articolo)   [Rizzi 1997]

In Italian, topics are not strictly ordered for Focus; they may precede or follow the unique Focused constituent:

(12)   a. Credo che QUESTO, a Gianni, gli dovremmo dire.
           'I believe that to Gianni, THIS, we should say'
        b. Credo che a Gianni, QUESTO, gli dovremmo dire   [Rizzi 1997]

Iatridou (1991) and Raposo (1996) propose that CLLDed topics are licensed by "rules of predication" (see Chomsky 1977), which require the topic to be 'base-generated' in a position of adjunction to the XP that is predicated of it. In such an analysis, CLLDed topics are freely adjoined to a clausal projection. Deriving the properties of Focus from movement theory and assuming that a unique focal head can project between C and IP, we can analyze (12a,b) in terms of free adjunction of the topic to IP or FocP:

(13)   a. [$_{CP}$che [$_{FocP}$QUESTO$_k$ [$_{Foc}$ ∅ [$_{IP}$ a Gianni [$_{IP}$ gli dovremmo dire t$_k$]]]]]
        b. [$_{CP}$che [$_{FocP}$[a Gianni [$_{FocP}$ QUESTO$_k$ [$_{Foc}$ ∅ [$_{IP}$ gli dovremmo dire t$_k$]]]]]

The different possibilities allowed follow from the fact that there are at least two clausal projections available to function as predicates in Italian: IP and FocP.[1]

Integrating Topic and Focus in the Force-Finiteness system defended in Rizzi (1997), we have the following maximally expanded CP layer for Italian:

(14) Force (Topics*) (Focus) (Topics*) Fin IP

For Rizzi, the Force-Finiteness system is always projected, but the Topic-Focus system is projected only when needed. With the hierarchical structure (14) in mind, we are now in a position to turn to the issue of the landing site of wh-movement in Romance.

2.   The Landing Site(s) of Question Operators in Romance

There is pretty robust evidence that question operators in Romance target a position that is lower than that filled by relative operators. As discussed in Raposo (1996), Rizzi (1997), Poletto (1997), and Sola (1992), relative operators must precede topics, but question operators must follow topics in main questions. The following examples illustrate the case of Italian, but the other Romance languages behave alike:

(15)   *Relative operator > Topic*
       Un uomo **a cui**, *il premio Nobel*, lo daranno senz'altro.
       'A man to whom, the Nobel Prize, they will give it indoubtedly.'

(16)   **Topic > Relative operator*
       *Un uomo, *il premio Nobel*, **a cui** lo daranno senz' altro.

(17)   *Topic > wh-phrase*
       a. *Il premio Nobel*, **a chi** lo daranno?
          The Nobel Prize to whom it gave.3pl
          'To whom did they give the Nobel Prize?'
       b. ***A chi**, *il premio Nobel*, lo daranno?

Since Force is the one CP head that cannot be preceded by topics, the contrasts above are explained under the assumption that relative operators target Spec-ForceP, whereas question operators target a lower position.

Martins (1994), Raposo (1994, 1996), Rizzi (1997), and Uriagereka (1995) suggest that question operators target the Spec of FocP, located between C and IP (or FinP, in Rizzi's more fine-grained analysis). Infl-to-Foc raising, triggered by the requirement to check the wh-feature, accounts for obligatory adjacency between the question operator and inflection in root clauses:

(18)   [$_{FocP}$ Q-operator [$_{Foc}$ Infl + V] [$_{IP}$ t] . . .]]
       |_____|

Assuming that in main questions the [wh] feature is located in T and that wh-movement targets Spec-Foc, then T must raise up to Foc to satisfy the wh-Criterion.

A long-standing problem for the Infl-raising approach to the phenomenon of obligatory adjacency between inflection and question operators in Romance is that the order Aux-Subject-V is often impossible, as illustrated below for Italian and French:

(19) *Italian*:
a. *Che cosa ha Maria detto?
What has M said M
b. Che cosa ha detto Maria?

(20) *French*:
a. *Où est Marie allée?
Where is M. gone?
b. Où est allée Marie?
'Where did Mary go?'

These examples have a very different pattern than Germanic. Whereas the latter freely allow the order wh-Aux-Subject, the Romance languages mentioned do not let the lexical subject immediately follow the inflected Aux. If inflection raises across the subject, one would expect the subject to be allowed to appear immediately after the auxiliary, as occurs in English.[2]

A quick survey of the restrictions on the placement of lexical subjects immediately to the right of auxiliaries in Romance reveals that the pattern observed in declaratives is systematically kept in interrogatives. Starting with Italian, we observe that the order Aux-Subject-Prt is barred in declaratives, as well as interrogatives:

(21) a. *Ha Mario accettato di aiutarci.
Has Mario accepted to help us   [Rizzi 1982]
b. *Che cosa ha Maria detto?
What has M said?

Turning to Spanish, where the availability of Aux-Subject-Prt order appears to depend on the form of the auxiliary, we observe that there is no asymmetry between questions and declaratives: The range of subject positions allowed in declaratives is kept in interrogatives. Consider the following examples:

(22) a. Ha (*Juan) leido el libro (Juan)?
Has J. read the book?
b. ?Habia Juan leido casi todo el libro.
Had J read almost all the book?
c. Esta Juan leyendo el libro (Juan)?
Is J. reading the book?   [Rivero, p.c.]

Aux-Subject-Prt order is unavailable with the third-person-present form of *haber*, *ha* (cf. 22a) but is marginally possible with the imperfect past, *habia* (cf. 22b), and is generally accepted when the auxiliary is *estar*. Now consider interrogatives:

(23) a. Que ha (*Juan) leído (Juan)?
What has J. read J.

b. ?Que había Juan leído ya?
   What had J read already?
c. Que esta (Juan) leyendo (Juan)?
   What is J. reading?   [Rivero, p.c.]

The restrictions on the distribution of subjects observed in declaratives are maintained in interrogatives. This lack of asymmetry between questions and declaratives casts doubt on the idea that inflection raises higher in questions.

Since there is no evidence for Infl raising in Romance, an alternative way of accounting for obligatory adjacency between inflection and question operators is to posit that question operators target the specifier position of the highest Infl head, as schematized below:

(24)   [$_{IP}$ Q-operator [$_{I'}$ [$_{I}$ Infl V] [$_{VP}$ subject]]]
       |_____|

The suggestion that question operators target Spec-IP has been made for Catalan (Bonet 1990; Sola 1992; Vallduví 1992), Iberian Spanish (Contreras 1991; Uribe-Etxebarria 1991; and Zubizarreta 1997), and Romanian (Dobrovie-Sorin 1994). In the next section, I briefly review some of the arguments presented by these authors, and in the sections that follow I argue that this approach should be extended to all of the other Romance languages.

2.1.   Catalan, Iberian Spanish, and Romanian

In this section I consider the Romance languages that show no embedded-root asymmetry in the adjacency requirement between inflection and a wh-fronted element, namely, Catalan, Iberian Spanish, and Romanian. The following examples illustrate the fact that in these Romance varieties, inflection must be adjacent to a wh-element even in an embedded question:

(25)   a.   *Catalan*: *V[wh-S-V]
            ¿No sé **què** (*en Joan) farà (en Joan)   [Sola 1992]
            Not know-1sg what (*Joan) will-do (Joan)
       b.   *Romanian*: *V[wh-S-V]
            Nu ne-a spus **unde** (*Ion) s'a dus (Ion).
            'They didn't tell us where has gone Ion.'   [Dobrovie-Sorin 1994]
       c.   *Spanish*: *V-wh-S-V
            No sabía **qué** (*esos dos) querían (esos dos).   [Torrego 1984]
            'I didn't know what those two wanted.'

The lack of root-embedded asymmetry observed in Iberian Spanish, Catalan, and Romanian for the adjacency requirement imposed between extracted arguments and inflection has led a number of linguists to suggest that Spec-IP is an A' position in these languages (see Bonet 1990, Sola 1992, and Vallduví 1992 for Catalan; Contreras 1991, Uribe-Etxebarria 1991, and Zubizarreta 1997 for

Iberian Spanish; Dobrovie-Sorin 1994 for Romanian). Here I review Vallduví´s (1992) treatment since it introduces yet another range of facts that will be useful in the discussion that follows.

Vallduví (1992) shows that in Catalan, negative quantifiers and certain other quantifiers must be string-adjacent to the verb when fronted. In this, they behave like fronted wh-phrases and differently from CLLDed phrases, which do not need to be string-adjacent to V. Consider a typical CLLD construction in Catalan (Vallduví 1992: 127):

(26) [El sou]$_1$ [a la gent]$_2$ no l$_1$'hi$_2$ regalen.
     the pay to the people not it to-them give-3Pl
     'They don't give the pay to people for free.'

The two fronted constituents can be freely switched around:

(27) [a la gent]$_2$ [el sou]$_1$ no l$_1$'hi$_2$ regalen.

Vallduví (1992) shows that if one of the two left-hand phrases is a negative quantifier, the linear order among the phrases is not free anymore (note that in Catalan a negative bare quantifier can be doubled by a clitic while still displaying this restriction):

(28) a. El sou a ningú (no) l'hi regalen.
         the pay to noone (not) it to him give
         'They don't give the pay to anyone for free.'
    b. *A ningú el sou (no) l'hi regalen.

Subject negative quantifiers behave alike, as shown by the comparison between (29) and (30) below. In (29), subject and object may be switched around freely:

(29) a. Els dolents l'empresa no els vol
         the bad-ones the company no them want
         'The company doesn't want the bad ones.'
    b. L' empresa els dolents no els vol

When the subject is a negative quantifier, as in the sentences below, left-adjacency to the verbal string is required again:

(30) a. Els dolents ningú (no) els vol
         No one wants the bad ones.'
    b. *Ningú els dolens (no) els vol

Vallduví (1992) concludes the following:

It is clear, then, that these negative quantifiers do not appear in the typical IP-adjunction slot left-detached phrases appear in, but rather in a position within IP which is left-adjacent to the verbal string. The left-adjacency requirement for *ningú* in (15) [our (30)] has nothing to do with the grammatical status as a subject, as shown by the fact that it also applies in (14) [our (28)], where *ningú* is an indirect object. It is rather its status as a quantificational operator that appears to determine its inability to allow other left-hand phrases between itself and the verbal string. (p. 328)

According to Vallduví, this adjacency requirement doesn't affect all QPs but a subset of them that includes *poques* N ('few N'), *alguna cosa* 'something', and *tothom* 'everyone', among others. Vallduví further observes that the QPs in question are in complementary distribution with a preverbal wh-phrase:

(31)   a.   Què$_i$ no regalen t$_i$ a ningú?
            what not give 3PL to no-one
            'What don't they give to anyone for free?'
       b.   *Què a ningú (no) li regalen?
       c.   *A ningú què (no) li regalen?

(32)   a.   Qui farà poques coses?
            who do-FUT-3SG few things
            'Who'll do few things?'
       b.   *Qui poques coses farà?
       c.   *Poques coses qui farà?

It is clear that these QPs and wh-phrases occupy the same position, which suggests that the QPs in question are extracted by A-bar movement. Thus, there is a subset of quantified expressions that are fronted by A-bar movement *without requiring contrastive Focus intonation*. Vallduví (1992) refers to these QPs as "quantificational operators" and describes them as being incapable of functioning as "links." A "link phrase" "points to the file card that it denotes in the file-structured knowledge-store of the hearer and selects it among the sentence participants as the sole point of information entry." Hence, Vallduví's "link phrases" stand for discourse topics. The expressions that cannot be discourse topics range over QPs without a lexical restriction, nonspecific indefinites, and [+affective] operators.

In view of the fact that the position that wh-phrases and fronted QPs occupy must be string-adjacent to the verb but lower than complementizers, Vallduví (1992) suggests that it is Spec-IP:

(33)   [$_{CP}$ C [$_{IP}$ XP [$_{IP}$wh + Op QP [$_{I'}$ [$_I$ V] [$_{VP}$ . . .]]]]]

Here XP stands for left-adjoined topics (which may be construed with an object clitic or with subject *pro*) and Spec-IP is filled by either a fronted wh-phrase or a "nonreferential" QP (subject or object). Vallduví follows previous proposals according to which Catalan's basic order is VOS (Adams 1987; Bonet 1990; Contreras 1991), so Spec-IP is empty and available for this role as a quantifier-related position.

The structure proposed in (33) also fits Iberian Spanish and Romanian. Recall that these are like Catalan in that they show no embedded-root asymmetry in the left-adjacency requirement imposed on wh-questions. Moreover, in these languages, a Focused phrase must also be adjacent to inflection in matrix, as well as in embedded, clauses (see Zubizarreta 1997 for Iberian Spanish; Bonet 1990 for Catalan; and Dobrovie-Sorin 1994 and Motapanyane 1994 for Romanian).

(34) a. Las ESPINACAS detesta **Pedro** (no las papas). [Zubizarreta 1997]
          The SPINACH hates P. (not the potatoes)
      b. *Las ESPINACAS **Pedro** trajo (no las papas)
          the SPINACH P. brought (not the potatoes)

Whenever a Focused phrase co-occurs with a topic, the latter must precede it [note that (35) contains a subject topic]:

(35) Estoy segura que Pedro, las ESPINACAS trajo (no las papas).
      I am sure that P. the SPINACH brought

(36) Spunea ca*, scrisorile, IERI le-a primit, (nu azi)
      said that letters-the them has received (not today)   [Motapanyane 1994]

Fronting of bare indefinites, indefinite QPs, and negative QPs displays a similar restriction, as shown in Zubizarreta (1997). Zubizarreta discusses the difference between QP fronting and Focus fronting, even though she labels the former type of movement "emphatic movement":

(37) a. ALGO debe haberte dicho Maria para que te hayas enojado tanto.
          Something must have-to-you said Maria so that you have been so annoyed
          'Something Maria must have told you, for you to be so annoyed.'
      b. ?*ALGO Maria te habrá dicho para que te hayas enojado tanto.

(38) a. Con NADIE compartió María su secreto.
          With no one shared Maria her secret
          'Maria shared her secret with no one.'
      b. ?*Con NADIE María compartió su secreto.

Under the assumption that there is only one A'-projection to the left of inflection, namely, the Spec of the highest Infl head, the left-adjacency requirement imposed on all kinds of A'-extraction is immediately accounted for without recourse to Infl raising. As a result of the configuration in (33), topics will always precede wh-phrases, foci, or nonspecific fronted QPs in matrix, as well as embedded, clauses.

The proposal that Spec-IP is the landing site for extraction in these languages is supported by the fact that there is no evidence for Infl raising. As noted previously, there is no asymmetry between questions and declaratives concerning the possibility of placing the subject immediately to the right of the verb or Aux.[3] Since there is no evidence for Infl raising, the left-adjacency requirement imposed on extraction can only be explained by means of raising of the question operator to the Specifier position of the head that contains inflection, IP. Hence, I conclude that Vallduví's (1992) clause structure in (33) is adequate for the subset of the Romance languages discussed in this section.

2.2. Standard Italian

Standard Italian differs from Iberian Spanish, Catalan, and Romanian in that it doesn't require strict adjacency between a fronted Focus and inflection:

(39)   (Domani,) QUESTO (a Gianni) gli dovrete dire.
       '(Tomorrow,) THIS (to Gianni) we should say'

Question operators, by contrast, obey the left-adjacency requirement in root questions:

(40)   (Domani) che cosa (*a Gianni) gli dovremmo dire?
       '(Tomorrow) what (to Gianni) we should say?'

Rizzi's (1997) main argument that question operators target Spec-Foc in Italian is based on the observation that in main questions they are incompatible with Focus-movement:

(41)   Focus and wh-phrase are incompatible
       a. *A GIANNI che cosa hai detto (, non Piero)?
           'TO GIANNI what did you tell (, not to P.)?'
       b. *Che cosa A GIANNI hai detto (, non Piero)?
           'What TO GIANNI did you tell (, not to Piero)?'

However, in a footnote, Rizzi observes that in embedded questions, a wh-element is marginally compatible with a focalized element:

(42)   ?Mi domando A GIANNI che cosa abbiano detto (, non a Piero)
       'I wonder TO GIANNI what they said (, not to Piero)   [Rizzi 1997]

Sentence (42) suggests that there is a position for question operators that is independent from Spec-Foc and in fact lower than Spec-Foc. Thus, the observed complementary distribution between Focus and wh-elements is only a root phenomenon. Now note that examples such as (42) open the way to an alternative account of the differences between Focus and question operators. We know that topics may immediately follow Focus in Italian. If question operators target a position that is lower than Focus, it is not surprising that topics should precede question operators:

(43) (Topics) [Focus (Topics) [wh . . .

Clearly, under (43) we lose an account of why Focus and question operators are incompatible in root questions, but there are other plausible explanations for this restriction that don't necessarily rely on competition for the same structural position (see note 5). At any rate, for the moment it is enough to observe that whenever a Focus and a question operator may co-occur in standard Italian, the latter appears lower than Focus and immediately adjacent to inflection, which suggests that there is an available landing site for question operators to the right of Foc.

Even though in embedded questions in Italian the preferred order is V-topic-wh, V-wh-topic order is not completely excluded:

(44) a. Mi domando, il premio Nobel, a chi lo potrebbero dare.
          'I wonder, the Nobel Prize, to whom we should give it.'
      b. ?Mi domando a chi, il premio Nobel, lo potrebbero dare.
          'I wonder to whom, the Nobel Prize, we should give it.'

Similar effects are observed with preverbal subjects:

(45) a. ??Mi domando cosa Gianni ha fatto.
          Me ask-1sg what John has done
          'I wonder what John has done.'
      b. Mi chiedo cosa Gianni faccia adesso.
          Me asked what John do-subj. now
      c. ?Mi chiedo cosa Gianni fara' in quel frangente
          me asked what John do-future now   [Poletto 1997]

In Rizzi's (1997) I-to-F approach, these violations of the left-adjacency requirement in Italian are due to the fact that I-to-Foc is weakened in embedded environments. Poletto (1997), however, discusses evidence that suggests that the marginal status of (44b) and (45a, c) is independent from verb movement. In some northern Italian dialects that have subject-clitic inversion in root questions, a complementizer is obligatory in embedded interrogatives and there is no subject-clitic inversion.

(46) a. Gianni quando vienlo?
          G. when comes-he
      b. I me ga domandà Gianni quando che el vien.
          SCL me have asked G. when that SCL comes
      c. ??Me domando cossa che Nane ga fato casa
          me ask-1sg what that N. has done at home

Clearly, the verb in (46b, c) has not raised to the CP system. However, with a subject intervening between the complementizer and the verb, (46c) is marginal. Poletto (1997) concludes that this effect on preverbal subjects is not connected to verb movement. Poletto also discusses examples with intervening topics:

(47)   a.   Ghe go domandà *el posto* **quando** che i ghe lo da
            To-her have asked the position when that SCL to-her it give
       b.   ??Ghe go domandà **quando** *el posto* che i ghe lo da

Sentence (47b), with the indicative mood and a topic immediately to the right of the question operator, is degraded—compare (47b) to its standard Italian counterpart (44b)—and becomes more acceptable "if the *Wh*-element is strongly focalized as the interpretation becomes one of correction as the wrong information has been given, i.e. I am asking when and not how" (Poletto 1997).

Clearly, these intuitions are entirely compatible with the assumption that the wh-element in (47b) is itself focalized (in Spec-Foc), with the topic to its right. In view of the fact that (47a) lacks the focused reading, I conclude that there the wh-element occupies a position that is distinct from Spec-Foc. With this conclusion in mind, we now turn to the standard Italian examples in (44). Apart from the absence of the complementizer and the difference in mood, which is probably responsible for the slightly more degraded status of (47b), the standard Italian example (44b) is parallel to (47b). I conclude that in standard Italian, too, the marginal availability of the order wh-topic is due to the marginal possibility of focusing the wh-element itself rather than to "weakening" of I-to-C movement. This conclusion entails that in the nonmarginal case (44a), the question operator occupies a lower position, to the right of the lowest position for topics, namely, XP in the schema in (43) above.[4]

Recall that Iberian Spanish and Romanian differ from Italian in requiring strict adjacency between a Focused phrase and inflection. Now suppose that the difference between Italian and Iberian Spanish, Catalan, and Romanian is that Italian has an independent Focus head above IP, whereas Spanish lacks a projecting head between Force and IP (see Zubizarreta 1997 for a somewhat similar proposal). In Spanish the Spec of the highest Infl head is the landing site for all sorts of A'-movement: wh-movement, Focus movement, and fronting of those expressions that cannot be discourse topics. In Italian, by hypothesis, Focus movement and QP fronting target Spec-Foc, in which case a topic or a subject may intervene between the phrase in Spec-Foc and inflection:

(48)   *Italian:*
       C [Topic* [**Focus/QP** [[Foc] [Topic* [$_{IP}$ [$_{I'}$ [$_I$ V] ...]]]]]

(49)   *Spanish/Catalan/Romanian:*
       [$_{CP}$ C [Topic* [$_{IP}$ **wh\+Op QP/Focus** [$_{I'}$ [$_I$ V] ...]]]]

Previously I suggested that whenever a subject or a topic is allowed to intervene between the wh-element and inflection in Italian, the wh-element is itself focalized, sitting in Spec-Foc. Under the hypothesis that the structure of the left periphery in Romanian and Iberian Spanish lacks FocP as an independent head, the absence of the order wh-topic/subject-V in these languages follows.

Now we turn to the issue of the landing site of nonfocalized wh-elements in Italian. As argued, this position is lower than Foc and adjacent to the inflected verb. Since, as discussed, there is no clear evidence from standard Italian that inflection raises up to the C-system in questions, it would appear that the logical move is to propose that the specifier position of the highest Infl head is the landing site for wh-movement in standard Italian too. In this proposal, the Italian example (50a), where a focalized phrase and a wh-phrase co-occur, would be analyzed as in (50b), with the wh-element sitting in Spec-IP and the Focused phrase sitting in Spec-Foc:

(50)   a. ?Mi domando A GIANNI che cosa abbiano detto (‚non a Piero)
            'I wonder TO GIANNI what they said (‚not to Piero)
        b. ?Mi domando [$_{FOCP}$A GIANNI [$_{Foc'}$ [$_{Foc}$ ø] [$_{IP}$ che cosa [$_{I'}$ abbiano . . .]]]]

Assuming that the wh-criterion holds in the syntax in Italian and that the locus of the wh-feature is Infl (as in fact is suggested for root clauses by Rizzi 1991), the wh-criterion is satisfied by attraction of the wh-operator to Spec-IP. This proposal has the advantage of unifying Italian and the other Romance languages discussed: The wh-criterion is satisfied against Infl in all cases. The superficial differences detected between Italian, on the one hand, and Catalan, Romanian, and Iberian Spanish, on the other hand, are due to independent differences in the structure of the left periphery. Italian has an intermediate Focus head between C and IP. Catalan, Romanian, and Iberian Spanish lack this intermediate head.[5]

The hypothesis that question operators are attracted to Spec-IP in Italian, Romanian, Iberian Spanish, and Catalan raises two issues. The first one is the status of Finiteness; the second, the status of Spec-IP. Recall that Rizzi (1997) argues in favor of a split-CP system for Italian, minimally consisting of a Force head and a Finiteness head. Topic and Focus occupy the space between C and Fin:

(51)   Force (Topics) (Focus) (Topics) Fin IP

According to (51), there are in principle two specifier positions to the left of inflection in Italian and below topics or focus, namely, Spec-IP and Spec-Fin. For Rizzi (1997), Spec-IP is an A-position and is immediately preceded by Fin. According to the structure that I have proposed for Italian in (48), there is only one specifier position to the left of inflection and below topics or focus, that is, the specifier position of the highest Infl head. Moreover, this position is the landing site for question operators. Up to now I have not addressed the status of Fin. None of the structures in (48) and (49) contemplate this position, so now the question arises of how Fin should be integrated into our system.

2.3. Finiteness and Inflection

In this section I examine the status on Finiteness in light of evidence from Romanian subjunctives, which are introduced by a particle that has the same distribution as Italian *di*. I argue, on the basis of distributional evidence, that the Romanian subjunctive particle *sa** is adequately analyzed as the lexicalization of Rizzi's (1997) Fin. The curious property of this particle is that, unlike Italian *di*, it occurs in finite environments, that is, in constructions that may take an overt subject. Thus, Romanian provides the environment needed to test Rizzi's hypothesis, according to which Fin selects an IP in whose specifier a preverbal subject may land. Rizzi's hypothesis predicts that a subject may intervene between Infl and Fin; if subjects raise to Spec-IP and Fin selects IP, nothing in principle would prevent the order Fin-Subject-Infl. Drawing on work by Dobrovie-Sorin (1994), we see that a subject may not intervene between the subjunctive particle and the verbal cluster. In effect, nothing except clitics may intervene between this particle and inflection. Thus, Rizzi's prediction is not met. I interpret these facts as an indication that Fin belongs to the inflectional system: it is the highest head in the inflectional system, so Spec-Fin should instead be analyzed as Spec-IP, with Fin belonging to a complex Infl. Spec-IP is the landing site for question operators and fronted Focus, so it is an A-bar position. I argue that the status of Spec-IP as an A-bar position is connected to the Null Subject Property.

Consider the following Romanian sentence:

(52)   As3 vrea *ca* mîine *să* vină Ion.
        (I) Would want that tomorrow *să* come-3sg-SUBJ John
        'I would want John to come tomorrow.'

In (52) there are what seem to be two complementizer particles: *ca* and *sa**. The particle *sa** has been the topic of much debate in the literature (see Dobrovie-Sorin 1994; Rivero 1987; Terzi 1993) since it appears to have some of the properties of a complementizer, as well as some of the properties of an Infl head.

Dobrovie-Sorin (1994) mentions a number of properties that distinguish *sa** from Infl particles and bring it closer to regular complementizers: (a) *sa** is invariable; (b) *sa** can head an embedded clause; (c) its position is leftmost, necessarily preceding clitics and negation. This is illustrated in (53):

(53)   a. Vreau *să* **nu-l** mai întîlnesti.
            [I] want *să* not him again meet-you
        b. *vreau **nu** *să-l* mai întîlnesti
        c. *vreau îl *să* mai întîlnesti*
        d. vreau **nu-l** *să* mai întîlnesti

In spite of sharing these properties with complementizers, *sa** bears a strong coherence with the verbal cluster. As (54a) shows, an overt subject may not appear between *sa** and the verbal cluster. It can appear postverbally (54b) or to the left of *sa** (54c):

(54) a. Vreau ca pîna mîine **să** *Ion* **termine** cartea asta.
      [I] want that until tomorrow *să* finish John this book.
      b. Vreau ca pînă mîine *să* **termine** *Ion* cartea asta.
      [I] want that until tomorrow *să* finish John this book.
      c. Vreau *ca Ion să* **vină**
      [I] want that John *să* come

Dobrovie-Sorin (1994) shows that *sa** necessarily precedes the other elements of the verb cluster; the maximal string that may separate it from the verb is Neg-cl-Adv-Aux, and these elements are themselves strictly adjacent to the inflected verb.[6] Thus the particle *sa** shares properties both with complementizers and with Infl elements. On the one hand, nothing except negation and clitics can intervene between it and the verb. On the other hand, we need to assume that *sa** is sufficiently high in the structure to precede all the other elements in the Infl cluster. For this reason, Dobrovie-Sorin proposes that *sa** heads its own projection and selects a Spec-less IP (and perhaps NegP).

Now note that the distribution of *sa** is remarkably similar to *di*, Rizzi's (1997) Finiteness head. *Di* also precedes negation, and according to Rizzi, nothing can intervene between it and the verb except negation:

(55) *Penso di, a Gianni, dovergli parlare.

Recall that the main piece of evidence that motivated Rizzi's (1997) distinction between Force and Finiteness was the distribution of topics. Topics obligatorily follow the declarative complementizer in Italian, but they obligatorily precede *di*. It is interesting to note that topics obligatorily appear between the complementizer and *sa**:

(56) Doresc *ca* pe Ion *să*-l examineze Popescu
      [I] wish that *pe* Ion *să*-him examine Popescu

Thus *sa** has the same distribution as *di*. For many authors, *sa** stands for mood and heads a Mood Phrase (Rivero 1987 and Terzi 1993). Elsewhere, I have argued that *sa** is adequately characterized as the lexicalization of Finiteness (Barbosa 1995), so it is quite plausible that it fills the same abstract head as the Italian or French *di* (see Wada 1998 for this claim). Taking Fin to be the spell-out of the feature [± Finite], we see that *sa** represents the positive value for this feature, whereas Italian *di* represents its negative value.

Without going into the question of whether Fin selects a Spec-less TP, I will simply assume that Fin is the highest head in the inflectional system. Recall Rizzi's (1997) insight that Fin establishes the interface between the inflectional system and the CP system. Based on the observation that in Romanian a lexical subject may not intervene between *sa** and the verbal cluster, I suggest that Fin is the highest head of the inflectional system, which is equivalent to suggesting that Fin selects a Spec-less IP or NegP. Taking I NFL to be a cover term for "set of inflectional heads," I include Fin in this set. Fin is the highest T-head in the inflectional system.

Now I address the issue of the status Spec-Fin. In addition to topics and subjects, *sa** can also be immediately preceded by focused expressions or question operators:

(57) a. Vreau ca **MÎINE** *să* vină Ion.
          [I] want tomorrow *să* come John.
          'I want John to come tomorrow.'
      b. Nu stia **unde** *să* plece.
          Not know-3SG where *să* go
          'He doesn't know where to go.'

We saw earlier that Focus and question operators require strict adjacency with inflection. Topics do not. Thus, it seems reasonable to conclude that Spec-Fin is the landing site for Focus and question operator movement. Now the question arises of whether preverbal subjects also raise to Spec-FinP in Romanian.

Romanian, it is interesting to note, has a test that clearly shows that preverbal nonfocalized subjects behave like topics: the distributional properties of the subjunctive complementizer *ca*. This particle has a very curious distribution. In the absence of any material in the front of *sa**, *ca* is preferably absent:

(58) a. ?? as3 vrea *ca să* -l examineze Popescu pe Ion.

Ca becomes obligatory if there is a subject (59), a sentential adverb (60a), or a dislocated object (60b) in front of *sa**:

(59) Vreau (ca) Ion *să* vină
      [I] want that John *să* come

(60) a. Vreau * (ca) mîine *să* vină Ion.
          [I] want tomorrow *să* come John.
          'I want John to come tomorrow.'
      b. Doresc (ca) pe Ion *să*-l examineze Popescu
          [I] wish pe Ion *să*-him examine Popescu

However, *ca* can be left out when the element preceding *sa** is focalized, and this observation also applies to subjects (61b, c):[7]

(61) a. Vreau (ca) MÎINE *să* vină Ion.
          [I] want tomorrow *să* come John.
          'I want John to come tomorrow.'
      b. Vreau (ca) ION *să* vină.
      c. As3 vrea (ca) numai Ion *să* vină la petrecere
          [I] want that only Ion *să* come to the party
          'I want only John to come to the party.'

Thus, we observe that preverbal (neutral) subjects form a pattern with dislocated elements and sentential adverbs in requiring the presence of *ca*. Preverbal focused subjects, on the other hand, form a pattern with Focalized adverbs or objects. The analysis developed by Vallduví (1992) for Catalan extends rather naturally to this paradigm. Recall that Vallduví adopted the VOS hypothesis for Catalan and argued that preverbal neutral subjects were 'left-detached', just like other 'left-detached' objects. The Spec-IP position was the landing site for A-bar movement. Extending Vallduví's proposal to Romanian, we have the following structure for (59), where *Ion* is a left-dislocated topic doubled by resumptive *pro*:

(62)   Vreau ca [$_{FinP}$ Ion$_1$ [$_{FinP}$ *sa** vina* *pro* $_1$]]

Sentence (61b), by contrast, is analyzed as an instance of subject extraction from the postverbal position to Spec-FinP (an A-bar position):

(63)   Vreau [$_{FinP}$ ION$_1$ [$_{Fin'}$ *sa** vina* t$_1$]]

This extension of Vallduví's (1992) analysis of Catalan to Romanian entails that the A-position for subjects in Romanian is to the right of the verb. Unlike Catalan, however, Romanian allows for VSO order. It is a well-known fact that the Romance languages vary in the position of postverbal subjects relative to other arguments (see Sola 1992 and Zubizarreta 1997 for an overview). This variation is not directly relevant, however. What matters for now is to show that in Romanian, as well as in Catalan, there is *a subject position* to the right of the verb. In both cases, the preverbal field is divided into the position that is adjacent to the verbal string, which is an A'-position and the recursive position for topics. Base-generated topics include CLLded subjects or objects and sentential adverbs. Example (64) represents the structure of the left periphery in Romanian:

(64)[C [$_{IP}$ topics [$_{IP}$ Focus/wh/QPs [$_{I'}$ Fin + I + V ... [ ]]]]

This is essentially the structure proposed in the previous section for Romanian, Catalan, and Iberian Spanish, except that Fin is now incorporated in the structure as the highest head in the inflectional system.

Now we turn to Italian. In the previous section we claimed that Italian differs from Catalan, Romanian, and Iberian Spanish in having an independent Focus head between C and the highest Infl head. Assuming that Fin is the highest Infl head, I suggest the following structure for Italian, where topics are base-generated to the left of FocP or to the left of IP:

(65)   [C [$_{FocP}$ topics [$_{FocP}$ [Foc] [$_{IP}$ [topics [$_{IP}$ [$_I$ Fin + I + V] ... [ ]]]]]

I have argued that question operators in Italian are attracted to Spec-IP, so now the question arises of whether Spec-IP is an A-position in Italian. Elsewhere, I have argued that Vallduví's observations about the status of Spec-IP as an A'-position in Catalan should be extended to all of the Null Subject Languages (NSL), Portuguese and Italian included (see Barbosa 1995, forthcoming). I argued that the real A-position for subjects in all of the NSLs is to the right of the raised verb and that preverbal subjects in the NSLs are either left-dislocated topics (doubled by a resumptive *pro* in postverbal position) or A'-moved to the front of the clause, in which case they must bear contrastive focus intonation unless they belong to the class of expressions that cannot be topics (i.e., if they are bare QPs or negative QPs).

Alexiadou and Anagnostopoulou (1998), Barbosa (1995), and Pollock (1997) suggest that agreement in the NSLs is +N/D, thus being capable of checking the EPP under incorporation with T. From this it follows that the lexical subject may remain in situ, which is why Spec-IP is never the landing site for A-movement in the NSLs. Here I have discussed evidence from Romanian, Iberian Spanish, and Catalan that reinforces this view. Since an argument in favor of this claim for Italian would take me too far afield, I refer the reader to Barbosa (1995, 1996b) for further discussion.

Under the view that subjects never raise to Spec-IP in the Null Subject languages, this position is available as the landing site for wh-movement and there is no need to assume V-to-C movement in Italian, too. If the locus of the wh-specification is the highest T-head (as in fact is suggested for root clauses by Rizzi 1991) then, by the shortest move, wh-elements raise to Spec-IP. Because Italian is an NSL, the EPP is checked against Fin under incorporation and Spec-IP is free to host wh-elements.

To complete my argument for the status of Spec-IP as the landing site for A'-movement in the NSLs, I now briefly turn to European Portuguese (EP).

2.4. European Portuguese

European Portuguese lacks Focus movement but has fronting of affective operators and 'nonreferential' quantified expressions of the kind discussed by Vallduví (1992) for Catalan. Moreover, QP fronting can be distinguished from *Topicalization* or CLLD by the position of object clitics (for detailed discussion see Barbosa 1996a, forthcoming; Duarte 1983; Martins 1994; Raposo 1994; Uriagereka 1995). Also, QP fronting forms patterns with wh-fronting in requiring the order cl-V. By contrast, CLLD and Topicalization trigger the order V-cl:

(66)   a. *QP-movement*:   **Cl -V**
           Algo **te** disseram para que te tenhas incomodado tanto.
           Something (Maria) to-you said (Maria) for you to be so upset.
           'Maria must have told you something for you to be so upset!

       b. *Wh-movement*:   **Cl-V**
           Quem **te** disse isso?

(67)   *CLLD*:   **V-Cl**
       a. A Maria apresento-**ta** amanhã.
          the Maria introduce-to-you-her tomorrow
          'Maria, I'll introduce her to you tomorrow.'
       b. *A Maria **ta** apresento amanhã.

(68) *Topicalization*: **V-Cl**

    a. [A Maria]$_i$ apresento-**te** ec$_i$ amanhã
       M. I'll introduce to you ec tomorrow
    b. *[A Maria]$_i$ **te** apresento ec$_i$ amanhã.
       M. I'll introduce to you tomorrow.

In Barbosa (1996a, forthcoming), I argue that the different patterns of clitic placement in EP can be accounted for once we assume that QP fronting and wh-movement involve A'-movement, whereas CLLD and Topicalization involve base-generation of the overt topic in a position of adjunction to the XP that is predicated of it. In the particular case of Topicalization, I assume Raposo's (1996) analysis, according to which the gap in argument position is the trace of an empty operator, which serves as an open position whose reference is fixed by the topic. The topic itself is directly merged in front of the clause (but see Duarte 1987 for an alternative analysis):

(69) [A Maria] [Op$_k$ [apresento-te t$_k$ amanhã]]

The QP fronting in EP forms patterns with Italian Focus movement in allowing a topic to intervene between the extracted phrase and inflection (Duarte 1987):

(70) Pouco afecto, aos meus filhos, nunca darei!
    little affection, to my children never will-give
    'Little affection, to my children, I will never give.'

In EP it is possible to have two fronted QPs in the left periphery of the clause, and the subject can appear to be sandwiched between the two:

(71) [Nem ao seu melhor amigo]$_1$ a Maria [alguma ajuda]$_2$ ofereceu t$_2$ t$_1$!
    not even to her best friend the Maria some help offered

Clearly, the subject in (71) is not sitting in Spec-IP. In view of examples such as (70), where a topic appears between a fronted phrase and inflection, nothing prevents (71) from being analyzed as an instance of subject dislocation (with the DP *a Maria* being base-generated as topic-doubled by a resumptive *pro* subject). In such an analysis the negative phrase occupies the Spec position of a higher head, the subject occupies the intermediate topic position, and the lower fronted object occupies a lower position. Thus, there are two landing sites for A-bar movement to the left of inflection, and topics may occupy the space between them. Example (71) is straightforwardly analyzed once we let A-bar movement target Spec-IP. The nonspecific indefinite raises to Spec-IP; the topic construed with the subject is adjoined to IP, and the higher negative phrase is in Spec-CP:

(72) [$_{CP}$ [Nem ao seu melhor amigo]$_1$[$_{C'}$ [ø][$_{IP}$ A Maria [$_{IP}$ [alguma ajuda]$_2$[$_{I'}$ ofereceu t$_2$ t$_1$]]]]]

Hence in Portuguese, too, Spec-IP can be the landing site for A-bar movement.

Non-d-linked question operators require strict adjacency with inflection in root clauses in EP:

(73)   Quando (*a Maria) chegou (a Maria)?
       when (the M.) arrived (the M.)

Since the specifier of the highest Infl head can be the landing site for A-bar movement in EP, nothing prevents a root question from being analyzed as involving movement of the question operator to Spec-IP. The subject sits in its base position:

(74)   [$_{IP}$ [quando]$_y$ [$_{I'}$ [$_I$ [chegou]$_k$] [$_{VP}$ t$_k$ a Maria t$_y$]]]

In Rizzi's (1991) hypothesis that the wh-feature in root clauses is located in Infl, obligatory adjacency between the fronted phrase and inflection follows from attraction of the wh-element to the specifier of the head that contains the wh-feature, and we do not need to assume V-to-C. Hence, Portuguese and the other languages discussed use the same strategy to check the wh-feature in root clauses.[8]

So far, I have discussed only the Null Subject languages. However, it can be argued that wh-elements may target Spec-IP in Romance even in a non-NSL such as French.

2.5.   French

French has a variety of ways in which to construct interrogative clauses (see De Wind 1995; Drijkoningen 1997; Hulk 1993; Kayne 1975, 1984; Kayne & Pollock 1978). Of interest to us here is the variety of standard French, where inversion of the subject is required in interrogatives. Three types of inversion can be distinguished in standard French: Complex Inversion, Pronominal Inversion, and Stylistic Inversion. Pronominal inversion is illustrated in (75):

(75)   Quand est-elle venue?
       when is-she come

In (75) the pronominal clitic subject appears between the auxiliary and the verb. In French, Aux-subject inversion is restricted to pronominal clitics. When the subject is nonpronominal, it can never invert with the auxiliary in French. It either appears in VP-final position or at the front of the clause, in which case it must be doubled by a clitic. These two constructions are illustrated below:

(76)   *Complex Inversion*:
       Quand Marie est-elle venue?
       when M. is-she come

(77)   *Stylistic Inversion*
       Quand est venue Marie?
       when is come M.

The variant without the clitic, Stylistic Inversion (SI), is different from Pronominal Inversion (PI) and Complex Inversion (CI). Stylistic Inversion has two
distinctive features: First, the subject, which is always nominal, is in VP-final
position; second, SI is permitted in root clauses, as well as in embedded clauses:

(78)   Je me demande quand est venue Marie.
       I me ask when is come M.

Pronominal Inversion and Complex Inversion, by contrast, are restricted to root
environments:

(79)   a. *Je me demande quand est-elle venue.
       b. *Je me demande quand Marie est-elle venue.

Kayne and Pollock (1978) proposed that SI is derived by a rule that moves
the subject to the right. More recently, a number of researchers have argued that
the subject in SI sits in its base position, inside the VP (see Deprez 1990 and De
Wind 1995). Since the evidence presented by these authors is rather compelling,
I adopt their proposal without further argument. Concerning the issue of the
landing site of the question operator in SI, there is some indication that the wh-
constituent in Stylistic Inversion targets Spec-IP. I review this evidence next.
    One of the most striking features of SI is that it depends on whether a con-
stituent is fronted in the syntax. Thus, SI is unavailable in yes-no questions but
is fine when an argument is fronted:

(80)   *Viendra Jean?
       will-come J.?

(81)   Qui a vu Jean?
       who has seen J.
       'Who did J. see?'

The contrast above suggests that the following generalization holds: SI is possible just in case the specifier position of some designated head is filled in overt
syntax (see Kayne 1984). Note that the ungrammaticality of (80) is not due to
the failure of the Nominative Case assignment to the postverbal subject: In (81)
the subject doesn't raise and yet it has Case. According to the Minimalist Program (Chomsky 1995, 1998), the principle that requires that the specifier of a
designated head be filled in overt syntax is the EPP, not Case. Note that equivalents to (80) are fine in the Null Subject (NS) Romance languages. In the view
of the *pro*-drop parameter sketched in the previous section, what characterizes
the *pro*-drop languages is the fact that agreement has the ability to check the

EPP. Thus, in the NS equivalents to (80), the EPP is checked. In French, however, agreement doesn't have this capacity, so (80) violates the EPP.

If we assume that (80) is out because the EPP fails to be checked, it follows that the fronted constituent is capable of checking the EPP in (81). In other words, it follows that the fronted constituent in (81) raises to the specifier position of the head that contains the EPP feature. According to standard assumptions, this head is the highest Infl head. Hence, I suggest that the question operator is attracted to Spec-IP, where it checks *both* the EPP and the wh-feature in Infl. In line with the Minimalist Program, I assume that the EPP and Nominative Case are dissociated. In (81) the Case and *phi*-features of the subject are checked at LF; the EPP is checked by the question operator.

Note that whenever SI applies in embedded questions, a topic may not intervene between the wh-item and inflection:

(82)   *Je me demande bien à qui, *de temps en temps*, téléphone Marie. [Deprez 1990]

The impossibility of (82) is parallel to the Romanian, Catalan, and Iberian Spanish examples discussed above. A common explanation can be given as soon as it is assumed that, in Romance in general, Spec-IP *can* be the target for wh-movement. This hypothesis captures a wide range of facts concerning wh-triggered inversion in this language family and immediately accounts for the absence of the cluster of properties typical of Germanic Aux-Subject inversion, namely, the lack of root and embedded asymmetries and the impossibility of the order Aux-Subject-V.

3.   Categorial Selection, Complementizers, and Parameterization

Even though French SI has properties that are common to wh-triggered inversion in Catalan, Romanian, Iberian Spanish, and Italian, these languages differ from French in one important aspect. In embedded questions in French the SI option (83a) coexists with the option with no inversion (83b):

(83)   a.   Je me demande bien à qui téléphone Marie.
       b.   Je me demande bien à qui, *de temps en temps*, Marie téléphone.

Recall that the counterparts to (83b) are bad in Iberian Spanish, Catalan, and Romanian and marginal at best in standard Italian. Portuguese is very much like French in this regard: In embedded questions, the order wh-subject-V is possible (see Âmbar 1988) and co-occurs with the inverted option (84a):

(84)   a.   Sabes **quando** *a Maria* chegou?
            Know-2sg when the M. arrived
       b.   Sabes **quando** chegou *a Maria?*
            Know-2sg when arrived the M.
            'Do you know when Mary arrived?'

In addition, a sentential adverb or a topic PP may appear immediately to the right of a question operator in embedded questions:

(85) a. Sabes **a quem**, *de vez em quando*, a Maria telefona?
          Know-2sg to whom, every now and then, the M. calls
          'Do you know who, every now and then, Mary calls?'
      b. Sabes **a que horas**, *ao Pedro*, mais lhe convirá lá ir?
          Know-2s at what time, for Peter, more to-him would-be-convenient to go there
          'Do you know at what time it is more convenient for Peter to go there?'

Sentence (84a) and (85a, b) can be analyzed only in terms of the attraction of the question operator to the CP system.

Recall Rizzi's (1991) wh-criterion. According to that formulation, a wh-phrase must be in a Spec-head relation with a clausal head marked +wh. For Rizzi, there are in principle two loci for the wh-specification on a clausal head: (A) the head that contains the *independent* tense specification of the +interrogative sentence; (B) the embedded C, where the occurrence of the wh-specification is determined by lexical selection.

This formulation of the wh-criterion enables Rizzi (1991) to account for the root and embedded asymmetry observed in Germanic. In root clauses, I must raise to C so that the required configuration is obtained. In embedded clauses, C is the head marked [+wh] through lexical selection.

Now consider French (or Portuguese) in light of this formulation of the wh-criterion. In root clauses, the head that contains the wh-feature is the highest T-head (Fin). Since, as argued, Spec-IP can host question operators, the wh-criterion is trivially satisfied at the IP level. In embedded clauses, however, two options appear to exist: C may be the locus of the wh-feature, in which case it attracts the wh-phrase:

(86) Je me demande bien [$_{CP}$ à qui [$_{C'}$ [C] [$_{IP}$ *de temps en temps*]
      [$_{IP}$ Marie téléphone t]]]]

or Fin/I is the locus of the wh-feature, in which case the wh-item is attracted to Spec-Fin/I, yielding SI:

(87) Je me demande bien [$_{IP/FinP}$ à qui téléphone Marie]

Now consider Catalan, Iberian Spanish, and Italian. In these varieties, embedded C doesn't seem to ever be the locus of the wh-feature, or we would expect to find the order wh-Topic/Subject-Fin, as we do in French and Portuguese. This order, however, is ungrammatical in Catalan, Romanian, and Iberian Spanish and marginal in Italian, as extensively discussed above. Instead, we find the order Topic-wh-Infl as the favored one:

(88)   a. Mi domando, *il premio Nobel,* **a chi** lo potrebbero dare?
           'I wonder, the Nobel Prize, to whom they could give it?'
       b. No sé *en Joan* **quan** el veuré.
           Not know.1s the J. when him will-I-see
           'Joan, I don't know when I'll see him.' [Sola 1992, p. 224]

We have seen that a topic may not immediately precede the subordinator complementizer *che* in Italian, so (88) can be analyzed only with the topic adjoined
to a projection that is lower than C:

(89)   Mi domando [$_{CP}$ [$_C$ ∅] [il premio Nobel [a chi lo potrebbero dare]]]?

Thus, it is fair to conclude that C is *not* the locus of the wh-feature in this
language set. In French and Portuguese, by contrast, embedded C can be the
locus of the wh-specification. Before we propose a formulation of the parameter responsible for this difference between French and Portuguese and Italian, Catalan, Romanian, and Iberian Spanish, the following question needs to
be addressed: When I is the locus of the wh-specification, is CP projected?
Recall that according to Rizzi (1991), Force and Fin are invariably projected.
This being so, the stylistic inversion example in (82a) is analyzed as in (89):

(90)   Je me demande bien [$_{CP}$ [$_{C'}$ C] [$_{IP/FinP}$ à qui téléphone Marie]]]]

For Rizzi (1991), the CP status of the embedded clausal projection is required by the selectional requirements of the main verb. However, one should
examine this argument more carefully and consider what is meant by "selection." Recall that in Rizzi's formulation of the wh-criterion, in embedded contexts C is [+wh] in virtue of selection. However, the wh-phrase in (90) is overtly
attracted to a projection that is lower than C, so it can't be the case that the wh-
feature is located in C. Selection for particular terminal nodes or features contained in them (*lexical* selection, in the sense of Pesetsky 1992) is generally
strictly local, so C should be the head that bears the selected feature, contrary
to fact. Thus, it is highly unlikely that l-selection is what imposes CP status on
an embedded question.

Semantic selection doesn't appear to be relevant either. Grimshaw (1979)
shows that semantic selection is satisfied at LF, so the issue of which of the clausal
heads, C or Fin, is specified as [+wh] is not relevant for semantic interpretation.
This observation entails that *categorial* selection is the only mechanism of the
grammar that requires embedded questions to be CPs. However, there is good
reason to doubt that c-selection plays a role as an autonomous mechanism in the
grammar (see Boskovic 1996; Pesetsky 1982, 1992).

Boskovic (1996), in particular, has argued explicitly that as long as CP
status is not required by lexical properties or other constraints independent of
c-selection, clausal complements may be IPs. One of the arguments he uses is

based on the Romanian facts discussed above. Recall the restrictions on the distribution of the subjunctive complementizer in Romanian. The generalization underlying the distribution of *ca* appears to be that *ca* is obligatory as long as there is a topic in the left periphery of the clause. Thus, *ca* is obligatory just in case a topic (including subject topics) precedes *sa**, even though it may be omitted with a preverbal focus in some dialects:

(91)　a.　Vreau **(ca)** mîine *să* **termine** *Ion* cartea asta.
　　　　　[I] want that tomorrow *să* finish John this book.
　　　b.　Vreau (ca) MÎINE *să* vină Ion.
　　　　　[I] want tomorrow *să* come John.
　　　　　'I want John to come tomorrow.'

In the absence of any material in the front of *sa**, *ca* is preferably absent:

(92)　Vreau *să* **termine** *Ion* cartea asta.

The contrast between Focalization and topics suggests that what is at stake here are the X-bar theoretical notions: *substitution* vs. *adjunction*. Relying on this difference and on the assumption that adjunction to an argument is banned (Chomsky 1986; McCloskey 1996), Boskovic (1996) suggests that the distribution of *ca* is captured once we let complements of volitionals in Romanian be bare IPs. Boskovic proposes that whenever *ca* is absent, CP doesn't project. Thus, in (92) the complement of the volitional verb is a bare IP:

(93)　vreau [$_{IP}$ *să* **termine** *Ion* cartea asta]

Assuming that FinP may be a complement of the volitional verb in Romanian and that topics are in a configuration of adjunction, we see that (94a) is straightforwardly ruled out by the ban on adjunction to an argument:

(94)　a.　Vreau mîine *să* **termine** *Ion* cartea asta.
　　　b.　Vreau [$_{IP}$ mîine [$_{IP}$ *să* **termine** *Ion* cartea asta]]

Example (95a), which contains a focused adverbial, is analyzed as in (95b), with substitution into Spec-FinP:

(95)　a.　Vreau MÎINE *să* vină Ion
　　　b.　Vreau [$_{FinP}$ MÎINE [$_{Fin'}$ *să* vină Ion]]

For a topic to appear in the left periphery of a selected subjunctive clause in Romanian, CP must be projected, yielding (96):

(96)　Vreau [$_{CP}$ ca [$_{IP}$ mîine] [$_{IP}$ *să* **termine** *Ion* cartea asta]]]
　　　[I] want that tomorrow *să* finish John this book.

This means that CP status is not imposed by selection but rather by an independent principle, namely, the ban on adjunction to an argument. Hence, I conclude that Boskovic's (1996) proposal to eliminate categorial selection as an autonomous mechanism of the grammar has strong empirical support.

Recall that Rizzi (1997) suggests that the Topic-Focus field is activated whenever needed, even though he assumed that ForceP status is imposed by selection. The Romanian data, however, suggest that selection imposes no categorial restrictions on clausal projections. Eliminating c-selection while incorporating Rizzi's idea that some projections are activated when needed, I adopt Boskovic's proposal according to which C is projected whenever needed. One such case in which C must project is when a topic is adjoined to IP. In this case, C must be part of the numeration so that the derivation doesn't violate the ban against adjunction to an argument.

With this conclusion in mind, we now turn to an analysis of embedded questions in Romance. Recall that French and Portuguese have two options in embedded questions, one with "inversion" and the other without "inversion." I use French for illustration:

(97)   a. Je me demande bien à qui téléphone Marie.
       b. Je me demande bien à qui Marie téléphone.

If we let embedded clauses be CPs or IPs, we account for the existence of both options. In (97b), C is projected and the subject is sitting in Spec-IP, where it checks the EPP. The wh-feature in C attracts the wh-phrase:

(98)   Je me demande bien [$_{CP}$ à qui [$_{C'}$ C$_{+wh}$] [$_{IP/FinP}$ Marie téléphone]]]]

In (97a) no CP is projected, the embedded clause is a bare FinP(= IP), Fin is specified +wh and the wh-phrase is attracted to Spec-IP:

(99)   Je me demande bien [$_{IP/FinP}$ à qui téléphone Marie]

Note that the configuration in (99) is also a possibility in all of the other Romance languages. As long as there is no topic adjoined to IP, nothing prevents a bare IP from being a complement of the higher verb, so the Portuguese example (100a)—as well as any of its equivalents in Iberian Spanish, Romanian, Italian, and Catalan—may very well be analyzed as in (100b), with the wh-item in Spec-IP and the subject in postverbal position:

(100) a. Sabes **quando** chegou *a Maria?*
           know-2sg when arrived the M.
           'Do you know when M. arrived?'
       b. Sabes [$_{IP}$ quando [$_{I'}$ [chegou] [$_{VP}$ . . . a Maria]

Whenever a topic is adjoined to IP (or Spec-IP is filled by a quantificational operator of the sort discussed by Vallduví 1992), CP must project, in which case the wh-element is attracted to Spec-CP:

(101)   a. Sabes **a que horas**, ao Pedro, mais lhe convirá lá ir?
            Know-2s at what time, for Peter, more to-him would-be-convenient to go
              there
            'Do you know at what time it is more convenient for Peter to go there?'
        b. Sabes [$_{CP}$ a que horas [$_{C'}$ [$_C$] [$_{IP}$ ao Pedro] [$_{IP}$ mais lhe convirá lá ir]]

Now recall that the order V-wh-topic/subject-Infl is bad in Catalan and Iberian Spanish and marginal in Italian. Instead, we find the order V-Topic-wh-Infl:

(102)   Mi domando, il premio Nobel, a chi lo potrebbero dare?

In (102) we see a topic in the left periphery of the clause in addition to a wh-phrase. This means that the embedded clause must be a CP, or else the topic would be adjoined to an argument:

(103)   Mi domando [$_{CP}$ [$_C$ ø] [il premio Nobel [a chi lo potrebbero dare]]]?

On the assumption that wh-movement is triggered by feature checking, the fact that C is not an attractor for wh-arguments in Italian, Iberian Spanish, and Catalan can only be due to its featural makeup. I suggest that the null complementizer in Italian, Iberian Spanish, and Catalan embedded interrogatives is unspecified with respect to the feature [±wh]. That certain complementizers appear to be "transparent" with respect to the wh-feature is shown by the complementizer *che* in Catalan (and also Spanish), which is compatible with an embedded question:

(104)   *Catalan*:
        a. Pregunten **que** la feina **qui** la farà.
            ask.3p that the work who it fut.3s.do
            Lit. 'They are asking that the work who will do?'
            'They are asking who will do the work'
        b. Pregunten **que** el Lluc **qui** va veure.
            Lit.'They are asking that Lluc who saw.'
            'They are asking who Lluc saw'   [Vallduví 1992, p. 118]

It can't be the case that *que* in (104) is [–wh] or there would be a feature mismatch at LF. This particular behavior of *que* appears to be an idiosyncrasy of Catalan and Iberian Spanish since examples such as (104) have not been described for most of the other Romance languages. I interpret this observation as an indication that the featural makeup of C may vary cross-linguistically. In Spanish and Catalan the overt complementizer *que* is not specified for the feature [-wh]. Now, by hypothesis, Italian has a null counterpart to Spanish and Catalan *que*. The Italian null C is not specified with respect to [±wh]. Hence, it is never an attractor for wh-phrases but is compatible with a question embedded under it:

(105)   Mi domando [$_{CP}$ [$_C$ ∅] [il premio Nobel [a chi [$_{I\,[+wh]}$ lo potrebbero dare]]]?

In (105) null C cannot be [–wh] since there would be a feature mismatch with [+wh] T. Our hypothesis here is that null C is not specified for [+wh] either, and hence it never gets to be an attractor for wh-phrases. Catalan and Spanish appear to also have a null counterpart to *que* since examples similar to Italian (105) are fine in Catalan and Spanish.

I have stated that C is a wh-attractor in French and Portuguese. This means that C in these languages is specified with respect to [+wh]. I propose that the parameter that distinguishes French and Portuguese from Italian, Catalan, and Iberian Spanish is the following: In the latter, null C is unspecified with respect to [±]wh; in the former, C must be specified as [±wh].

Now consider what happens when C in French or Portuguese is [–wh]. In theory, there are two possibilities: Either –wh-C is spelled out or –wh-C can be null. In either case, C, being specified as [–wh], should not be able to embed an IP with a +wh phrase in its Spec because of feature mismatch. This observation predicts that French or Portuguese should not have equivalents to Italian (105) or to Catalan (104). In effect, this prediction is borne out:

(106)   a.   *Je me demande à Jean, ce que lui a donné Marie.
             I me ask to John, what to him has given M.
             'I wonder, to John, what has given M.'
        b.   *Je me demande que à Jean, ce que lui a donné Marie.

(107)   a.   *Sabes *ao Pedro* **quando** mais lhe convirá lá ir?
             know-2SG to-the P. when more to-him is convenient to go there
             'Do you know, for Peter, when it is more convenient to go there?'
        b.   *Pergunto-me que, ao Pedro, quando mais lhe convirá lá ir.

Sentences (106a) and (107a) show that a topic may not immediately precede an embedded wh-question in French or Portuguese. I have argued that a topic can only precede IP when C projects. If C projects, it must be specified as [±wh]. Suppose C is [+wh]. Then it should attract the wh-phrase, and (106a) and (107b) crash because the wh-feature in C fails to be checked in overt syntax. Now suppose that C is –wh and null. Examples (106a) and (107a) are also predicted to be bad because of feature mismatch: that is, [–wh] C is incompatible with [+wh] I. Finally, suppose that [–wh] C must be spelled out, yielding (106b) and (107b). Such a configuration should also be ruled out because of feature mismatch.

Thus, the hypothesis that the featural content of C is what distinguishes French and Portuguese from Italian, Catalan, and Spanish rightly predicts that the possibility of wh-attraction to Spec-CP should correlate with the impossibility of adjunction to an IP with a wh-phrase in its Spec.[9]

The only question that remains to be addressed now is how C is endowed with the wh-feature in embedded environments in EP and French on the assumption that categorial selection plays no role in the grammar. Pesetsky (1992) notes that regardless of whether or not c-selection is eliminated, we need selection for terminal elements, which he refers to as *lexical selection* (L-selection). This term does not refer to syntactic categories but rather to individual lexical items, such as particular prepositions or specific features like [±finite]. Thus, I suggest that once C is part of the numeration, [+wh] C is selected by the verbs that semantically select Question [Q]. Lexical selection for [+wh] C occurs only in those languages in which null C is specified for [±]wh, such as EP, French, or English. In Italian, Spanish, or Catalan, null C is unspecified with respect to [±wh], so the question of selection for a particular value of this feature on null C doesn't arise.

4. When Root Questions Are CPs

Even though the featural content of subordinating C brings French and Portuguese together, the non-*pro*-drop nature of French sets it apart from all the other Romance languages discussed, including Portuguese. Since French is non-*pro*-drop, preverbal subject constructions are genuine instances of subject raising to Spec-IP. Thus, in a question, a conflict arises between the requirement to check the wh-phrase and raising of a non-wh-subject in the overt syntax. A non-wh-subject checks the EPP but cannot check the wh-feature in Fin. This conflict even more problematic in those cases in which the subject is a pronominal clitic. French weak pronouns (in the sense of Cardinaletti & Starke 1994) cannot stay in situ, so whenever the numeration contains a weak subject pronoun, Stylistic Inversion is not an option:

(108)   *Quand est venu-t-il?
         when is come he

According to the framework of assumptions developed so far, the only wh-questions in which a non-wh-subject is allowed to raise in the syntax are those in which C is part of the numeration. In French, as argued, lexically selected C is always specified as [±wh]. Consequently, CPs embedded under a verb that semantically selects [Question] will always involve checking of the wh-feature against [+wh] C. This enables the subject to raise in overt syntax, as occurs in (109a):

(109)   a. Je me demande bien à qui elle téléphone.
         b. Je me demande bien [$_{CP}$ à qui [[$_C$ +wh] [$_{IP}$ elle téléphone]]]

Now consider the predictions that our theory makes in the case of root questions with a weak pronoun as subject or a preverbal lexical non-wh-subject. Recall that in root questions, I is the locus of the wh-feature (lexical selection fails to license a +wh-C), so even when C projects and the wh-phrase raises up to C, the wh-criterion will not be satisfied:

(110)   [$_{CP}$wh [[$_C$ ø] [$_{IP}$ Subject/pronoun [[$_{I\ [+wh]}$]]]]]

In (110) the wh-criterion fails to be checked, so the derivation doesn't converge, yielding the following sentence, which is bad in standard French, the
variety we are analyzing:

(111)   *Quand Marie/elle est venu?
        when M. /she is come

Now (110) is exactly the context that yields Subject-Aux inversion in English.
However, Infl raising doesn't appear to be an option in French, as shown by
the fact that (112) is unacceptable:

(112)   *Quand est Marie venue?

Instead of (112) or (111), what we find is the construction known as Complex Inversion:

(113)   *Complex Inversion*
        Quand Marie est-elle venue?

The impossibility of (112) has led a number of authors to the conclusion that
I-to-C movement does not apply in French (De Wind 1995; Drijkoningen 1997;
Hulk 1993; Noonan 1989). The main idea behind the analyses of Complex
Inversion developed by these authors is that it arises whenever both the wh-
operator and the subject need to check their features against the features of the
same functional head (Infl, according to my analysis). Here I will not propose
an analysis of this construction. For my present purposes it suffices to observe
that Complex Inversion (as well as Subject Clitic Inversion) is the instantiation
of the option of expanding a C-node.[10] This option has a different guise in root
questions as opposed to embedded questions, because in the former C is not
the locus of the wh-feature. The fact that the other Romance languages discussed lack Complex Inversion follows from the Null Subject property: Since
subjects do not raise to Spec-IP to check an L-related feature, the configuration in (110) does not arise in a Null Subject language.[11]

5. Conclusions

In this chapter, I argue that the crucial property that distinguishes Romance
from Germanic is that [+wh] Infl does not raise up to the C. I argue that the
wh-criterion *can* be checked against the highest Infl head in all of Romance
and that the wh-feature may be located in Infl in root, as well as in embedded,
clauses. In addition, I present evidence in support of Boskovic's (1996) proposal, according to which clausal projections may be bare IPs unless further

structure is independently required. Since the wh-criterion can be satisfied at the IP level in Romance, root questions may be bare IPs. Obligatory adjacency between Infl and the wh-constituent follows.

Following recent proposals (Alexiadou & Anagnostopoulou 1998; Barbosa 1995; Pollock 1997) according to which the Null Subject Languages are languages in which rich agreement checks the EPP and the N-features of Infl, I claim that in these languages Spec-IP is not an A-position. In the absence of A'-movement to Spec-IP, Infl doesn't project a specifier. This property accounts for certain differences between French and the other Romance languages. In the latter, Spec-IP doesn't necessarily need to be filled in overt syntax. In French, however, the EPP can only be satisfied by overt raising to Spec-IP.

One important difference distinguishes French from English, however. In French, the EPP feature doesn't necessarily need to be checked by a subject: A wh-phrase in Spec-IP may satisfy *both* the wh-criterion and the EPP. Hence, both root and embedded questions may be bare IPs in French as long as the subject is allowed to stay in situ.

Embedded questions can in principle be bare IPs in all of the Romance languages under discussion (wh-checking can be done against the highest T-head). They can also involve additional layers, depending on whether the Topic or Focus layer is activated. The cross-linguistic variation detected for the relative position of the lexical subject and the wh-constituent is due to variation in the structure of the 'left-periphery', combined with the featural makeup of complementizers in the inventory of each language. I argue that in Italian, Catalan, and Spanish, null C is underspecified for the feature [±] wh. Consequently, it is never the locus of the feature [+wh] and hence it is never an attractor for wh-arguments; on the other hand, the presence of a null C in these languages doesn't interfere with semantic selection since C is "transparent" with respect to the feature [±wh]. As a result, wh-arguments must invariably raise to Spec-IP, including in those derivations in which the clausal argument is a CP. This accounts for the obligatoriness of subject inversion in embedded questions in Catalan and Spanish. The marginal acceptability of Italian embedded questions with wh-S-V order is due to the availability in this language of a FocusPhrase between C and IP, which may under certain conditions host a wh-phrase in its Spec. In Portuguese and French, subordinating C is fully specified for the feature [±wh], so whenever embedded questions project up to the CP level, [+wh] C is lexically selected, thus attracting the wh-operator and yielding the order wh-S-V.

Even though root questions may be bare IPs in Romance, additional structure (a CP layer) may be required. In French, root questions must be CPs whenever a non-wh-subject raises overtly and checks the EPP feature in Infl. Since Spec-IP is not available for the wh-element, CP must project to host the wh-element in its Spec. This yields the constructions known as French Complex Inversion and Subject Clitic Inversion.

If these conclusions are right, the question arises of why, in English (or in Germanic, quite generally), the option of checking the wh-feature against the highest Infl head is not available. I leave this problem for further research.

NOTES

1. Rizzi (1997) adopts a different take on the matter of topics. In the spirit of Kayne's (1994) proposal, according to which mutual c-command is excluded from the grammar, Rizzi postulates a recursive Top node that projects its own X' schema. This Top node "defines a kind of 'higher predication.'" The differences between Topic and Focus are due to the kind of relation established between the phrase in an A'-position (Topic or Focus) and the element in argument position. As a configuration, there is no difference between Topic and Focus. Interpretive constraints prevent FocusP from being recursive and allow recursion of TopicP. In section 3, we see that a configurational difference between Focus and Topic is crucial in the analysis of the distribution of the subjunctive complementizer *ca* in Romanian (Boskovic 1996). We see that the distribution of *ca* depends on the assumption that Topics are in a position of adjunction, whereas Focus fronting involves substitution into a specifier. For this reason, I adopt the analysis described in the text instead of Rizzi's.

2. This problem is noted in Rizzi (1991) and Rizzi and Roberts (1989). In view of the observation that adverbs and floating quantifiers may appear immediately to the right of Aux, these authors conclude that the restriction in question cannot be due to incorporation of the Aux with the participle, and they propose a case-theoretic solution. In particular, they suggest that I-to-C movement destroys the context of Nominative Case assignment, which in Romance would be limited to the Spec-head configuration with Agr. Hence (7a), (8a) and (9a) are ruled out because the subject fails to be checked for Case. This solution, however, is clearly unsatisfactory. First, it raises the question of why I-to-C movement should interfere with Case checking in Romance but not in Germanic. Second, it immediately runs into problems when we consider other cases that arguably involve I-to-C and yet allow the order Aux-Subject-Participle. The relevant paradigm is the following (from Rizzi 1982):

(i)　a.　Se lui avesse capito al volo, tutto sarebbe andato bene.
　　　　 "If he had understood immediately, everything would have gone
　　　　 smoothly."
　　　b.　*Se avesse lui capito al volo, tutto sarebbe andato bene.
　　　c.　Avesse lui capito al volo, tutto sarebbe andato bene.
　　　d.　*Se lui avesse capito al volo, tutto sarebbe andato bene.

This paradigm shows that the order Aux-Subject-Participle is possible just in case the complementizer is absent [compare (ib) with (ic)]. Taking complementary distribution with an overt complementizer as a test for I-to-C, we conclude that this movement does not interfere with nominative Case checking in Italian. Hence the Case-theoretic solution presented in Rizzi and Roberts (1989) is untenable (see Poletto 1997 for a similar point).

3. In Catalan the only possible order in questions is VOS, so there is no evidence that V raises:

(i)　*Què ficarem nosaltres al calaix?
　　　 what put-FUT-1p we in-the-drawer
　　　 What will we put in the drawer?'

4. The northern Italian examples show without question that the landing site for the question operator is not the Spec of the Infl head that contains the verbal cluster.

Below I argue that in standard Italian question operators target the Spec of highest Infl head. However, the dialects require additional structure in view of the fact that they have obligatory subject clitics that need to be in the checking domain of Infl (see note 8 for discussion).

5. In the analysis developed in the text, we lack an explanation for why Focus and question operators are incompatible in root questions in Italian:

(i)   *A GIANNI che cosa hai detto (, non Piero)?
      'TO GIANNI what did you tell (, not to P.)?'

However, it is not unreasonable to assume that, for a root sentence to have interrogative force, the propositional content of the sentence must be under the scope of the head marked [+wh]. According to the analysis proposed in the text, (i) is analyzed as follows:

(ii) [A GIANNI [$_{Foc'}$ [$_{F\,oc}$] [che cosa [$_{I'}$ [$_{I\,+wh}$ hai] [$_{VP\ldots}$]]]]]

In (ii) the highest head is [+Focus], not [+wh], so (ii) doesn't have interrogative force and violates Full Interpretation. In the case of an embedded question, matters are different because of semantic selection. Since the main verb semantically selects [Q], it suffices that the embedded clause satisfies the wh-criterion for Full Interpretation to be satisfied.

6. According to Dobrovie-Sorin (1994), the Aux position is occupied by the perfect auxiliary *fi* 'be', and under Adv we find a restricted class of clitic adverbs: *mai* 'again', *prea* 'too'.

7. These examples are from Manuela Ungureanu (personal communication). Similar data can also be found in Rivero (1987). There appears to be some dialectal variation in the possibility of dropping *ca* in front of Focus. Although some speakers may drop *ca* in front of focused elements (but cannot drop it in front of topics), some others cannot drop it in front of focus either. I thank an anonymous reviewer for pointing this out to me.

8. The assumption that preverbal "subjects" in the NSLs are topics doubled by subject *pro* predicts that a subject should be able to precede question operators in root questions. This prediction is fulfilled:

(i)   A Maria quando virá?
      the Maria when will-come

In addition, this hypothesis predicts that whenever the subject is one of those expressions that cannot be discourse topics, it should not be allowed to precede the question operator. Recall that I argue that these expressions are extracted by A'-movement when they appear preverbally, so they should be in complementary distribution with a fronted question operator. This prediction is also fulfilled:

(ii) a. *Alguém quando virá?
          someone when will-come
          Quando virá alguém?
          When will-come someone

9. This generalization can be phrased as a conditional:

(i)   If a language has overt wh-movement to Spec-CP and to Spec-IP, it
       shouldn't allow adjunction to an IP with a wh-phrase in its Spec.

Note that (i) is not a biconditional; that is, the impossibility of adjunction to an IP with
a wh-phrase in its Spec doesn't necessarily entail that the language in question also
has overt movement to Spec-CP, for example, Romanian *sa** subjunctives. Romanian
has a complementizer that is exclusively used in subjunctives: *ca*. This complementizer
is incompatible with an embedded question:

(ii)   Nu stia (*ca) unde *să* plece.
       Not know-3SG that where *să* go
       He doesn't know where to go.'

Example (ii) shows that *ca* must be negatively specified for the wh-feature. When
ca is omitted, the embedded clause is a bare IP, so we predict that a topic should not be
allowed to adjoin to the embedded subjunctive. The difference between Romanian
subjunctives and Italian, Catalan, and Spanish is that the latter have a null C that is
underspecified for the feature [±wh]; Romanian lacks such a null complementizer, at
least in subjunctives.

10. Other Romance varieties that have Subject Clitic Inversion are the northern
Italian dialects discussed in Poletto (1997). These have *obligatory* Subject Clitic Inversion in root questions even though they lack Complex Inversion. In embedded clauses
the clitic may be preverbal. These dialects differ from French in that subject clitics are
invariably present and do not alternate with a lexical subject. Elsewhere (Barbosa 1995),
I argue that preverbal subject constructions in these languages are instances of left
dislocation of the lexical subject: The clitic itself is a sort of incorporated pronoun,
which checks the EPP feature. In this light, it is not surprising that these varieties lack
Complex Inversion (the lexical subject itself doesn't raise to Spec-IP for feature checking). Since in these varieties subject clitics are obligatory and, by hypothesis, need to
check their nominal features against Infl, wh-movement may not target Spec-IP. Hence,
wh-questions in these varieties must project up to the CP level regardless of whether
they are root questions or embedded questions. An analysis of the dialects is obviously
outside the scope of this chapter. In any case, the major point I wish to make here is
that in the dialects both root and embedded questions cannot be bare IPs because of
the obligatory presence of subject clitics

11. Even though the NSLs lack Complex Inversion, there are cases in which root
questions project up to the CP level. This is the case of root questions in which the wh-
consituent is a partitive phrase or an adjunct:

(i)   *Portuguese* (Âmbar 1988):
       Em que dia a Maria chegou?
       On what day the Maria arrived:

(ii)   *Spanish* (Torrego 1984)
       ¿Cómo Juan ha conseguido meter allí a su hijo?
       'How has John managed to get his son in there?'

De Wind (1995) and Dobrovie Sorin (1990) suggest that partitive wh-phrases are base-generated directly in Spec-CP. Rizzi (1990) makes the same claim for certain wh-adjuncts. Thus, in these particular constructions, the CP layer is projected, in which case a topic subject may intervene between the wh-phrase and the wh-phrase in Spec-CP. In sum, root questions in Romance may be bare IPs unless a CP layer is independently required.

REFERENCES

Adams, M. (1987). "From Old French to the Theory of *Pro*-Drop. *NLLT* 5, 1–32.
Alexiadou, A., & H. Anagnostopoulou. (1998). "Parameterizing AGR: Word Order, V-movement and EPP Checking." *NLLT* 16, 491–539.
Âmbar, M. (1988). "Para uma Sintaxe da Inversão Sujeito Verbo em Português." Ph.D. diss., University of Lisbon.
———. (1998). "Towards a Definition of CP—Evidence from TopicFocusP and EvaluativeP." Talk presented at *Going Romance 1997*, Groningen.
Barbosa, P. (1993). "Clitic Placement in Old Romance and European Portuguese." *CLS 29: Papers from the Twenty-ninth Regional Meeting of the Chicago Linguistic Society*. CLS, Chicago, Ill.
———. (1995). "Null Subjects." Ph.D. diss., MIT, Cambridge, Mass.
———. (1996a.) "Clitic Placement in European Portuguese and the Position of Subjects." In A. Halpern & A. Zwicky (eds.), *Approaching Second: Second Position Clitics and Related Phenomena*. CSLI Publications, Stanford, Calif., 1–40.
———. (1996b). "In Defense of Right Adjunction for Head-movement in Romance." In A.-M. Di Scullio (ed.), *Configurations: Essays on Structure and Interpretation*. Cascadilla Press, Somerville, Mass., 160.
———. (1996c). "A New Look at the Null Subject Parameter." In J. Costa, R. Goedemans, & R. van de Vijver (orgs.). *Proceedings of ConSole IV*. Leiden, 375–395.
———. (forthcoming). "Clitics: A Window into the Null Subject Property." In J. Costa (ed.), *Essays in Portuguese Comparative Syntax*. Oxford University Press, New York.
Belleti, A. (1990). *Generalized Verb Movement*. Rosenberg & Sellier, Torino.
Bonet, E. (1990). "Subjects in Catalan." *MIT Working Papers* 13, 1–26.
Boskovic, Z. (1996). "Selection and the Categorial Status of Infinitival Complements." *NLLT* 14, 269–304.
Cardinaletti, A., & M. Starke. (1994). "The Typology of Structural Deficiency: On the Three Grammatical Classes." Ms., University of Venice and University of Geneva/MaxPlanck, Berlin.
Chomsky, N. (1977). "On *Wh*-movement." In P. Culicover, T. Wasos, & A. Akmajian (eds.), *Formal Syntax*. Academic Press, New York, 71–132.
———. (1986). *Barriers*. MIT Press, Cambridge, Mass.
———. (1995). *The Minimalist Program*. MIT Press, Cambridge, Mass.
———. (1998). *Minimalist Inquiries: The Framework*. MIT Working Papers in Linguistics, MIT, Cambridge, Mass.
Cinque, G. (1990). *Types of A'- dependencies*. MIT Press, Cambridge, Mass.
Contreras, H. (1991). "On the Position of Subjects." *Syntax and Semantics* 25.
Deprez, V. (1990). "Two Ways of Moving the Verb in French." *MIT Working Papers in Linguistics* 13, 47–85.
De Wind, M. (1995). "Inversion in French." Ph.D. diss., Groningen Dissertations in Linguistics, Groningen.

Dobrovie-Sorin, C. (1990). "Clitic Doubling, *Wh*-movement, and Quantification in Romanian." *Linguistic Inquiry* 22, 1–25.

————. (1994). *The Syntax of Roumanian: Comparative Studies in Romance*. Foris Publications, Dordrecht.

Drijkoningen, F. (1997). "Morphological Strength: NP Positions in French." In D. Berman, D. LeBlanc, & H. van Riemsdijk (eds.), *Rightward Movement*. John Benjamins, Amsterdam.

Duarte, I. (1983). Variação Paramétrica e Ordem dos Clíticos. *Revista da Faculdade de Letras de Lisboa* 50, 158–178.

————. (1987). "A construção de topicalização na gramática do português: regência, ligação e condições sobre movimento." Ph.D. diss., University of Lisbon.

Grimshaw, J. (1979). "Complement Selection and the Lexicon." *Linguistic Inquiry* 10, 279–326.

————. (1993). "Minimal Projection, Heads and Optimality." Ms., Rutgers University, New Brunswick, N.J.

Holmberg, H., & Ch. Platzack. (1988). "The Role of Inflection in Scandinavian Syntax." *Working Papers in Scandinavian Syntax* 42, 25–43.

Hulk, A. C. J. (1993). "Residual V2 and the Licensing of Functional Features." *Probus* 5, 127–154.

Hulk, A. C. J., & A. van Kemenade. (1990). "Licensing V2, Case Systems and Prodrop." Paper presented at the First Generative Diachronic Syntax Conference, New York.

Iatridou, S. (1991). "Clitics and Island Effects." Ms., MIT, Cambridge, Mass.

Kayne, R. (1975). *French Syntax: The Transformational Cycle*. MIT Press, Cambridge, Mass.

————. (1984). *Connectedness and Binary Branching*. Foris Publications, Dordrecht.

————. (1994). *The Antisymmetry of Syntax*. MIT Press, Cambridge, Mass.

Kayne, R. S., & J. Y. Pollock. (1978). "Stylistic Inversion and Successive Cyclicity and Move NP in French." *Linguistic Inquiry* 9, 595–621.

Klima, E. (1964). "Negation in English." In J. Katz & J. Fodor (eds.), *The Structure of Language*. Prentice Hall, Upper Saddle River, N.J.

Laka, I. (1990). "Negation in Syntax: On the Nature of Functional Categories and Projections." Ph.D. diss., MIT, Cambridge, Mass.

Law, P. (1991). "Effects of Head Movement on Theories of Subjacency and Proper Government." Ph.D. diss., MIT, Cambridge, Mass.

Martins, A. M. (1994). "Foco e Clíticos no Português Europeu." Ph.D. diss., University of Lisbon.

McCloskey, J. (1996). "On the Scope of Verb Movement in Irish." *NLLT* 14, 47–104.

Motapanyane, V. (1994). "An A-position for Romanian Subjects." *LI* 25/4, 729–734.

Noonan, M. (1989). "Operator Licensing and the Case of French Interrogatives." In Fee & Hunt (eds.), *Proceedings of the 8 West Coast Conference on Formal Linguistics*, 315–330.

Ordónez, F. (1995). "Post-verbal Asymmetries in Spanish." *NLLT* 16, 313–346.

Pesetsky, D. (1982). "Paths and Categories." Ph.D. diss., MIT, Cambridge, Mass.

————. (1992). "Zero Syntax, Volume 2." Ms., MIT, Cambridge, Mass.

Poletto, C. (1997). "The Higher Functional Field in the Northern Italian Dialects." Ms., University of Padova.

Pollock, J.-Y. (1986). "Sur la Syntaxe de *en* et le Paramètre du Sujet Nul." In D. Couquaux & M. Ronat (eds.), *La Grammaire Modulaire*. Editions Minuit, Paris, 211–246.

———. (1997). *Langage et Cognition: Introduction au Programme Minimaliste de la Grammaire Générative*. Presses Universitaires de France, Paris.

Radford, A. (1994). "The Nature of Children's Initial Clauses." Ms., Essex University, Colchester, England.

Raposo, E. (1986). "On the Null Object in European Portuguese." In O. Jaeggli & C. Silva-Corvalán (eds.), *Studies in Romance Linguistics*. Foris Publications, Dordrecht.

———. (1994). "Affective Operators and Clausal Structure in European Portuguese and European Spanish." Ms., University of California, Santa Barbara.

———. (1996). "Towards a Unification of Topic Constructions." Ms., University of California, Santa Barbara.

———. (1997). "Definite/zero Alternations in Portuguese: Towards a Unified Theory of Topic Constructions." Ms., University of California, Santa Barbara.

Rivero, M. L. (1987). "La teoría de las barreras y las completivas del rumano. In V. Demonte & M. Fernández Lagunilla (eds.), *Sintaxis le las lenguas Románicas*. Textos Universitarios, Madrid, 329–354.

Rizzi, L. (1982). *Issues in Italian Syntax*. Foris Publications, Dordrecht.

———. (1986). "Null Objects in Italian and the Theory of *Pro*." *Linguistic Inquiry* 17, 501–557.

———. (1990). *Relativized Minimality*. MIT Press, Cambridge, Mass.

———. (1991). "Residual Verb Second and the *Wh*-Criterion." *Technical Reports in Formal and Computational Linguistics* 2. Faculté des Lettres, Université de Genève.

———. (1997). "The Fine Structure of the Left Periphery." In I. Haegeman (ed.), *Elements of Grammar*. Kluwer, Dordrecht, 281–337.

Rizzi, L., & I. Roberts. (1989). "Complex Inversion in French." *Probus* 1/1, 1–30.

Schneider-Zioga, P. (1994). "The Syntax of Clitic Doubling in Modern Greek." Ph.D. diss., University of Southern California, Los Angeles.

Sola, J. (1992). "Agreement and Subjects." Ph.D. diss., Universitat Autònoma de Barcelona.

Speas, M. (1994). "Null Arguments in a Theory of Economy of Projection." *University of Massachusetts Occasional Papers* 17, 179–208.

Terzi, A. (1993). "*Pro* in Finite Clauses, A Study of the Inflectional Heads of the Balkan Languages." Ph.D. diss., City University of New York.

Torrego, E. (1984). "On Inversion in Spanish and Some of Its Effects." *LI* 15, 103–129.

Tsimpli, I. M. (1994). "Focusing in Modern Greek." In K. Kiss (ed.), *Discourse-configurational Languages*. Oxford University Press, New York.

Uriagereka, J. (1995). "Aspects of the Syntax of Clitic Placement in Western Romance." *LI* 26, 79–123.

Uribe-Etxebarria, M. (1991). "On the Structural Positions of the Subject in Spanish, Their Nature and Their Consequences for Quantification." Ms., University of Connecticut, Storrs.

Vallduví, E. (1990). "The Informational Component." Ph.D. diss., University of Pennsylvania, Philadelphia.

———. (1992). "A Preverbal Landing Site for Quantificational Operators." *CTWPL*, Universitat Autònoma de Barcelona.

Wada, M. (1998). "The Position of Subjects in the Clause Structure of the Null-Subject Romance Languages." *Journal of the Faculty of Letters* (Okayama University) 29.

Zanuttini, R. (1989). "The Structure of Negative Clauses in Romance." *NELS* 20, 517–530.

Zubizarreta, M. L. (1997). *Word Order, Prosody and Focus.* MIT Press, Cambridge, Mass.

3

"Inversion" as Focalization

ADRIANA BELLETTI

The main empirical area studied in this chapter concerns Inversion structures with a subject that linearly follows the inflected verb, displaying the word order VS. Seemingly unrelated structures that involve reordering of complements (in the sense of Belletti & Shlonsky 1995; henceforth B&S) are also considered and are assumed to involve the same derivational process at work in Subject Inversion. Both are argued to be instances of clause-internal Focalization.[1] The term "Subject Inversion" is thus a purely descriptive label, referring to a subset, albeit an important one, of a more general clause-internal process.

The descriptive term "Inversion," with reference to Subject Inversion structures, implicitly capitalizes on the idea that the order VS reverses the canonical order SV(O). However, that Subject Inversion configurations cannot be derived through a lowering operation, moving the preverbal "high" subject to some clause-internal position, has been assumed ever since Romance Subject Inversion phenomena have undergone serious examinations in Government and Binding (GB) terms. Lowering operations of this sort are not admitted in principle, as they necessarily produce a violation of the proper binding requirement that holds within chains. Without attempting to faithfully reconstruct the details of the different analyses proposed in the literature during the 1980s and the 1990s, I suggest that they all share the idea that the inverted subject is allowed to fill some position in the VP area and that a relation is established with an associate (overt or nonovert) expletive, filling the preverbal "high" subject position. It is precisely by virtue of such a relation (sometimes called CHAIN) that the subject is allowed to be found in the low VP area.[2] The spirit of this traditional GB-style account[3] is essentially preserved in recent treatments of Inversion-type phenomena developed under minimalist assumptions, with the necessary changes due to the adoption of the VP-internal subject hypothesis (Koopman & Sportiche 1991; Kuroda 1988; compare the analysis of the so-called Transitive Expletive Construction (TEC) of Icelandic (Bobalijk & Jonas 1996; Chomsky (1995). The account here shares with traditional ones the idea that there is no literal Inversion process that moves the subject from the preverbal subject position to the right, past the inflected verb. However, the existence of a relation with an associate expletive in the preverbal subject position is not considered crucial in the licensing of the inverted/postverbal subject. Such a relation may well exist for independent reasons, and I actually assume that it does, but the subject, as well as reordered complements in the intended sense, is licensed in situ in a position rather low in the clause-functional structure. This position is identified with the specifier of the projection of a clause-internal Focus feature.

Let me make the proposal precise, first, by considering how low in the clause structure the postverbal subject appears to be. Second, I move to the analysis of more complex VPs, containing different kinds of complements. Third, the topic of complement reordering is taken up and reconsidered within the system developed. Finally, the implications of the proposal are also considered with respect to structures that contain unaccusative verbs.

The data taken into account come from Italian. Some comparative reference is occasionally made to other Romance languages. The following crucial "reading instruction" holds: Unless otherwise specified, all the sentences under investigation here are evaluated with respect to a neutral, noninterrupted intonation.[4]

1. Position and Licensing of Inverted, Postverbal Subjects

1.1. How "Low" in the Clause Structure Is the Inverted/Postverbal Subject?

Although the sentences in (1) are not perfect in status, with an interesting difference internal to the paradigm between (1a, b), on the one side, and (1c), on the other, they certainly are definitely better than (2):

(1) a. ?Capirà completamente Maria
         will understand completely Maria
     b. ?Capirà bene Maria
         will understand well Maria
     c. Capirà tutto Maria
         will understand everything Maria

(2) a. *Capirà Maria completamente
         will understand Maria completely
     b. *Capirà Maria bene
         will understand Maria well

c. *Capirà Maria tutto
will understand Maria everything

Both (1) and (2) are pronounced with normal, noninterrupted intonation, not implying any sort of "rescuing" strategy through intonation.[5] According to Cinque's (1998) typology, which I adopt without discussion as a point of departure, the adverbs and the quantifier in (1) and (2) are those filling the Specs of the lowest different functional projections that build up clause structure. The contrast between (1) and (2) indicates a strong preference for the V-Adv-S order over the alternative V-S-Adv.

The sentences in (1) show a kind of "interference" effect that can be held responsible for their slightly degraded status. The effect is interestingly absent in (1c), which indicates that what is at stake here is not just linear interference but some more structured notion. Something can "intervene" between the verb and the postverbal subject provided that certain structural conditions are met. Suppose that the relevant structural conditions require that a certain "distance" in the tree is present between the Adv/quantifier and the postverbal subject. We can speculate that the quantifier nature of *tutto* allows it to move to some higher (Spec) position than those occupied by the adverbs in (1a, b), thus becoming more "distant" from the subject in the relevant sense and consequently interfering "less."[6]

If we assume the VP-internal subject hypothesis and abstract from the gradation manifested by (1), the contrast between (1) and (2) allows us to conclude that in Subject "Inversion" structures either the subject remains in its original VP-internal position or it raises to a very low position in the clause structure, lower than the lowest Spec that is hosting an adverb.

1.2. "Inversion" as Focalization

If the above conclusion is correct, one then wonders how the subject is licensed in the low position. A frequently made observation in the literature (cf. Antinucci & Cinque 1977 for some of the first structured observations in this connection; see also, e.g., B&S and Zubizarreta 1998 for more recent analyses) is that a postverbal subject is focalized; that is, concerning the "old" vs. "new" informational organization of the clause, it carries the new information. Pairs like the following illustrate the point:

(3) a. Chi è partito/ha parlato?
who has left/has spoken
b. E' partito/ha parlato Gianni
has left/has spoken Gianni
c. #Gianni è partito/ha parlato
Gianni has left/has spoken

The oddness of (3c) is due to the fact that the subject is not appropriately located: When it is located preverbally it is interpreted as the "old" ("topic") information and cannot function as the "new" ("focus") information. But since question (3a) precisely concerns the subject, (3c) is not an appropriate answer to it.[7] Sharp contrasts along similar lines are provided by the examples in (4):

(4) a. (Pronto, chi parla?)
         (Hello, who speaks?)
     b. Parla Gianni
         speaks Gianni
     c. *Gianni parla.
         Gianni speaks.
     d. (Chi è?)
         (Who is (there)?)
     e. i. Sono io
             am I = it's me
         ii. Sono Gianni
             am Gianni = it's Gianni
         iii. E' Gianni
             It's Gianni.
     f. *Io/Gianni sono/è
         I/Gianni am/is

Examples (4b) and (4e) i, ii, iii, illustrate the typical sentences utilized in answering (the often implicit question of) phone calls or a (possibly implicit) request of identification in typical situations, for example, after knocking at somebody's door. The word order in this case is consistently and only VS. Having the subject in preverbal position gives a sharply ungrammatical result in these situations, as (4c, f) indicate.[8] In (4), exactly as in (3), the well-formed sentences have the subject as the new information focus. It then seems plausible to hypothesize that Focalization plays the crucial role in the licensing of the (low) postverbal subject.

I pointed out in 1.1 that the postverbal subject fills a very low position in the clause. A natural hypothesis would be to assume that it is as low as its original VP-internal position.[9] If this is the case, the obvious question arises of how it is licensed in such a low position. It is currently assumed that Case is the (morpho)syntactic feature that is crucial in the licensing of overt noun phrases. Unless we allow nominative Case to be accessible to the VP-internal subject position, possibly through the relation with an associate expletive, it is clear that Case is not available VP-internally for the postverbal subject. If we want to try to maintain Case assignment and checking to be as local a process as possible, as seems desirable,[10] we are in fact forced to conclude that no Case is available for the subject in its original VP-internal position. As we have just determined that the postverbal subject fills a very low position in the clause structure, we seem to be forced to conclude that this position cannot coincide with the VP-internal original one because the subject could not be licensed through Case there. Furthermore, given current assumptions on the distribution of functional projections in the clausal architecture, in particular of those responsible for Case assignment and checking, it seems that no other (nominative) Case position is likely to be available for the subject in the very low area where it is found. The question of the licensing of the postverbal subject thus remains open.

Suppose that not Case but Focus plays the role of the licenser of the postverbal subject. From the interpretive/informational point of view, the hypothesis seems entirely justified. But what is the status of Focus in this view? To make the proposal technically more precise, I assume that Focus is a syntactic feature that is heading a functional projection in the clause structure, thus creating a regular checking configuration. In this proposal, the syntactic feature in question has licensing abilities. In a broader perspective, we can assume that Case is not the only licenser of overt DPs in the clause. It is probably the most typical and widespread one, but others are available as well. Focus is one of them in this view.

The proposal that a Focus Phrase is present in the clause has been made various times in the recent literature on functional projections. Typically, the FocusP is located in the left periphery of the clause, as in Brody (1990), Rizzi (1997), and Puskas (1996). I assume that such a position exists. It is the one that is hosting "contrastive" focus in Italian:

(5)   Il LIBRO ho letto, non il giornale
      THE BOOK I have read, not the newspaper

As in the analysis developed in B&S, I take the FocusP that is hosting postverbal subjects to be a different one, as is clear from the distribution, and to be clause-internal. In contrast to the left-peripheral focus position, the clause-internal one is not associated with any special contrastive intonation: no contrast is implied, as (3) and (4) show. Indeed, the pragmatics of the two focus positions are quite different. A left-peripheral focus cannot function as an appropriate answer to a pure question of information; (5) cannot answer a question like (6).[11]

(6)   Che cosa hai letto?
      What have you read?

Nor can (7b) answer a question like (3a), repeated in (7a):

(7)   a. Chi è partito/ha parlato?
          Who has left/has spoken?
      b. (*) GIANNI è partito/ha parlato.
          GIANNI has left/has spoken.

Example (7b) is pronounced with the typical intonation associated with left-peripheral focus in Italian, indicated by capital letters.

Given the considerations prompted by the respective position of low adverbs and postverbal subjects, we are led to conclude that the clause-internal FocusP is very low in the clause. Assume that it is the first functional projection above VP:[12]

(8)   FocusP
         1
         Foc'
         1
         Foc   VP

The subject moves to the specifier of FocusP and the Verb raises higher up producing the order VS.[13] In this approach, Focus has no special status: it is a feature that gives rise to a regular checking configuration. Its licensing property does not need to appeal to special external conventions. The only hypothesis needed is the one attributing to the Focus feature a licensing ability for overt DPs comparable to that of a Case feature and, as such, a possible alternative to it.[14]

In Subject Inversion sentences in standard Italian, the verb agrees with the postverbal subject and the latter carries nominative case. This is overtly visible in examples like (9):

(9)   Sono arrivata io
        have arrived I

A fairly traditional interpretation of this kind of data[15] might assume that a relation between the postverbal subject and the preverbal subject position is established, possibly with a nonovert expletive that fills the latter position (the CHAIN relation referred to above), and that all pronounceable features in the chain are (by necessity) realized on the "overt" elements. They are then realized in the inflectional affixes and in the morphological case of the postverbal subject. The chain relation would then be held responsible for both case and agreement. As for the presence of the nominative, however, an account of this kind appears to be insufficiently general and should be refined to incorporate cases like (10):

(10)   Penso di [- parlare io a Gianni]
          (I) think to speak I to Gianni

In (10) the relation should be established between the postverbal "io" and the embedded preverbal subject position of the infinitival clause. But no association with nominative case is granted here through this relation because null case is the only case related to the infinitival subject position (Chomsky & Lasnik 1993). Moreover, null case is incompatible with overt elements. Suppose instead that the postverbal embedded subject "io" is licensed in situ within the clause-internal Focus phrase.[16] Its realization as a first-person singular can be attributed to the relation with the preverbal subject, PRO, controlled by the matrix subject.[17] Its realization as a nominative must be due to the independent necessity of choosing a morphological realization for a pronounceable overt element, if available. In this view, the nominative would count as a default realization. If an account along these lines is tenable, examples like (10) illustrate a situation in which Case and Focus are dissociated. The same account could then naturally extend to examples like (9), in which the nominative on the postverbal pronoun should not necessarily be interpreted as a consequence of the established relation with the preverbal subject position.[18] Examples like (11) complete the paradigm with cases in which both the preverbal subject and the postverbal pronominal subject are overt:

(11)   Gianni parlerà lui con Maria
       Gianni will speak he with Maria

In these examples, the postverbal pronominal subject is usually interpreted as having a strengthening function, often called "emphatic." Note that if the postverbal pronominal subject is licensed in FocusP, this directly explains why it must necessarily be realized as a strong pronoun. The weak pronoun version of the third-person singular pronoun "egli" is totally excluded in these constructions:

(12)   *Gianni parlerà egli con Maria
       Gianni will speak he with Maria

If weak pronouns are "deficient" in Cardinaletti and Starke's (1994) sense, it is natural that they are incompatible with a saliency feature like Focus. Note finally that the detectable anaphoric behavior of the emphatic postverbal subject pronoun in (11) could be analyzed along similar lines as those assumed for the "Floated Quantifiers" (FQ) phenomenon in Sportiche (1988). It could be an indirect consequence of the movement of a portion of the Noun Phrase that contains the lexical subject to some preverbal subject position, leaving behind the DP portion that contains an explicit determiner. Because the latter is licensed through focus, it necessarily corresponds to the strong version of the pronoun, as discussed above.[19]

1.3.   V S XP (V S O, V S PP, V S CP)

Once we assume that the postverbal subject is licensed in the specifier of the Focus Phrase, the natural question that arises is what happens if a complement of V is also present in the VP. Let us consider three cases in turn: (A) the complement is a direct object (O, henceforth); (B) the complement is a prepositional object (PP); (C) the complement is a clause (CP).

1.3.1.   VSO (Case A)

Once S moves to the specifier of FocusP and V moves to some inflectional head above it, a direct object O would still need to be licensed in some functional Spec position. The specifier of FocusP is filled by the subject; hence O could (only) be licensed through Case. To perform Case checking, it should move to the Spec of its Case-checking projection, which is located above the Focus Phrase, this being the lowest functional projection of the clause by hypothesis. I assume that such crossing of the object over the subject is not allowed because of Relativized Minimality (RM). I also assume that in clauses with a preverbal subject, the same problem does not arise since the subject continues its movement and in the final representation it ends up higher than the object. Indeed, the relevant constraint requires that the initial hierarchical order of constituents is preserved in the final structure.[20]

Note that the excluded movement of the direct object to the specifier of its Case-checking projection would yield the word order VOS. This order is not a felicitous one, as is illustrated by examples like (13):[21]

(13) a. ??Capirà il problema Gianni
          will understand the problem Gianni
      b. ??Ha spedito la lettera Maria
          has sent the letter Maria
      c. ??Ha chiamato Maria Gianni
          has called Maria Gianni

The VOS order has often been seen as a violation of an adjacency constraint that no material must interrupt the VS sequence. The status of this adjacency requirement has been assimilated to Case adjacency (Rizzi 1996 and related works, including B&S and Friedemann 1995), assuming that the postverbal subject could be directly Case-marked in the low, inverted position under the government of a nominative Case assigner functional head, sometimes identified with T. However, in a more recent conception of clause structure with a richer and more articulated functional skeleton than the original analysis by Pollock (1989), it does not seem very likely that the nominative Case assigner (assume it to be T) could really be the functional head closest to the low/inverted subject. Furthermore, the Case adjacency analysis does not make one expect a VSO sequence to be seen as completely impossible in Italian, in fact much worse than VOS, as I discuss at some length:[22]

(14) a. *Capirà Gianni il problema
          will understand Gianni the problem
      b. *Ha spedito Maria la lettera
          has sent Maria the letter

As in all the cases throughout, the reported judgments refer to the sentences pronounced with continuous, noninterrupted, normal intonation. It would seem that, all things being equal, if Case adjacency were the relevant notion, (14) should be more acceptable than (13), possibly totally acceptable (with the qualification of note 22), contrary to fact.

It is natural at this point to raise the following question: What does the proposed analysis have to say on the detected impossibility of the VSO order in Italian? In fact, in this analysis, VSO cannot be generated altogether: With S licensed in the specifier of the Focus Phrase, O is blocked within VP, where no licenser is present. Hence the structure is eliminated. Thus, VOS and VSO are ruled out for essentially the same reason: impossibility of properly licensing both S and O in the low area of the clause. Note, for completeness, that if we wanted to license O in the specifier of the Focus Phrase, leaving the subject VP-internal and yielding VOS once again, we would be left this time with S licensed neither through Case nor through Focus (hence unlicensed), expectedly an unacceptable outcome.[23]

Speakers tend to attribute a slightly less marginal status to the VOS order than to order VSO in Italian, provided that a particular intonation is utilized (note 21) and certain pragmatic conditions are met. On the other hand, it is well known that there are languages, in particular languages of the Romance family, for example, Spanish (Ordóñez 1997; Zubizarreta 1998) and Romanian (Motapanyane 1995), which appear to allow for the order VSO rather freely. I delay until after discussion of points (B) and (C) some reflections on the possible reasons behind these contrasts.

1.3.2.   VSPP (Case B)

Let us now consider the case in which the VP-internal complement of V is a prepositional object. Suppose that S is licensed in the specifier of the Focus Phrase and PP remains in the VP-internal position. In combination with verb movement, this yields the order VSPP. Recall that in the case of a direct object, this order yields an impossible output in Italian since, as we have just seen, the direct object O cannot be licensed VP internally (nor can S with O in the specifier of FocusP). It appears that the situation is remarkably different if the object is a PP. Consider the following quasi-minimal pairs in this respect:

(15)   a.   (?) Ha telefonato Maria al giornale
              has phoned Maria to the newspaper
        b.   *Ha comprato Maria il giornale
              has bought Maria the newspaper
        c.   (?) Ha parlato uno studente col direttore
              has spoken a student to the director
        d.   *Ha corrotto uno studente il direttore
              has bribed a student the director
        e.   (?) Ha sparato il bandito al carabiniere
              has shot the gangster at the policeman
        f.   *Ha colpito il bandito il carabiniere[24]
              has hit the gangster the policeman

Why should this difference exist? If the proposed interpretation of the reasons that rule out VSO is on the right track, the contrast between direct objects and prepositional objects naturally suggests the following interpretation. Assume that S fills the specifier of the Focus Projection. Assume that, in contrast to DPs, PPs are autonomously licensed and do not need to move to a VP-external position. Rather, PPs are licensed in situ. If this is the case, the VSPP order is obtained by leaving the PP in its base VP-internal position. The output is expected to be acceptable.

Why should PPs be licensed in situ? An obvious reason suggests itself. Note that, in fact, only DP arguments need licensing (usually performed through Case). Thus, a PP can be taken to contain the licenser of its DP complement internal to its own projection. Suppose that such a licenser is recognized in the preposition itself. We could execute the idea by assuming that checking of the P feature is done through movement of the DP complement to the specifier of PP or through movement of some relevant feature (Chomsky 1995) or through the establishment of an agreement relation in Chomsky's (1998) sense. This line of analysis captures a fact often observed in both traditional accounts and more theoretically oriented ones according to which prepositions "play the role" of Case.

1.3.3.   VSCP (Case C)

In the generative literature, clauses have occasionally been assumed not to need Case.[25] In the terms adopted here, this should mean that they do not need to move to a Case-checking position but can remain in situ, in the VP-internal complement position. Assume that this is what occurs. We then expect that the order VSCP should be a possible one, with S in the specifier of the Focus Projection and the CP complement VP-internal, much as in the case of VSPP. This is indeed what we find in various cases:

(16)   a.   Ha detto la mamma che ha telefonato Gianni
            has said the mother that has telephoned Gianni
       b.   Ha detto la mamma di andare a letto
            has said the mother to go to bed

It should be pointed out, however, that the order VSCP is not felicitous with all verbal choices, thus suggesting that other factors are involved in making the order appropriate. Examples like those in (17) provide a sample of cases in which the order VSCP, pronounced with the usual continuous intonation, is bizarre and essentially unacceptable:

(17)   a.   *?Ha cominciato Gianni a non capire più niente
            has started Gianni to not understand anything anymore
       b.   *?Ha pensato/pensa la mamma che Gianni non capisca più niente
            has though/thinks the mother that Gianni doesn't understand anything
            anymore
       c.   *?Crede Maria che Gianni sia partito
            believes Maria that Gianni has left
       d.   *?Ha deciso Gianni di parlare con Maria
            has decided Gianni to speak with Maria

I leave open here the development of an accurate hypothesis for the deviance of sentences like (17).[26]

Summarizing, I propose that the VS order is obtained through movement of the subject into the specifier of a clause-internal Focus-Functional Projection, with the verb filling some higher functional head. All other things being equal, other arguments of the verb are allowed to linearly follow S only if they can remain in their (original) VP-internal complement position. This possibility is available to PPs and CPs but not to direct object DPs. This rules out the VSO order, with O a direct object DP. If O raises out of VP to its Case-checking position, it necessarily crosses over the low subject in the specifier of the Focus Phrase, giving rise to an illegitimate derivation, because of RM (and since the subject does not raise further up). This rules out VOS. All the judgments refer to the sentences pronounced with normal, noninterrupted intonation.

1.4.   More on VOS

We are now ready to take up the issue left open—why the speakers' intuitions give VOS as a word order slightly more acceptable than VSO. I have reproduced this intuition by attributing two "??" to the former order and a straight "*" to the latter. Nevertheless, the analysis developed above rules out both VOS and VSO, with no attempt to express a difference. Indeed, I suggest that no real "grammatical" difference is at stake here; rather, interfering factors account for the subtle differentiation made by speakers. I intend now to make these factors explicit within the terms of the general analysis proposed.

One context in which VOS appears to be a possible (although somewhat redundant and slightly unnatural) word order is the one where it shows up as the answer to a question for which the whole "given" information is repeated, this being precisely constituted by V and O. Consider in this respect the following question-answer pairs:

(18)   a. Chi ha capito il problema?
           Who has understood the problem?
       b. Ha capito il problema Gianni
           Has understood the problem Gianni
       c. Chi spedirà la lettera?
           Who will send the letter?
       d. Spedirà la lettera Maria[27]
           Will send the letter Maria

Of course the most natural answers to questions (18a, c) would have O expressed in the form of a pronoun:

(19)   b'. L'ha capito Gianni.
            It + has understood Gianni.
       d'. La spedirà Maria[28]
            It + will send Maria.

More natural examples of an acceptable VOS order are typically found in special contexts that belong to a particular register, such as that of live radio and TV reports of, say, football matches.[29] Some examples are given in (20):

(20) a. Mette la palla sul dischetto del rigore Ronaldo
          puts the ball on the penalty point Ronaldo
      b. Protegge l'uscita di Marchegiani Nesta
          protects Marchegiani's coming out Nesta

Note that sentences of this kind are only possible if the VO part of the clause that immediately precedes S can be interpreted as describing a member of a set of prototypical situations (predicates) in the context of a (football) match. As soon as VO is not interpretable in this way, VOS becomes once again (essentially) unacceptable [cf. (13)]:

(21) a. ??Spinge l'arbitro Ronaldo
          pushes the referee Ronaldo
      b. ??Ferisce il guardialinee Nesta
          hurts the linesman Nesta

We can conclude that what the acceptable sentences with the order VOS have in common is the fact of introducing a VO sequence that constitutes the "given" part of the information provided by the sentence.

Suppose that this only possible interpretation is associated with the following syntactic analysis: The "given" constituent that contains V + O moves to the specifier position of a Topic Projection. A position of this type is assumed in the analysis of the left periphery by Rizzi (1997), where it is located immediately above the clause-external Focus Projection. Another Topic Projection is located right under Focus, which is thus surrounded by two Topic Phrases. Let me make the proposal that—much as for the peripheral, clause-external projections—the clause-internal ones involve not only a Focus Projection (above VP) but also a Topic Projection right above it and one right under it.[30] We can assume that the moved constituent is the XP (VP?) that contains the trace of the subject moved to the specifier of the Focus Phrase.[31] As in the analysis proposed by Ordóñez (1997), this topicalization can be considered the analog of the process in the Germanic languages, which has come to be known as "Remnant Topicalization," although I am assuming that the process here is clause-internal. I then suggest that the order VOS tends not to be totally excluded by speakers because of interference with this possibly topicalized construction.[32]

In the proposed analysis I have assumed that the subject fills the clause-internal specifier of the Focus Projection. Notice that, so far, we have considered sentences like (18b, d) to be pronounced with regular intonation, not involving any particular stress on any constituent. It is clear to any speaker of Italian that a special stress on the postverbal subject makes the VOS order uncontroversially acceptable. This stress is contrastive stress:

(22) a. Ha capito il problema GIANNI (non tutta la classe)
          has understood the problem GIANNI (not the whole class)
      b. Ha spedito la lettera MARIA (non sua sorella)
          has sent the letter MARIA (not her sister)

The remnant VP that is preceding S is still interpreted as the Topic; the Focus of the clause is the contrastively stressed subject. Note now that also a preverbal contrastively stressed subject counts as Focus:

(23) a. GIANNI ha capito il problema (non tutta la classe).
          GIANNI has understood the problem (not the whole class).
      b. MARIA ha spedito la lettera (non sua sorella).
          MARIA has sent the letter (not her sister).

A reasonable analysis of clauses like (23) locates the subject in the clause-external specifier of the Focus Phrase, the same position filled by the focalized constituents in (24a, b) and the same position that, according to Rizzi (1997), also hosts wh-interrogative operators[33] (24c):

(24) a. IL PROBLEMA Gianni ha capito (non l'equazione)
          THE PROBLEM Gianni has understood (not the equation)
      b. LA LETTERA Maria ha spedito (non il pacco)
          THE LETTER Maria has sent (not the parcel)
      c. Che cosa ha capito Gianni?
          What has understood Gianni?

The proposed analysis for the sentences in (23) thus assumes that the preverbal subject does not fill the preverbal clause-internal subject position[34] but is instead clause-external in the specifier of the Focus Phrase. If this analysis seems reasonable and coherent with current assumptions, I suggest that one could extend exactly the same analysis to the sentences in (22). Hence, when contrastively stressed, the postverbal subject of these clauses should have the subject in the left-peripheral specifier position of the Focus Projection. The remnant VP would fill the specifier of the Topic Projection above the clause-external Focus Phrase. I assume that this is the analysis of (23).[35]

1.5.   What Could Allow for VSO in Some Romance Languages

Several studies on postverbal subjects have repeatedly indicated that VSO is a possible word order in Spanish. See the discussions in Ordóñez (1997) and Zubizarreta (1998) in particular. As illustrated in Motapanyane (1995), VSO is also a possible word order in Romanian:

(25) a. Todos los días compra Juan el diario   [Zubizarreta 1998]
          Every day buys Juan the newspaper
      b. Espero que te devuelva Juan el libro   [Ordóñez 1997]
          I hope that cl-you return Juan the book
          (I hope that Juan returns the book to you.)
      c. O invita cam des Ion pe fata aceasta   [Motapanyane 1995]
          her invites quite often Ion 'pe' girl the-that
          (Ion invites that girl quite often.)

It appears that, in contrast to the situation in Italian, a postverbal subject in VSO order is not (or not necessarily) the new information focus of the clause in languages like Spanish. Suppose that this could indicate that it fills a position different from the specifier of the clause-internal Focus Projection.[36] The question then arises of what makes a further (higher) position available for a postverbal subject in Spanish but not in Italian. If Focus is not the licenser of the postverbal subject, there must be another licenser. The only suggestion I can make here essentially adopts and rephrases the proposal made by Zubizarreta (1998). Assume the licenser to be Case. Languages like Spanish would dispose of an extra Case position, different from the preverbal one(s), in which (nominative) Case can be assigned/checked. This position should be relatively high in the clause, higher than the VP-external position where the direct object is licensed. Hence, both S and O would be licensed in Spanish and similar languages in VSO clauses through Case.[37]

Why doesn't Italian have this extra Case position? Does this difference between the two kinds of languages correlate with some other difference? One could speculate that this is probably the case if another frequently pointed-out difference between the two kinds of languages is considered, namely, the fact that the finite verb seems to raise higher in Italian than in Spanish, taking the position of equivalent adverb classes to be revealing in this respect (see Motapanyane 1995 on Romanian). Consider the contrast between Spanish and Italian in (26):

(26) a. La vijeita apenas/siempre/nunca puede leer los periodicos.   [Suñer 1994]
          the dear old lady barely/always/never can read the newspaper.
      b. *?La vecchietta appena/sempre/mai può leggere i giornali.
          the old lady barely/always/never can read the newspaper.

Of course, what remains to be understood is how a lower verb could activate a further Case position below it. I leave this question open at this speculative stage.[38]

2. Multiple Complements Reordering and Subject Inversion

Let us assume a VP-internal structure like the one in (27):

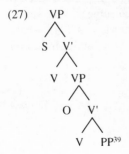

(27)

Consider now the following sentences, involving a verb like *dare*, which takes both a direct and an indirect prepositional object; beside the "unmarked"/basic VOPP order, the VPPO order is also admitted, as discussed in detail in B&S:

(28) a. Ho dato un libro a Gianni.
          (I) have given a book to Gianni.
      b. Ho dato a Gianni un libro.
          (I) have given to Gianni a book.

The authors provide a rich list of multiple complement verbs, all manifesting the same paradigm, with both orders of complements possible and the order VOPP normally considered the "unmarked"/basic one. Note now that both orders are perfectly acceptable when a preverbal overt subject is also present:

(29) a. Gianni ha dato un libro a Maria.
          Gianni has given a book to Maria.
      b. Gianni ha dato a Maria un libro.
          Gianni has given to Maria a book.

As observed in B&S, complement reordering interacts in interesting ways with Subject Inversion. The order VOPPS is (marginally) acceptable, with the only interpretation having VOPP, the "remnant" VP, as the "given" information and the postverbal subject as the "new" one. Consider the sentences in (30) in this respect [cf. B&S, (24a, c)]:

(30) a. Ha dato un libro a Maria Gianni
          has given a book to Maria Gianni
      b. Ha messo il libro sul tavolo Maria
          has put the book on the table Maria

These sentences can be given the same status as the possible Subject Inversion clauses that display the order VOS, discussed in 1.4 above [cf. (18b, d), for which I did not adopt any diacritic, as I do here for the sake of simplicity]. Given this similarity, as well as the observation that the whole VP has to be considered "given" information in order for the sentences to attain the level of marginal acceptability, it seems natural to attribute to them the same analysis as that attributed to VOS clauses. The sentences in (31) should then be analyzed as involving a topicalized "remnant" VP and a focalized subject in the specifier of the Focus Projection. Example (30) sharply contrasts with (31), where complement reordering has taken place in combination with Subject Inversion [B&S, (24b, d)]:

(31) a. *Ha dato a Maria un libro Gianni
          has given to Maria a book Gianni
      b. *Ha messo sul tavolo il libro Maria
          has put on the table the book Maria

Why should there be such a sharp degradation? To answer this question, the appropriate analysis of the complement-reordering phenomenon must be first spelled out. As noted in B&S, complement reordering appears to be a further case of clause-internal focalization. Consider the following question-answer pair, from B&S:

(32) a. Che cosa hai restituito a Maria?
          What have you given back to Maria?
      b. Ho restituito a Maria le chiavi.[40]
          (I) have given back to Maria the keys.
      b'. #Ho restituito le chiavi a Maria.
          (I) have given back the keys to Maria.

Sentence (32b') is pronounced with normal, noninterrupted intonation (cf. note 42). If an overt lexical subject is also present in the question, it shows up as preverbal subject in the answer:

(33) a. Che cosa ha restituito a Maria Gianni?
          What has given back to Maria Gianni?
      b. Gianni ha restituito a Maria le chiavi.
          Gianni has given back to Maria the keys.

The direct object "le chiavi" constitutes the "new" information. Assume that it is then associated with the specifier of the Focus Phrase in both (32b) and (33b). I take the latter sentence, containing a preverbal subject, to be a clear indication that Focalization is clause-internal here. Recall that no special intonation is associated with these clauses. Suppose that sentences like (32b) and (33b) involve clause-internal Topicalization of the remnant VP, overtly containing V and PP;[41] the direct object is focalized in the specifier of the Focus Phrase, and the preverbal subject is in the appropriate preverbal subject position. Schematically, the derivation in (34) is as follows (disregarding details):[42]

(34) [Gianni$_i$ ... ha. ... [$_{TopicP}$ [$_k$ e_i restituito e_j a Maria] [$_{FocusP}$ [$_j$le chiavi]
      [$_{TopicP}$ [$_{VP}$ e_k]]]] ...]
      Gianni ... has ... given back to Maria the keys

Consider now the possibility of a sentence like (35):

(35) C'è qualcosa che [restituito a Maria] Gianni ancora non ha: le chiavi
      There is something that given back to Maria Gianni hasn't yet: the keys

For reasons that do not concern us here, this kind of preposing, discussed in Cinque (1990), requires the presence of negation in the clause. A sentence like (35) can be analyzed as involving further movement of the clause-internal Topic to the clause-external one, present in the periphery.[43] Note that here the preverbal subject and the auxiliary remain in the same clause-internal positions as in (34). The natural assumption is that the direct object, too, fills the same position as in (34), that is, the clause-internal Focus position:

(36)   ... [$_k$ e_i restituito e_j a Maria] ... [Gianni$_i$ ... ancora non ha ... [$_{TopicP}$ [$_k$ e]
         [$_{FocusP}$ [$_j$le chiavi] [$_{TopicP}$ [$_{VP}$ e_k]]]] ...]
         ... given back to Maria ... Gianni ... hasn't yet ... the keys

In conclusion, I can make the hypothesis that complement reordering is an instance of clause-internal Focalization of the object, combined with (usually clause-internal) Topicalization of the remnant VP, containing V and PP. I am now ready to provide an interpretation of the reasons for the sharply degraded status of the sentences in (31) that involve complement reordering combined with Subject Inversion.

Intuitively, what rules out (31) should be the fact that both complement reordering and Subject Inversion are instances of clause-internal Focalization. If we admit, as in standard X' theory, that only one specifier position is available for X' Projection, it follows that either the object or the subject can be focalized, but not both. This is the same line of explanation developed by B&S.[44] Since we have assumed that Focus is a syntactic feature that licenses DPs if multiple specifiers are admitted (Chomsky 1995, 1998), the same effect is obtained under the natural assumption that the same syntactic feature (here Focus) cannot license more than one DP argument. Let us see how the computation works to rule out VPPOS. Indeed, in the system developed here, this order is not derivable. It cannot be derived with (remnant) VP Topicalization of V + PP, combined with movement into the specifier of the Focus Phrase of both O and S, since as I just said, we assume that Focus can license at most one argument in its specifier(s). An alternative derivation would be one in which O would move to the specifier of the Focus Phrase and the subject would remain within the VP in its base position. But we already know that such a derivation is not permitted.

An alternative order for (31), where the subject would precede the direct object, is also ruled out. As (37) shows, this order is equally impossible [B&S (24e)]:

(37)   *Ha dato a Maria Gianni un libro
         has given to Maria Gianni a book

A sentence like (37) is not derivable. It does not seem to be possible to topicalize V + PP, leaving OVP internal and moving S into the specifier of the Focus Phrase, as the linear order would require. Such a topicalization would necessarily pick up O as well.[45] Note that the linear order could be obtained if O is also topicalized into the lower Topic Phrase that surrounds the Focus Phrase. In this case the object acquires the status of a "marginalized" constituent in Antinucci and Cinque's (1977) sense. This derivation correlates with an interruption right before the marginalized object and a downgrading intonation on it:

(38)   Ha dato a Maria Gianni # un libro[46]
         Has given to Maria Gianni # a book

3.   Remarks on "Unaccusatives"

The unaccusative/ergative hypothesis as formulated in the 1980s assumes that verbs of this class do not have an external argument; rather, all arguments are VP-internal. The surface preverbal subject of unaccusatives is in fact a deep object, and even more important, the postverbal subject of unaccusatives is in fact not only a deep but also a surface object. This is, we may say, the core of the hypothesis. Note, however, that once the assumption is made that all subjects, which can appear as preverbal subjects, originate VP-internally, independently of the class to which the verb belongs, the natural question arises of where the difference between unaccusatives, on the one side, and transitives and unergatives, on the other side, should be located.

I address the question by considering unaccusatives that also select a prepositional argument beside the direct one. Note, incidentally, that this is the most common situation.[47] If a VP-internal structure like the one in (27) is assumed for transitive verbs that select both a direct and an indirect argument, it would appear that the most direct updating of the unaccusative hypothesis should hypothesize a structure along the lines of (39):

(39)

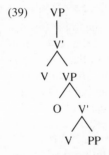

No argument is associated with the nonthematic VP-internal subject position. Adapting traditional accounts, I assume that O needs licensing and that this can be done VP-internally with unaccusatives (Belletti 1988). Suppose that licensing is done through Case in the VP specifier filled by O in (40).[48] Notice now that once V moves outside the VP into some functional head, this immediately yields the linear order VOPP. The structure being unaccusative, we know that O is in fact S, which is the argument that can also appear as a preverbal (agreeing) subject. In 1.3.2 we observed that VSPP structures are fairly acceptable, with S licensed in the specifier of the clause-internal Focus Projection and PP licensed in situ, VP-internally, for V-unergative intransitive. We are now phrasing the unaccusative hypothesis in such a way that the same VSPP linear sequence is given a different syntactic representation, with all arguments licensed VP-internally in the described way. Can we detect different behaviors of the two kinds of postverbal subjects?

As has been frequently pointed out in the literature, VSPP is a perfectly acceptable order with unaccusatives when S is indefinite. Within the terms of this analysis, we can claim that there is an indefinite requirement for VP-internally licensed subjects. Sentences like (40) are usually considered the most natural occurrences of unaccusative structures:

(40) a. E' arrivato uno studente al giornale
          has arrived a student at the newspaper
      b. E' entrato un ladro dalla finestra
          has come in a thief from the window

In 1.3.2 I attributed to the sentences (15a, c, e) a slightly marginal status, indicated as (?). The proposed analysis, however, does not make one expect any marginality. Let me now comment on this. Suppose that the slight marginality of sentences like (15a, c), repeated here, is due to the existence of a certain tendency whereby there is a preference in having the focused constituent in the clause-final position.[49]

(15) a. ?) Ha telefonato Maria al giornale
          has phoned Maria to the newspaper
      c. (?) Ha parlato uno studente col direttore
          has spoken a student with the director

We can make the hypothesis that the marginality of (15) is due to the fact that this tendency is not respected. Since the structure does not violate any deep constraint, it is ruled in but acquires a marginality flavor. Note now that no marginality whatsoever is associated with the sentences in (41). The different analysis attributed to these sentences, with a VP-internal postverbal indefinite subject not involving focalization, provides a natural interpretation for the contrast.

If the VP-internal position for the unaccusative postverbal subject is reserved to indefinite noun phrases, a definite subject should fill a different position. Such a position can be identified with the one filled by postverbal subjects of nonunaccusative verbs, which we have identified with the specifier of the clause-internal Focus Phrase. If this assumption is correct, we expect that sentences containing a definite subject and an unaccusative verb should be given essentially the same level of marginality as the marginal sentences of (15). I think that this describes the situation in a fairly accurate way:[50]

(41) a. ?E' arrivato lo studente al giornale
          has arrived the student at the newspaper
      b. ?E' entrato Mario dalla finestra
          has come in Mario from the window

No marginality is now detectable if no prepositional complement follows the postverbal subject, as no violation of the tendency to locate the focused constituent in the last position is produced:

(42) a. E' arrivato lo studente
          has arrived the student

b. E' entrato Mario
    has come in Mario

It is well known that *ne* cliticization gives a perfect output when it takes place from a postverbal unaccusative subject[51] but a marginal output when it takes place from an unergative one. Example (43) illustrates the contrast:

(43) a. (?) Ha telefonato uno studente al giornale
          has phoned a student to the newspaper
      b. ??Ne ha telefonato uno al giornale
          of-them+has telephoned one at the newspaper
      c. E' arrivato uno studente al giornale
          has arrived a student at the newspaper
      d. Ne è arrivato uno al giornale
          of-them+has arrived one at the newspaper

Updating Belletti (1988), I interpret the contrast between (43b) and (43d) as due to the fact that (*ne*) extraction is possible from the VP-internal (subject) position but does not work equally well from the VP-external Focus position.[52]

The natural question to ask now is this: What is the status of clauses that contain a reordering of the postverbal subject and the prepositional object of an unaccusative verb? We note first that such a reordering is possible:

(44) a. E' arrivato al giornale uno studente
          has arrived at the newspaper a student
      b. E' entrato dalla finestra un ladro
          has come in from the window a thief

These sentences can be given the same status as the double-complement sentences that involve reordering. The null assumption is that they receive the same analysis with a topicalized (remnant) VP and a focalized subject.[53] Note that if this analysis is on the right track, we expect *ne* cliticization to have the same status in both cases. This status should be a marginal one because extraction from a Noun Phrase in the specifier of the Focus Phrase gives rise to marginality. This is indeed what we find. Example (45a, b), containing an unaccusative verb, and (45c), containing a double-complement verb, are all rather marginal. Their status compares with that of (43b):

(45) a. ??Ne è arrivato al giornale uno
          of-them+has arrived at the newspaper one
      b. ??Ne è entrato dalla finestra uno
          of-them+has come in from the window one
      c. ??Ne ho dato a Gianni uno
          (I) of-them+have given to Gianni one

NOTES

Versions of this work were presented at the workshop Inversion in Romance, University of Amsterdam, May 1998; in lectures at the Australian Linguistic Institute (ALI, July 1998); at the IX Colloquium on Generative Grammar, Universitat Autònoma de Barcelona, April 1999; and in seminars at the Scuola Normale Superiore di Pisa and at the University of Siena. I wish to thank the audiences for these events for their comments and reactions, which engendered significant improvements. For insightful comments on a previously written version, I owe special thanks to Andrea Calabrese, Anna Cardinaletti, Carlo Cecchetto, Aafke Hulk, Richard Kayne, Andrea Moro, and Luigi Rizzi.

1. This argument preserves the spirit of B&S although various aspects of the implementation, some more crucial than others, differ in various ways, as will be pointed out in the course of the discussion.

2. Case is often considered to be the licensing feature held responsible for this distribution of the subject and is made available through the established relation, with possible differences according to whether the verb is a transitive/unergative or an unaccusative.

3. The topic has been widely investigated; some representative items in the literature include Belletti (1988), Burzio (1986), Lasnik (1992, 1995), Pollock (1983), Rizzi (1982), and Safir (1984).

4. It is well known that intonation may "save" or simply change the status of various sentences in interesting ways, some of which will be considered in some detail when relevant to the analysis.

5. This should be considered an explicit sign of a change in the syntactic structure.

6. Note that *tutto* is higher than *bene* and lower than *completamente* in Cinque's (1998) clausal map. The quantifier should then be allowed to raise higher than the latter adverb if the proposed interpretation of the contrast is on the right track (see Rizzi 1996 for a similar conclusion). Movement of *tutto* should be assimilated to the visible syntactic movement of the equivalent French *tout* and negative *rien*. It is frequently suggested that an adjacency requirement operates to the effect that a verb and a postverbal subject should be adjacent to each other and that nothing should intervene between them (Friedemann 1995; Rizzi 1996; see also the observations below). Of course the relevant constraint, usually assimilated to Case adjacency, should be able to capture the subtle distinctions in (1) and to account for the total impossibility of (2), despite the apparent satisfaction of the requirement. Conceivably, as a reviewer suggests, the VP (or bigger constituent) that contains V + Adv could be topicalized in the clause-internal Topic Phrase, to be discussed below, or in the clause-external one (Rizzi 1997). If so, these data would not indicate the low location of the inverted (focalized) subject. Although a derivation of this kind could not be excluded in principle, it seems that nothing in the interpretation would force it (contrary to the data to be discussed in 1.4). Hence, a derivation not involving topicalization should also be admitted. As a consequence, the contrast between the orders in (1) and (2) can indeed be taken as an explicit indication of the clausal map, with the postverbal subject lower than the lowest adverbs. Note furthermore, that a derivation that involves topicalization would not easily be able to draw the relevant distinction in the hierarchy of grammaticality judgments.

7. In the same vein, consider the further fact that (3b) can also be the appropriate answer to a question about the clause as a whole, such as *cosa è successo?*; or it can be pronounced in a so-called "out of the blue" context, in both cases with no presupposition about the subject. Sentence (3c) would not be equally appropriate in similar contexts.

8. It is possible that the judgment is so sharp because these "answers" have become *figées* expressions. Furthermore, the impossibility of (4f) is also due to the fact that a predicate is necessary in copular sentences. See Moro (1997) for a discussion of similar data in which the good cases are assumed to be "inverse copular" sentences that contain a low clause-internal subject. This is an analysis interestingly convergent with the one to be developed here.

9. See Cardinaletti (1998), where data like those in (1) and (2) are also presented and precisely this assumption is made.

10. In addition to subject inversion structures, no other cases appear to require a similar kind of nonlocal assignment/realization. See Belletti (1988) and Lasnik (1992, 1995); see also the discussion in note 16.

11. For a distinction between peripheral (often contrastive) Focus and new information Focus, see Kiss (1998), where only the first type is associated with a designated syntactic head.

12. This is a proposal to be refined below (cf. 1.4).

13. In contrast to B&S, I now assume that FocusP always displays a regular left-branching Spec position. This eliminates one unsatisfactory aspect of that analysis that stipulates a parametrical difference between languages with respect to the direction of the location of the specifier of FocusP while keeping its fundamental leading intuition. I believe that the comparative insights of B&S's analysis can be preserved within the set of new assumptions developed here, but I do not attempt a close examination of the comparative issue.

14. Case and Focus are not necessarily alternative licensing features. They can combine with no clash being created: The clearest case is probably peripheral Focus (under a movement analysis of Focalization).

15. This is the "standard" view in GB (cf. Burzio 1986; Rizzi 1982; Safir 1984). See Alexiadou and Anagnostopoulou (1998) for a recent different view, which does not imply the presence of a nonovert expletive in the preverbal subject position (of null subject languages).

16. Its status as "new information" is confirmed by the following question-answer pairs:

(i) a. Chi pensa di parlare a Gianni?
         Who thinks to speak to Gianni?
     b. Penso di parlare io a Gianni (= (10))
         (I) think to speak I to Gianni
     b'. Penso di parlarci io
         (I) think to speak to him I

"A Gianni" in (ib) could fill the low Topic position to be introduced in 1.4. Note that no "long-distance agreement" of the type advocated in Chomsky (1998) could be established in (10) between the matrix T and the postverbal pronoun in the embedded clause and held responsible for both Case on the pronoun and Agreement, given the control status of the infinitival clause. Cases like (10) are thus crucially different from raising cases such as *There was a man in the room* or, possibly, *Sembrano essere arrivati molti ragazzi* (*there seem to have arrived many children*), discussed in Chomsky and in previous literature on inversion (see the references in note 3). I thank E. Raposo and an anonymous reviewer for implicitly raising the issue of a comparison between the two types of structures. It should also be noted that structures like those in (10) do not necessarily involve agreement between the matrix subject and the embedded nominative pronoun, as in cases such as (ii), thus confirming the conclusion that "long-distance agreement" is not the relevant notion here anyway:

(ii)   Maria mi ha chiesto [di parlare io a Gianni]
        Maria asked me to speak I to Gianni

17. In this analysis PRO is then an argumental subject, not an expletive PRO. This is a welcome conclusion, given the often observed lack of an expletive PRO in infinitival clauses, which examples such as the following illustrate:

(i)   *?E' difficile rispondere senza PRO sembrare impossibile.
       It is difficult to answer without seeming impossible.

(ii)   *Maria è partita senza PRO essere certo che fosse necessario.
       Maria has left without being certain that it was necessary.

18. This should be held responsible for verbal agreement only.

19. Contrary to emphatic pronouns, FQ does not need licensing in Focus Phrase— whence the different status of FQ and emphatic pronouns for Focalization. An emphatic function is also associated with the overt embedded pronoun of (10). The same analysis should account for the (apparent) anaphoric behavior of the personal pronoun "io." Here the moved portion of the noun phrase should correspond to a nonovert PRO. The fact that the emphatic pronoun can be realized as different persons and numbers suggests that it corresponds to various functional positions of the DP. Thus, the proposal hinted at in the text of simply calling it "D" must be viewed as a simplification. Note that for the proposed account to work, a sufficiently rich internal structure must be attributed to the noun phrase to allow for more than one D-type position. This is necessary in order to derive cases like (i):

(i)   *Il* responsabile parlerà *lui* della situazione.
       The responsible person will speak he of the situation.

Here both the article and the strong emphatic pronoun are present. In the analysis in the text, the emphatic constructions share crucial structural properties with clitic-doubling constructions (Belletti forthcoming; Sportiche 1996; Uriagereka 1995). This is also true from the point of view of the ϑ roles involved, as in both cases one single ϑ role is shared by the two related elements: the lexical noun phrase and the pronoun. The emphatic construction is, in a sense, the "mirror image" of clitic doubling. In clitic doubling the moved portion is the D-portion, whereas it is the portion that contains the lexical noun phrase in the emphatic construction. I leave these considerations for further development.

20. No similar problem arises if movement involves a QP rather than a direct object DP, as facts about the quantifier "tutto," like those in (1c), indicate. The different categorial status should be at the source of this difference. See Haegeman (1993) and Watanabe (1992) on the operation of the constraint, which appears also to be generally respected in "object shift" constructions (Vikner 1995).

21. The two "??" in (13) refer to the sentence pronounced with normal, noninterrupted intonation. The sentences have a reading in which VO is taken as the given/presupposed information, related to a slightly different intonation, with VO pronounced as a unit, which makes them acceptable. We address this possible reading in the following discussion. If cliticization of O takes place, the output is straightforwardly well formed:

(i)   Lo capirà Gianni
       It+will understand Gianni

I propose that, if cliticization starts out as head movement of the clitic (D) from the object Case-checking specifier position (Belletti forthcoming), (i) would not violate RM under the assumption that the clitic DP moves to the object Case-checking specifier from the specifier of a clause-internal Topic Phrase, as in the analysis of VOS in 1.4, and thus not directly crossing over the subject. Movement of the object DP from the specifier of the Topic Phrase should be assumed anyway, as Case checking of the object should be performed in VOS.

22.   This is, of course, under the assumption that O could be licensed in this structure, a matter to which we return shortly.

23.   The RM would possibly be violated here as well, although it might be suggested that if S does not move the violation of RM would not arise in the same way. See in this connection VOS in object shift, with S indefinite, and hence, possibly, in its VP-internal base position.

24.   The variety of subjects utilized—definite, indefinite, and proper name—is meant to indicate that the contrast is detectable independently from this variable. As pointed out in Kayne and Pollock (1978) and as is discussed in detail in Friedemann (1995), VSPP is also a possible order in French stylistic inversion constructions such as (i) (see Friedemann for the discussion of subtle gradations in acceptability judgments in these structures; see also Kampers-Manhe 1998 for restrictions on VSPP in subjunctive stylistic inversion contexts):

(i)   Qu'a dit Jean au jardinier?
       What has said Jean to the gardener?

Both VSO and VOS are excluded in the same constructions. Although the judgment is fairly subtle, VSPP tends to be more acceptable than VSO also in embedded control infinitival clauses that contain an emphatic (noncontrastive) nominative pronoun of the kind discussed in (10):

(ii)   a.   (?) Quello studente/ - ha/ho deciso [di parlare lui/io col direttore]
            that student/(I) decided to talk he/I to the director
       b.   ??Quello studente/ - ha/ho deciso [di corrompere lui/io il direttore]
            that student /(I) decided to bribe he/I the director

The judgments refer to the sentences pronounced with continuous, neutral intonation, in particular, with no "marginalization" of the direct object in the sense of Antinucci and Cinque (1977), which would make both sentences perfectly acceptable.

25.   A stronger requirement has been proposed by Stowell (1981), namely, that clauses "resist" Case. Given the framework for the proposal, where Case was taken to be assigned under government in the complement position, Stowell also assumes that clauses are necessarily extraposed. The analysis required supplementary assumptions to distinguish between complement clauses and adjunct clauses, which display very different behaviors, most notably in extraction. The fundamental intuition that distinguishes between clauses and nominal arguments is on the right track, I believe.

26.   To the extent that the sentences become acceptable with the alternative order V CP S, they could be amenable to the same analysis as the possible VOS orders to be discussed in 1.4:

(i)   a. Ha cominciato a non capire più niente Gianni
          has started to not understand anything anymore Gianni
      b. Ha pensato/pensa che Gianni non capisca più niente la mamma
          has thought/thinks that Gianni doesn't understand anything anymore
          the mother
      c. Crede che Gianni sia partito Maria
          believes that Gianni has left Maria
      d. Ha deciso di parlare con Maria Gianni
          has decided to speak with Maria Gianni

Note, furthermore, the following interesting contrast:

(ii)   *?Ha deciso di parlare Gianni con Mario
       has decided to speak Gianni with Mario
(iii) Gianni ha deciso di parlare lui con Mario.
       Gianni has decided to speak he with Mario.

Judgments refer to situations in which no special (contrastive) intonation is associated
with "Gianni" or "lui." Example (iii) should be analyzed as discussed in 1.2 in the text,
with the pronoun licensed in the specifier of the embedded Focus Phrase, "doubling"
the PRO raised to the subject position of the infinitival. A similar analysis could not be
extended to (ii) as PRO and "Gianni" would plausibly compete for the same position
within the original DP. Example (ii) contrasts with (iv):

(iv)   [ha deciso di PRO parlare t] GIANNI con Mario
       has decided to speak GIANNI with Mario

The preposed portion of the clause is topicalized in the clause-peripheral position,
"Gianni" is contrastively focalized in the clause-peripheral Focus Phrase, and the PP
is "marginalized" in a clause-internal Topic position (Belletti 1999); in the simplified
representation "t" stands for the original location of the PP.
    27. A similar judgment applies to sentences in which the VP contains a PP comple-
ment, displaying the order V PP S:

(i)   a. Chi ha parlato con Maria?
          Who has spoken with Maria?
      b. Ha parlato con Maria Gianni
          Has spoken with Maria Gianni

    28. Given the appropriate set of presuppositions, the following would also
be more natural answers to the questions in (18a, c):

(i)   Ha capito il problema solo Gianni.
       Has understood the problem only Gianni.
(ii)   Spedirà la lettera proprio Maria.
       Will send the letter precisely Maria.

"Solo" and "proprio" act as constituent focalizers, thus leaving as a "topic"/"given"
information everything that precedes them.

29. I thank L. Rizzi for bringing these quite typical data to my attention in this connection.

30. The role of the latter is analyzed in Belletti (1999) in the context of the discussion of the so-called process of "marginalization" (Antinucci & Cinque 1977).

31. An analysis along similar lines is proposed in Ordóñez (1997) for similar data. However, in contrast to Ordóñez, I assume that the process is clause-internal. I leave the clause-external Focus (and the related Topics) as the designated position for contrastive focus. See also the discussion below. For the idea of a clause-internal Topic Phrase position, see the recent analysis of right dislocation proposed by Cecchetto (1998).

32. I must consequently assume that the violation of the proper binding requirement (induced by the subject trace) is "rescued" in the same way as the same violation of "remnant topicalization" structures (through "reconstruction"). It can furthermore be assumed that O can then move out of the Topic Phrase to reach its Case-checking specifier. See note 21 for a related discussion. Moreover, V could also move out to perform checking of its φ features.

33. This is an updating and refinement of Chomsky's (1977) analysis of various "left-peripheral" constructions in terms of the unifying process of wh-movement.

34. That is, "one" of the clause-internal positions available to preverbal subjects; see Cardinaletti (1997) and related work in the same direction, according to which there are at least two, and possibly more, positions available to preverbal subjects, each specialized for different interpretations and hosting different kinds of subjects.

35. Ordóñez's (1997) analysis is then adopted for these cases only. I leave open for now a close discussion of the question of whether the clause-external Focus Projection is the only one designated for assignment of contrastive stress or whether, in some cases, the clause-internal one would also qualify. What is important to underscore is that only the clause-internal Focus Projection is compatible with regular stress/intonation, and it is the site of simple new information focus; the clause-external one is compatible with contrastive stress. What remains to be seen is whether the clause-internal Focus Projection can also be compatible with contrastive stress and, if yes, in what circumstances. For the time being, I make the strongest assumption that only the clause-external Focus Projection is specialized for contrast, as in the discussion in the text.

36. It is possible that this latter position is accessible to the direct object.

37. The processes involved are assimilated to those at work in VSO languages in general (cf. Semitic, Irish, etc.).

38. In the spirit of this kind of account, the same DP position could be available and possibly host the subject in all languages. The difference should be whether the DP is allowed to remain in such a position, whether it is licensed there or not. It would be licensed in Spanish and not in Italian. I speculate that agreement with the closest governing V could be the relevant factor. As pointed out in Picallo (1998; see also Solà 1992), VSO is excluded in Catalan (Picallo's diacritics):

(i) (??)*Fullejava en Joan el diari
    leafed Joan through the newspaper

Because Catalan displays an order of adverbs closer to Spanish than to Italian, this seems to suggest that a "shorter V-movement" should at most be considered a necessary but not a sufficient condition for the licensing of the extra "low" subject position anyway.

39. In contrast to B&S, I make the assumption that, as in the uniform base of Kayne (1994), the direction of the location of the Specs is uniformly on the left of

the head projection. I have made the same change as for the location of the Specifier of the Focus Projection. (See also note 13.) In B&S the hierarchy of the arguments has the PP in the Spec of the low VP and O in its complement position. If this is the case, the assumption must be made that RM is not violated by the crossing of O over the PP in its movement to the case-checking position. Plausibly, a PP would not interfere in the movement of a DP. The constraint on the preservation of the hierarchy of arguments might be more problematic, though. This suggests that a more appropriate representation should have O in the Spec of the lower VP and PP in the complement position, as in the representation in (28). The issue concerning RM does not arise, nor does the one concerning the preservation of the hierarchy of arguments. See Larson (1988) and the representation adopted in section (3) for unaccusatives. Nothing changes with either assumption in the execution of the proposal to be discussed below.

40. The usual feeling of redundancy and slight unnaturalness is associated with (33b), as in the case of (18b, d). A more natural answer would not repeat the lexical PP but would utilize a dative pronoun:

    (i)   le ho restituito le chiavi
         (I) to-her+gave back the keys

The crucial observation here does not concern this relatively subtle fact but rather the sharp contrast between (33b) vs. (33b').

41. The auxiliary should fill its regular position within the relevant inflectional head that normally hosts it. If checking of the past participle features needs to take place, we could assume that the relevant heads (Asp, at least) should immediately dominate the VP before the Topic-Focus Phrases. Alternatively, movement to the checking head could start out from the Topic Phrase, as already assumed for the direct object in VOS (cf. notes 21 and 31).

42. Note that an alternative answer to (34a), could be

    (i)   Gianni ha restituito le chiavi # a Maria.
         Gianni has given back the keys #to Maria.

There is a clear interruption between the direct object and the following PP. (The pause can be enriched with contrastive stress on the direct object, but contrast is not necessary here.) Sentence (i) involves Topicalization/Marginalization of the PP (more on that in Belletti 1999). Given the organization of the information structure of the clause, I assume the object to also be in the specifier of the Focus Phrase in this case.

43. As in Rizzi's (1997) articulated CP structure, the Topic Phrase is found below the relative complementizer, which is the highest C-level.

44. More generally, every clause allows for just one constituent to be focalized (Calabrese 1992). Thus, not only clause internal focalization can involve one constituent at most, but clause external focalization as well:

    (i)   *IL LIBRO, A MARIA, Gianni non ha ancora dato.
         THE BOOK, TO MARIA, Gianni hasn't given yet.

It is interesting that clause-internal and clause-external Focalization cannot combine either:

(ii)   *IL LIBRO, le darà Gianni
         THE BOOK to-her+will give Gianni.

"Gianni" should be construed as a new information Focus and "il libro" as a contrastive Focus. This might suggest that at the interpretive level, clause-internal and clause-external Focalization are indeed a unified phenomenon, despite the differences that they manifest in their distribution, as well as in their informational pragmatics. In the spirit of Chomsky (1977), one could suggest that at LF, all instances of Focalization are reduced to one single process. I do not attempt to provide a formalization of this idea here. See Rizzi (1997) for a relevant discussion.

45. O cannot independently move to its (Case)-checking position since this position is higher than both the Topic Phrase and the Focus Phrase, by assumption.

46. The peak of the intonation here is on S. For a closer discussion of marginalization in this connection see Belletti (1999).

47. Possibly, all unaccusatives do in fact select a prepositional argument, which can remain silent. See also the discussion in Moro (1997).

48. It may be that such a VP-internal, as such an inherent (partitive?) Case position, is systematically available for (certain) indefinite objects. This updates Belletti's (1988) analysis. According to Longobardi (1998), unmodified bare plural subjects in the existential interpretation are allowed to remain VP-internal with both unaccusative and intransitive verbs. We could speculate that they should qualify for VP-internal licensing through the VP-internal Case, which severely limits the choice of possible DPs. As a general approach, I assume that verbal agreement is obtained through the relation with the associate expletive in the preverbal subject position. See note 18 in this connection.

49. Note that the last constituent is often also the most embedded one, and thus the one receiving nuclear stress, which makes it the most prominent. There seems to be a tendency/preference to have matching between Focus and prominence. See in this connection Cinque (1993) and the line of research in Zubizarreta (1998).

50. These data illustrate the so called "Definiteness Effect" (DE), which has often been reported to give rise to a relatively subtle and often difficult violation in which different factors come into play that are related to the interpretation, the informational organization of the clause, and the intonation. This is at the source of a complex gradation in the grammaticality judgments associated with the relevant sentences. Note that the marginality of (42) is a bit stronger than that of (15). This could be related to the fact that the first/unmarked location for the postverbal subject of unaccusatives is the VP-internal one. Since this position is compatible only with indefinite subjects, this requires that sentences like (42) be reanalyzed to involve not a VP-internal but a VP-external, focused subject.

51. This is comparable to the status of the same cliticization process out of a direct object of a transitive verb (Belletti & Rizzi 1981; Burzio 1986). At least for indefinite direct objects we can assume the same structural analysis as the one assumed for the postverbal subject of unaccusatives. (See note 47.)

52. It gives rise to a CED-type effect (see the discussion in B&S). I assume that the specifier of the Focus Phrase is an impossible extraction site since it is a derived, not L-marked, position. On the other hand, like the preverbal subject position, it can be considered an A-position (in contrast to the clause-external Focus Phrase). This is suggested both by the fact that DPs are licensed there according to the proposed analysis and by the empirical phenomenon of verbal agreement, which holds with a focalized inverted subject (through the relation with the associate expletive in the preverbal subject position; see notes 18 and 47).

53. This occurs because we are systematically interpreting reordering as Focalization in the specifier of the Focus Phrase. This assumption excludes the possibility of leaving the indefinite subject in the VP-internal position in this case.

REFERENCES

Alexiadou, A., & E. Anagnostopoulou. (1998). "Parametrizing AGR: Word Order, V-Movement and EPP Checking." *Natural Language and Linguistic Theory* 16, 491–539.
Antinucci, F., & G. Cinque. (1977). "Sull'ordine delle parole in italiano, L'emarginazione." *Studi di grammatica italiana* 6, 121–146.
Belletti, A. (1988). "The Case of Unaccusatives." *Linguistic Inquiry* 19, 1–34.
———. (1999). " 'Inversion' as Focalization and Related Questions." Ms., University of Siena, to appear in *Catalan Working Papers in Linguistics*.
———. (forthcoming). "Italian/Romance Clitics: Structure and Derivation." In H. van Riemsdijk (ed.), *Clitics in the Languages of Europe*. Mouton de Gruyter, Berlin.
Belletti, A., & L. Rizzi. (1981). "The Syntax of *Ne*: Some Theoretical Implications." *Linguistic Review* 1, 117–154.
Belletti, A., & U. Shlonsky. (1995). "The Order of Verbal Complements: A Comparative Study." *Natural Language and Linguistic Theory* 13, 489–526.
Bobaljik, J. D., & D. Jonas. (1996). "Subject Position and the Roles of TP." *Linguistic Inquiry* 27/2, 195–236.
Brandi, L., & P. Cordin. (1981). "Dialetti e italiano: Un confronto sul parametro del soggetto nullo." *Rivista di Grammatica Generativa* 6, 33–87.
Brody, M. (1990). "Some Remarks on the Focus Field in Hungarian." *UCL Working Papers* 2, 201–225.
Burzio, L. (1986). *Italian Syntax: A Government-Binding Approach*. Reidel, Dordrecht.
Calabrese, A. (1992) "Some Remarks on Focus and Logical Structures in Italian." *Harvard Working Papers in Linguistics* 1, 19–27.
Cardinaletti, A. (1997). "Subjects and Clause Structure." In L. Haegeman (ed.), *The New Comparative Syntax*. Longman, London, England, 33–63.
———. (1998). "A Second Thought on Emargination: Destressing vs. 'Right Dislocation.'" Ms., Università di Venezia.
Cardinaletti, A., & M. Starke. (1994). "The Typology of Structural Deficiency: A Case Study of the Three Classes of Pronouns." In H. van Riemsdijk (ed.), *Clitics in the Languages of Europe*. Mouton de Gruyter, Berlin.
Cecchetto, C. (1998). "A Comparative Analysis of Left and Right Dislocation in Romance." *Studia Linguistica* 53, 40–67.
Chomsky, N. (1977). "On Wh-Movement." In A. Akmajian, P. Culicover, & T. Wasow (eds.), *Formal Syntax*. Academic Press, New York, 71–132.
———. (1995). *The Minimalist Program*. MIT Press, Cambridge, Mass.
———. (1998). "Minimalist Inquiries." Ms., MIT, Cambridge, Mass.
Chomsky, N., & H. Lasnik. (1993). "The Theory of Principles and Parameters." In A. von Stechow, W. Sternefeld, & T. Vennemann (eds). *An International Handbook of Contemporary Research*. De Gruyter, Berlin.
Cinque, G. (1990). *Types of A' Dependencies*. MIT Press, Cambridge, Mass.
———. (1993). "A Null Theory of Phrase and Compound Stress." *Linguistic Inquiry* 24, 239–298.
———. (1998). *Adverbs and Functional Heads*. Oxford University Press, New York.

Friedemann, M. A. (1995). "Sujets Syntaxiques: Position, inversion et pro." Thèse de doctorat, Université de Genève.

Guasti, M. T. (1996). "On the Controversial Status of Romance Interrogatives." *Probus* 8, 161–180.

Haegeman, L. (1993). "Some Speculations on Argument Shift, Clitics and Crossing in West Flemish." In W. Abrahm & J. Bayer (eds.), *Linguistiche Berichte, Dialectsyntax*, 131–160.

Kampers-Manhe, B. (1998). "'Je veux que parte Paul'. A neglected construction." In A. Schwegler, B. Tranel, & M. Uribe-Extebarria (eds.), *Romance Linguistics, Theoretical Perspectives*. John Benjamins, Amsterdam, 129–141.

Kayne, R. (1994). *The Antisymmetry of Syntax*. MIT Press, Cambridge, Mass.

Kayne, R., & J. Y. Pollock. (1978). "Stylistic Inversion, Successive Cyclicity, and Move NP in French." *Linguistic Inquiry* 9, 595–621.

Kiss, K. E. (1998). "Identificational Focus versus Information Focus." *Language* 74/2, 245–273.

Koopman, H., & D. Sportiche. (1991). The Position of Subjects. *Lingua* 85, 211–258.

Kuroda, Y. (1988). "Whether We Agree or Not: A Comparative Syntax of English and Japanese." In W. Poser (ed.), *Papers from the Second International Workshop on Japanese Syntax*. Stanford University, Stanford, Calif.

Larson, R. (1988). "On the Double Object Construction." *Linguistic Inquiry* 19, 335–391.

Lasnik, H. (1992). "Case and Expletives: Notes toward a Parametric Account." *Linguistic Inquiry* 23, 381–405.

———. (1995). "Case and Expletives Revisited: On Greed and Other Human Failings." *Linguistic Inquiry* 26, 615–633.

Longobardi, G. (1998). "Two Types of 'Postverbal' Subjects in Italian." Ms., University of Trieste.

Moro, A. (1997). *The Raising of Predicates*. Cambridge University Press, Cambridge.

Motapanyane, V. (1995). *Theoretical Implications of Complementation in Romanian*. Unipress, Padua, Italy.

Ordóñez, F. (1997). "Word Order and Clause Structure in Spanish and Other Romance Languages." Ph.D. diss., City University of New York.

Picallo, C. (1998). "On the Extended Projection Principle and Null Expletive Subjects." *Probus* 10, 219–241.

Pollock, J. Y. (1983). "Accord, chaines impersonnelles et variables." *Linguisticae Investigationes* 7, 131–181.

———. (1989). "Verb Movement, Universal Grammar, and the Structure of IP." *Linguistic Inquiry* 20, 365–424.

Puskas, G. (1996). "Word Order in Hungarian. The Synatx of A' positions." Thèse de doctorat, Université de Genève.

Rizzi, L. (1982). *Issues in Italian Syntax*. Foris Publications, Dordrecht.

———. (1990). *Relativized Minimality*. MIT Press, Cambridge, Mass.

———. (1996). "Residual Verb Second and the *Wh*-Criterion." In A. Belletti & L. Rizzi (eds.), *Parameters and Functional Heads*. Oxford University Press, New York, 63–90.

———. (1997). "The Fine Structure of the Left Periphery." In L. Haegeman (ed.), *Elements of grammar*. Kluwer, Dordrecht, 281–337.

Safir, K. (1984). "Syntactic Chains and the Definiteness Effect." Ph.D. diss., MIT, Cambridge, Mass.

Solà, J. (1992). "Agreement and Subjects." Ph.D. diss., Universitat Autònoma de Barcelona.

Sportiche, D. (1988). "A Theory of Floating Quantifiers and Its Corollaries for Constituent Structure." *Linguistic Inquiry* 19, 425–449.

———. (1996). "Clitic Constructions." In J. Rooryck & L. Zaring (eds.), *Phrase Structure and the Lexicon*. Kluwer, Dordrecht, 213–276.

Stowell, T. (1981). "Origins of Phrase Structure." Ph.D. diss., MIT, Cambridge, Mass.

Suñer, M. (1994). "Verb Movement and the Licensing of Argumental Wh-Phrases in Spanish." *Natural Language and Linguistic Theory* 12, 335–372.

Uriagereka, J. (1995). "Aspects of the Syntax of Clitic Placement in Western Romance." *Linguistic Inquiry* 26, 79–123.

Vikner, S. (1995). *Verb Movement and Expletive Subjects in the Germanic languages*. Oxford University Press, New York.

Watanabe, A. (1992). "Wh-in-situ, Subjacency and Chain Formation," *MIT Working Papers in Linguistics*, 2.

Zubizarreta, M. L. (1998). *Prosody, Focus and Word Order*. MIT Press, Cambridge, Mass.

4

Marked versus Unmarked Inversion and Optimality Theory

JOÃO COSTA

The basic word order of a language is often determined in terms of markedness of discourse contexts. Accordingly, an unmarked word order is one in which all elements of the sentence are equal in discourse: Either they are all new information or they are all old information. A context in which all elements may have the same status in discourse is the answer to a question such as 'what happened?' This question does not presuppose any of the elements that appear in the answer; all of them will, therefore, constitute new information.

The unmarked word order differs cross-linguistically. In this chapter, I am interested in finding out why inverted constructions, in which the subject follows the verb, may be unmarked in some languages but obligatorily marked in others. I focus on the following languages: Portuguese, Spanish, and Greek.[1]

I suggest that variation at the base may be explained and formalized in terms of Emergence of the Unmarked (cf. McCarthy & Prince 1994). In section 1, I present the data to be discussed and the issues raised by the cross-linguistic variation to be observed. In section 2, I introduce the theoretical background: emergence of the unmarked in Optimality Theory. In section 3, I provide an analysis for the facts previously discussed within the premises of Optimality Theory. In section 4, I consider Italian inversion.

1. Data and Questions

As mentioned, and following standard literature, I consider that unmarked word orders may be identified in answers to the question 'what happened'? (Dik 1978;

Li 1976). Different languages display different word orders in this context. In Portuguese (Ambar 1992; Duarte 1987; Mateus et al. 1989; etc.), in this context, only SVO is possible:[2]

(1) *Portuguese:*
     O João comeu o bolo.
     João ate the cake.

In a variety of Spanish, which will be identified throughout as Spanish A, described, for example, in Hernanz and Brucart (1987), the unmarked word order is also SVO:

(2) *Spanish A* (Hernanz & Brucart 1987):
     Juan ha visto a Maria.
     Juan has seen to Maria.

Both Portuguese and Spanish A permit inverted orders, as is well known. However, these are illegitimate answers to the question 'what happened?':

(3) *Portuguese:*
     a. Comeu o Paulo a sopa.
         ate Paulo the soup

     Spanish A:
     b. Comió Pedro los guisantes.
         ate Pedro the peas

In contrast to the variety of Spanish just presented, in Spanish B (as described in Ordoñez & Treviño 1995, and Zubizarreta 1995), the inverted word order VSO is the unmarked one:

(4) *Spanish B:*
     Comió Juan los guisantes.
     ate Juan the peas

The same behavior is found in modern Greek. According to Alexiadou (1995) and Alexiadou & Anagnostopoulou (1995), only subjects that behave as topic occur preverbally:

(5) *Greek:*
     Pandreftike o Petros tin Ilekttra.
     Married the Petros-NOM the Ilektra-ACC
     'Petros married Ilektra.'

Greek and Spanish B also allow SVO orders, but not in unmarked contexts. Those may be analyzed as instances of subject left dislocation (see Barbosa 1995 and Alexiadou & Anagnostopoulou 1995 for details):

(6) *Greek:*
   a. O Petros pandreftike tin Ilektra.
     the Petros married the Ilektra

  Spanish B:
   b. Pedro comió los guisantes.
     Pedro ate the peas.

These cross-linguistic differences raise the following questions:

A. What does it formally mean to be the unmarked word order of a language?
   That is, how can it be determined that a given word order is the unmarked one for a given language? Is it possible to formalize the notion of unmarkedness?
B. Why is there variation at the base? Why isn't inversion universally (un)marked?
   In other words, once it is found that a given word order is unmarked for a given language, how can it be explained that the same word order is marked in other languages. What is the difference between inversion in Portuguese and inversion in Greek that makes it marked in the former and unmarked in the latter?

In the next sections, these two questions are answered through an Optimality-theoretical analysis.

2. Theoretical Background

The analysis I propose for the differences presented above is couched in the framework of Optimality Theory (OT) (Prince & Smolensky 1993). The following set of assumptions underlie this model:

A. The grammar is a set of universal and violable constraints.
B. Constraint ranking determines violability.
C. Particular grammars are rankings of constraints.
D. Cross-linguistic variation reflects different rankings.

A crucial difference between OT and parametric approaches is that OT predicts that in some contexts the effects of dominated constraints are visible. The visibility of dominated constraints is called the *Emergence of the Unmarked* (McCarthy & Prince 1994). In parametric approaches, the effects of a switched-off parameter are predicted not to be relevant.

    My proposal is that the unmarked word order of a language with a fair amount of discourse-based flexibility is the one emerging when the effects of the top-ranked discourse-related constraints are controlled for. In the next section, I illustrate how this proposal works for Portuguese.

3.   Derivation of Unmarked Word Order in Portuguese

Although it is an SVO language, Portuguese (Costa 1996b) allows for other word orders (VSO, OSV, OVS, and VOS). Discourse context determines the adequacy or felicity of each possible word order, as (7)–(9) illustrate:

(7)   O que é que aconteceu? ('What happened?')
   a. Paulo partiu a janela.
      Paulo broke the window.
   b. #Partiu a janela o Paulo.
   c. #Partiu o Paulo a janela.

(8)   Ninguém partiu nada. ('No one broke anything.')
   a. #O Paulo partiu a janela.
   b. #Partiu a janela o Paulo.
   c. Partiu o Paulo a janela.

(9)   Quem partiu a janela? ('Who broke the window?')
   a. #O Paulo partiu a janela.
   b. Partiu a janela o Paulo.
   c. #Partiu o Paulo a janela.

In previous work (Costa 1996b), I proposed that this dependency on context is the result of a tension between syntactic constraints and discourse constraints.

   In simple terms, the constraint on Case requires that subject NPs go to Spec-IP, moving leftward. On the other hand, Focus requires that focused constituents surface as rightmost as possible to receive nuclear sentence stress, in accordance with the algorithms proposed in, for example, Cinque (1993), Frota (1994, 1997), Nash (1995), Nespor and Vogel (1986), and since the subject NP may not occupy the two positions at the same time, the conflict is solved in a Optimality-theoretical way: In a language like Portuguese, Focus will be higher ranked, enabling the NP to stay low. In a language like English, Case will be higher ranked than focus, making the NP move to the focused position in spite of its discourse role.

   These and the other constraints used in the analysis of the interaction between focus and syntax are listed in (10):

(10)   ALIGNFOCUS: Focused constituents are rightmost in the sentence
      (Grimshaw & Samek-Lodovici 1995, 1996).
      SUBJ-CASE: Subject NPs license Case in Spec-IP (Chomsky 1986, 1989, 1995).
      OBJ-CASE: Object NPs license Case in Spec-AgrOP (Chomsky 1989, 1995).
      STAY: Don't move (Chomsky 1989; Grimshaw 1997).
      TOP-FIRST: The first element of the sentence is its topic (Li 1976).[3]

As a reviewer points out, the view on constraint interaction that I am assuming here implies that there may be a direct conflict between syntactic and discourse constraints, which goes against some assumptions about autonomous syntax. Note that this does not imply that the definition of the constraints must not be found in a modular way. That is, syntactic constraints must be defined within a theory of syntax, and discourse constraints must be defined within a theory of discourse. The only prediction made by the OT framework is that these independently formalized constraints may interact and conflict if they impose contradictory requirements on one single output (see Costa forthcoming for a comparison among several analyses of this problem).

The ranking proposed for Portuguese is the following:

(11)   {ALIGNFOCUS, TOP-FIRST} >>Subj-Case>>STAY>>Obj-Case

This ranking makes the following predictions:

A. It is more important to satisfy discourse constraints than to license nominative case.
B. In Portuguese, there is no movement to Spec-AgrOP (only scrambling via adjunction to VP).
C. When subjects are not the focus of the sentence, they may raise to Spec-IP.

A crucial aspect for the discussion in this chapter is that this type of ranking, in which discourse-related constraints dominate syntactic constraints, predicts that there is a correspondence between different word orders and different information structures. In other words, since the discourse requirements that force focused constituents to be rightmost are higher ranked than the syntactic constraints, all the outputs will be faithful to the input specifications for information status. This will trigger one-to-one correspondences between word orders and information structures.

The only case in which one single information structure may be mapped onto several word orders is in the sentence-focus context, as in answers to the question 'what happened?' In this context, all the elements of the sentence are focused. Therefore, as long as the sentence stress falls on the rightmost constituent and may project (Nespor & Vogel 1986; Selkirk 1984), any word order will satisfy the constraint ALIGNFOCUS.

In that case, since ALIGNFOCUS is satisfied by all candidates, the choice will have to be made by the other constraints, the effects of which are normally not visible because of the dominance of ALIGNFOCUS. The visibility of the effects of constraints that are usually dominated is called in OT *Emergence of the Unmarked* (cf. McCarthy & Prince 1994). In other words, unmarked patterns may be the result of the evaluation by constraints whose effect is generally invisible because of the constraint ranking of the language. In contexts in which the dominating constraints are inoperative, the role of the low-ranked constraints in making decisions between candidates becomes visible.[4]

The following table (T1) illustrates the emergence of SVO as the unmarked word order in Portuguese, in accordance with the ranking proposed in (11).

(T1) Portuguese Unmarked Word Order

	Align-Focus	Top-First	Subj.-Case	Stay	Obj-Case
☞A. $[_{IP}$ S V $[_{VP}$ t t O]]		*		**	*
B. $[_{IP}$ S V $[_{AgrOP}$ O $[_{VP}$ t t t]]]		*		***!	
C. $[_{IP}$ V $[_{VP}$ S t O]]		*	*!	*	*
D. $[_{IP}$ V $[_{AgrOP}$ O $[_{VP}$ S t t]]]		*	*!	**	

In (T1), all word orders satisfy ALIGNFOCUS, provided that in all of them
stress falls on the rightmost position and projects over the whole IP. Likewise,
all candidates violate TOP-FIRST since all of them have an element in first
position that is not to be interpreted as a topic. The inverted orders (candidates
C and D) are excluded since the subject stays in Spec-VP, violating the next
constraint in the hierarchy: SUBJ-CASE. The grammatical candidate will then
be SVO without movement of the object to Spec-AgrOP since this option is
more economical than the one involving movement.

The Optimality-theoretical framework forces us to answer two questions:
Do rerankings of these constraints derive other languages? Can we observe the
effects of the Emergence of the Unmarked in other languages? One premise of
the theory is that language variation follows from the reranking of a similar set
of constraints. It is thus predicted that the reranking of these constraints will
derive other languages. In the next section, I show that the difference between
marked and unmarked inversion may be explained in such terms.

4. Derivation of Unmarked Word Orders in Other Languages

In the preceding section, I show how OT may explain the fact that SVO is the
unmarked word order in Portuguese. In this section, I demonstrate that the
reranking of the set of constraints proposed for Portuguese is able to derive
the fact that inversion is the unmarked pattern in other languages. Note that
whatever reranking is proposed, the difference for Portuguese should be minimal since Portuguese and Spanish A, on the one hand, and Spanish B, on the
other hand, are related languages. Postulating a radically different constraint
profile between these two languages might predict some major differences
between the two sets of languages.

As mentioned before, Spanish B and Greek are languages with unmarked
VSO word order:

(12)   *Spanish B:*
       Comió Juan los guisantes.
       ate Juan the peas

(13)   *Greek:*
       Pandreftike o Petros tin Ilekttra.
       married Petros Ilektra

I suggest that the crucial difference between these languages and Portuguese and Spanish A may be found in the behavior of preverbal subjects. According to most authors, preverbal subjects in the latter languages are in Spec-IP (see Ambar 1992; Costa 1996a, 1997; Duarte 1987; Martins 1994; Mateus et al. 1989; and Raposo 1987 for Portuguese and Hernanz & Brucart 1987 for Spanish; for a different position, see Barbosa 1995).

Some of the tests leading to the conclusion that preverbal subjects in Portuguese are in Spec-IP are presented in (14)–(16):

A. The preverbal position does not trigger A-bar minimality effects:

    (14) *No A-bar minimality effects* (Ambar 1992):
        a. Que livro o João leu?
            which book João read
        b. *Que livro, ao Paulo, o João leu?
            which book to Paulo J. read

B. The preverbal position does not trigger multiple topicalization effects. In other words, sentences with a preposed constituent and a preverbal subject are not marginal, unlike sentences with two preposed complements (cf. 15a'):[5]

    (15) *No multiple topicalization effects:*
        a. Esse livro, deram ontem à Maria.
            that book (they) gave yesterday to Maria
        a'. ?(?)Esse livro, à Maria deram ontem.
            that book to Maria (they) gave yesterday
        b. Esse livro, leu o Paulo ontem.
            that book read Paulo yesterday
        b'. Esse livro, o Paulo leu ontem.

C. In cases of (marginal) multiple topicalization, the order between multiple topics may be reversed. If preverbal subjects were left-dislocated rather than in an A-position, their relative ordering with respect to a topicalized constituent might be switched. However, that is not the case (cf. 16b):

    (16) *No changes between topics:*
        a. (?)?Sobre tempestades, com o pescador, eles falaram ontem.
            about storms with the fisherman they talked today
        a'. (?)?Com o pescador, sobre tempestades, eles falaram ontem.
            with the fisherman about storms they talked today
        b. O que é que o Pedro fez ao chocolate?
            What did P. do to the chocolate?
        b'. O chocolate, o Pedro comeu.
            the chocolate, P. ate.
        b". #O Pedro, o chocolate comeu.

The tests above lead to the conclusion that preverbal subjects in Portuguese are in Spec-IP, which makes this language different from Spanish B and Greek. According to Barbosa (1995), Ordoñez and Treviño (1995), and Zubizarreta (1995) for Spanish B and Alexiadou and Anagnostopoulou (1995) for Greek, in these languages preverbal subjects are left-dislocated.[6]

To achieve the goal of explaining the difference between these two sets of languages in terms of constraint reranking, it is necessary to find out what the crucial difference is between left dislocation and movement to Spec-IP and its consequences for the constraints proposed. Several authors have suggested that this difference in the Romance languages, in addition to the type of chain formed, is whether movement or base generation is involved. Accordingly, movement of the subject to Spec-IP involves movement, whereas left dislocation involves base generation of the dislocated constituent (Cinque 1990).

Let us consider two arguments recently developed for Portuguese in favor of the view that no movement is involved in left-dislocation constructions. Duarte (1987, 1996) proposes an analysis of topic promotion in Portuguese in terms of long-distance scrambling rather than movement. She argues in favor of a base-generated analysis, based on differences between this construction and cases of real A-bar movement. For instance, as pointed out above, it is marginally possible to obtain sentences with multiple topics (17a), but it is completely impossible to obtain sentences with multiple wh-movement. If topic promotion were just A-bar movement (17b), there would be no principled reason for this asymmetry.

(17)   *Multiple topics, but no multiple wh:*
    a. (?)?Sobre tempestades, com o pescador, falaram ontem.
        about storms with the fisherman they talked yesterday
    a'. *Sobre o quê com quem falaram ontem?
        about what with whom they talked yesterday

A second argument by Duarte is that clitic placement is sensitive to A-bar movement. Clitics are enclitic in general. In A-bar contexts, they are proclitic (18a). In contexts of topicalization, they remain enclitic. If proclisis is a diagnostic for A-bar movement, (18b) shows that this type of movement is not involved in left-dislocation constructions in Portuguese:

(18)   *Clitic placement:*
    a. O que é que a Maria te deu/*deu-te?
        what did Maria you$_{DAT}$ gave/gave you$_{DAT}$
    a'. Esse livro, a Maria deu-me/*me deu
        that book Maria gave me$_{DAT}$/me$_{DAT}$ gave

Similarly, Raposo (1996, 1997) argues that treating left dislocation in terms of base generation allows for an equal analysis of null object constructions and topic promotion. In neither case is there movement, and in both cases there is base generation of the topic. The only difference is that in the case of null object constructions, the base-generated topic is a null operator:

(19) a. Muito whisky, comprei para o capitão.
           A lot of whisky I bought for the captain.
      b. Comprei **ec** para o capitão.
           I bought for the captain.

Thus, by assuming that the difference between left dislocation and movement to Spec-IP lies in whether movement is involved or not, it is legitimate to claim that it is more economical to base-generate the subject in topic position than to move it to Spec-IP. A similar conclusion is reached in Barbosa (1995).

This difference between moving the subject to Spec-IP or left-dislocating it may be captured through a minimal reranking of what has been proposed for Portuguese:

(20) *Portuguese and Spanish A:*
       {ALIGNFOCUS,TOP-FIRST} >>**Subj-Case**>>**Stay**>>Obj-Case
       Spanish B and Greek:
       {ALIGNFOCUS,TOP-FIRST} >>**Stay**>>**Subj-Case**>>Obj-Case

It has been proposed above that in Portuguese and Spanish A Subj-CASE outranks STAY—which would explain why subjects move to Spec-IP in the unmarked case instead of staying in their base position. In (20), it is proposed that in Greek and Spanish B STAY outranks Subj-CASE. This ranking predicts that obtaining a more economical representation is more important than moving the subject to Spec-IP. Since there is a construction in which subjects may be promoted to the topic-sentence-initial position without movement, that is, through left dislocation, this will be the option for these languages.

The diagrams in (T2) and (T3) illustrate how the difference in ranking derives the different options for topic promotion of the subject:[7]

(T2) Greek and Spanish B—Context: Subject Is the Topic

	Stay	*Subj-Case*
☞A. $[_{C/IP}$ S $[_{IP}$ V $[_{VP}$ pro t O]]]	*	*
B. $[_{IP}$ S V $[_{VP}$ t t O]]	**!	

(T3) Portuguese and Spanish A—Context: Subject Is the Topic

	Subj-Case	*Stay*
A. $[_{C/IP}$ S $[_{IP}$ pro V $[_{VP}$ t O]]]	*!	*
☞B. $[_{IP}$ S V $[_{VP}$ t t O]]		**

In Greek and Spanish B (T3), STAY outranks Subj-CASE. The representation in which the subject is not moved to Spec-IP involves one violation of STAY, because of V-to-I movement, and a violation of the dominated constraint Subj-CASE. The candidate in which there is movement of the subject to Spec-IP involves two movements: subject-to-Spec-IP and V-to-I. The second violation is fatal.

In Portuguese and Spanish A, the decision between the two candidates is made by Subj-CASE. The only candidate that satisfies these two constraints is the least economical one. In neither language would a VSO candidate be the optimal one since the sentence-initial position of the verb would violate TOP-FIRST in this context.

Let us now see how these rankings derive the fact that inversion is the unmarked word order in Greek and Spanish B. In (T4), I repeat the derivation of the unmarked word order of Portuguese:

(T4) Portuguese and Spanish A—Context: Sentence Focus

	Alignfocus	Top-First	Subj-Case	Stay	Obj-Case
A. $[_{CP}$ S $[_{IP}$ V $[_{VP}$ t O]]]		**!	*	*	*
☞B. $[_{IP}$ S V $[_{VP}$ t t O]]		*		**	*
C. $[_{IP}$ V $[_{VP}$ S t O]]		*	*!	*	*

Because it fatally violates Subj-CASE, VSO is not selected. Also, SVO with left dislocation of the subject is not the optimal candidate since left dislocation is contingent on topichood; in this context, there is no topic. The optimal candidate is thus the SVO word order with movement of the subject to Spec-IP.

The derivation of the unmarked word order in Greek and Spanish B is shown in (T5):

(T5) Greek and Spanish B—Context: Sentence Focus

	Alignfocus	Top-First	Stay	Subj-Case	Obj-Case
A. $[_{CP}$ S $[_{IP}$ V $[_{VP}$ t O]]]		**!	*	*	*
B. $[_{IP}$ S V $[_{VP}$ t t O]]		*	**!		*
☞C. $[_{IP}$ V $[_{VP}$ S t O]]		*	*	*	*

With left dislocation of the subject, SVO is not the optimal candidate since it involves topicalization of a nontopic. The decision between SVO (with movement to Spec-IP) and VSO is once again made in terms of economy. STAY will choose the candidate that has inversion since this candidate has one less movement operation.

This difference in constraint rankings explains why inversion may be marked in some languages but unmarked in others. The difference between the two groups is the reflex of the tension between an economical representation and compliance to Subj-CASE.

5. Different Types of Inversion: VOS in Italian

Before concluding, I note an asymmetry in behavior between Portuguese and Italian. In Portuguese, inversion is possible independently of the order between the subject and the object. In Italian, inversion is possible only if the subject is sentence-final.

(21) *Portuguese*: SVO   *Italian*: SVO
                    VSO   *VSO
                    VOS   VOS

It would be desirable to derive the absence of VSO in Italian in terms of a reranking of the constraints proposed for the other sets of languages.

A possible analysis of VOS in Italian is presented in (22):

(22) $[_{IP}$ V $[_{AgrOP}$ O $[_{VP}$ S tt]]]

According to this analysis, proposed by Cinque (1997) and Pinto (1997), the object has been moved to Spec-AgrOP. Since SVO is ambiguous between (23a) and (23b), it is legitimate to suppose that in Italian the movement of the object is obligatory and not discourse-dependent:

(23) a. $[_{IP}$ S V $[_{VP}$ t t O]]
      b. $[_{IP}$ S V $[_{AgrOP}$ O $[_{VP}$ t t t]]]

The obligatoriness of the movement of the object may be captured in the following ranking:

(24) Top-First>>Obj-Case>>Alignfocus>>Subj-Case>>Stay

The difference between (24) and the ranking proposed for Portuguese is just that Obj-CASE is ranked higher than ALIGNFOCUS and STAY, making the movement of the object to Spec-AgrOP more important than discourse requirements and more important than obtaining an economical representation.

The different predictions of the two rankings are illustrated in (T6) and (T7):

(T6) Portuguese—Context: S and O Focused

	Align Focus	Top-First	Subj-Case	Stay	Obj-Case
☞A. $[_{IP}$ V $[_{VP}$ S t O]]			*	*	*
B. $[_{IP}$ V $[_{AgrOP}$ O t $[_{VP}$ S t t]]]	*!		*	***	
C. $[_{IP}$ V $[_{VP}$ O $[_{VP}$ S t t]]]	*!		*	**	*

If the subject and the object are focused in Portuguese, the only word order that satisfies ALIGNFOCUS is VSO.[8] Note that VOS involves defocusing of the object, which is against the input specification of this constituent for its input status.[9]

(T7) Italian—Context: S and O Focused

	Top-First	Obj-Case	AlignFocus	Subj-Case	Stay
A. $[_{IP}$ V $[_{VP}$ S t O]]		*!		*	*
☞B. $[_{IP}$ V $[_{AgrOP}$ O t $[_{VP}$ S t t]]]			*	*	***
C. $[_{IP}$ V $[_{VP}$ O $[_{VP}$ S t]]]		*!	*	*	**

As shown in (T7), VSO is impossible in the same context because the high-ranked constraint Obj-CASE will filter out all candidates in which the object does not move to Spec-AgrOP. It is important to note that the same ranking predicts that Italian is SVO in the unmarked case:

(T8)

	Top-First	Obj-Case	AlignFocus	SubjCase	Stay
☞A. $[_{IP}$S V $[_{AgrOP}$O t $[_{VP}$ t t t]]]	*				****
B. $[_{IP}$S V $[_{VP}$ t t O]]	*	*!			**
C. $[_{IP}$ S V $[_{VP}$ O $[_{VP}$ t t t]]]	*	*!			***
D. $[_{CP}$ S $[_{IP}$ V$[_{AgrOP}$ O t $[_{VP}$ t t]]]	**!			*	***
E. $[_{CP}$ S $[_{IP}$ V $[_{VP}$ t O]]]	**!	*		*	*
F. $[_{CP}$ S $[_{IP}$ V $[_{VP}$ O $[_{VP}$ t t]]]	**!	*		*	**
G. $[_{IP}$ V $[_{VP}$ S t O]]	*	*!		*	*
H. $[_{IP}$ V $[_{AgrOP}$ O t $[_{VP}$ S t t]]]	*			*!	***
I. $[_{IP}$ V $[_{VP}$ O $[_{VP}$ S t t]]]	*	*!		*	**

As in Greek, Spanish, and Portuguese, all candidates that have left dislocation of the subject (D, E, and F) are ruled out by TOP-FIRST since there is topicalization of a nontopic. Next, all candidates without movement of the object to Spec-AgrOP (B, C, G, and I) are filtered out by Obj-CASE. The decision between SVO and VOS as unmarked word order is made by the crucial ranking between Subj-CASE and STAY. As in Portuguese, since Subj-CASE is ranked higher than STAY, the inverted candidate (H) is not selected as the unmarked one. Note that within one language family, only one constraint was crucially reranked.

6. Conclusions

In this chapter, I try to explain why inversion is not universally (un)marked. I argue that this type of cross-linguistic variation at the base may be formalized in Optimality Theory. In the specific case of inversion, I argue that the difference between languages that have inversion as the unmarked word order and languages with SV as the unmarked value may be explained as a consequence of a tension between constraints on economy (STAY), favoring inversion, and constraints on the surface representation of subjects (Subj-CASE), favoring A-movement of the subject to Spec-IP.

I hope I have shown that dialectal variation and differences between genetically related languages may be captured by minimal rerankings of constraints, as well as that OT is empirically adequate and explanatorily powerful as a theory of language variation.

NOTES

1. For an extension of this analysis to other languages, see Costa (1998, forthcoming).

2. With unaccusative verbs, VS is also possible in unmarked contexts. This possibility is related with an ongoing change in the properties of these verbs in colloquial European Portuguese. For instance, postverbal subjects do not necessarily agree with unaccusative verbs. Since in this chapter I am only considering patterns of word order variation in which the verbal morphology remains constant, I leave aside this verbal class. For a description of the data and an analysis compatible with my conclusions here, see Costa (1998, 1999).

3. At this stage, I am not able to find an adequate explanation for why topic must be sentence-initial. This contrasts with the explanation for the behavior of foci, which must be rightmost because that is where the main stress of the sentence falls. A potential explanation is to define a scale of information-bearing elements, according to which the newest element must appear as far as possible from the oldest.

4. The notion of *Emergence of the Unmarked* is more often used to express relations between faithfulness constraints and markedness constraints. As pointed out by Geraldine Legendre (personal communication), since there is not much work on the distinction between faithfulness and markedness constraints in Optimality-theoretical syntax, it is possible to restrict the use of this term to the case discussed in the text.

5. It must be noted that the (15a') improves if the first preposed element is not interpreted as a simple topic (see Ambar 1998) for a description of the interpretation associated to what she terms topic/focus.

6. For reasons of space, I do not repeat the authors' arguments here. Their conclusion that preverbal subjects are left-dislocated comes from V-second effects, minimality effects, and the possibility of coindexation as a bound variable. I refer the reader to the works cited for the actual examples.

7. As a reviewer points out, there must be some interaction between these constraints and the constraint that forces V-to-I. As far as I know, there is no example in which V-to-I movement does not take place, in order for the subject to stay inside VP in the leftmost position. For this reason, I do not add constraints on V-to-I to the discussion. See Vikner (1997).

8. Thus VSO satisfies ALIGNFOCUS, given the appropriate algorithm for identification of the focus set of the sentence. The hearer has to look for the most prominent element and everything it dominates. Since in VSO sentences, the subject is the most prominent element, both subject and object are interpreted as focus. Because these two elements are rightmost in the sentence, ALIGNFOCUS is satisfied.

9. For details about the compliance of the different word orders with ALIGNFOCUS, see Costa (1998). Even if VOS in Italian is able to satisfy ALIGNFOCUS, by virtue of heavy stress on the object, candidate B will be the winner since the decision will be made by OBJ-CASE.

REFERENCES

Alexiadou, A. (1995). "Word Order Alternations in Modern Greek." Paper presented at the 5th Colloquium on Generative Grammar, Coruña.

Alexiadou, A., & E. Anagnostopoulou. (1995). "SVO and EPP in Null Subject Languages and Germanic." *FAS Papers in Linguistics*, University of Potsdam, Potsdam, Germany.

———. (1996). "Symmetries, Asymmetries, and the Role of Agreement." Paper presented at GLOW XIX, Athens.

Ambar, M. (1992). "Para uma Sintaxe da Inversão Sujeito Verbo em Português." Ph.D. diss., University of Lisbon.

———. (1998). "The Syntax of Focus in European Portuguese." Ms, University of Lisbon.

Barbosa, P. (1995). "Null Subjects." Ph.D. diss., MIT, Cambridge, Mass.

———. (1996). "A New Look at the Null Subject Parameter." In J. Costa, R. Goedemans, & R. van de Vijver (eds.), *Proceedings of ConSOLE IV*. Leiden University, 375–395.

Battistella, E. (1996). *The Logics of Markedness*. Oxford University Press, New York.

Belletti, A. (1990). *Generalized Verb Movement*. Rosenberg & Sellier, Torino.

Bobaljik, J. (1995). "Morphosyntax: The Syntax of Verbal Inflection." Ph.D. diss., MIT, Cambridge, Mass.

Burzio, L. (1986). *Italian Syntax: A Government-Binding Approach*. Reidel, Dordrecht.

Calabrese, A. (1991). "Some Remarks on Focus and Logical Structures in Italian." *Harvard Working Papers in Linguistics*, 19–27.

Carnie, A. (1995). "Nonverbal Predication and Head Movement." Ph.D. diss, MIT, Cambridge, Mass.

Choi, H.-W. (1996). "Optimizing Structure in Context: Scrambling and Information Structure." Ph.D. diss., Stanford University, Stanford, Calif.

Chomsky, N. (1986). *Knowledge of Language. Its Nature, Origin, and Use*. Praeger, New York.

———. (1989). "Some Notes on Economy of Representations and Derivations." In Chomsky (1995).

———. (1995). *The Minimalist Program*. MIT Press, Cambridge, Mass.

Cinque, G. (1990). *Types of A-bar Dependencies*. MIT Press, Cambridge, Mass.

———. (1993). "A Null Theory of Phrase and Compound Stress." *Linguistic Inquiry* 24, 239–297.

———. (1997). "Adverbs and the Universal Hierarchy of Functional Projections." Oxford University Press, New York.

Costa, J. (1996a). "Scrambling in European Portuguese." *Proceedings of SCIL 8*, MIT Working Papers in Linguistics.

———. (1996b). "Word Order and Constraint Interaction." *Seminários de Linguística*.

———. (1997). "Positions for Subjects in European Portuguese." *Proceedings of the West Coast Conference on Formal Linguistics XV*.CLSI. Stanford, Calif.

———. (1998). "Word Order Variation. A constraint-based Approach." Ph.D. diss., HIL/Leiden University.

———. (1999). "Postverbal Subjects and Agreement in Unaccusative Contexts in European Portuguese." Ms, Universidade Nova de Lisboa.

———. (forthcoming). "Parameters vs. Soft-constraints in the Analysis of Discourse-Configurationality." *CLS 34 Proceedings*. University of Chicago.

Dik, S. (1978). *Functional Grammar*. Foris Publications, Dordrecht.

Duarte, I. (1987). "A Construção de Topicalização na Gramática do Português." Ph.D. diss., University of Lisbon.

———. (1996). "A Topicalização em Português Europeu: Uma análise comparativa." In I. Duarte & I. Leiria (eds.), *Actas do Congresso Internacional sobre o Português*, Vol. 1. Colibri, Associação Portuguesa de Linguística, Lisbon.

Frota, S. (1994). "Is Focus a Phonological Category in Portuguese?" In P. Ackema & M. Schoorlemmer (eds.), *Proceedings of ConSOLE 1*. The Hague.

———. (1997). "Focus in the Prosodic Interface: Evidence from European Portuguese." Talk presented at the University of Lisbon.

Givón, T. (1984). *Syntax: A Functional-typological Introduction*. John Benjamins, Amsterdam.

Grimshaw, J. (1997). Projections, Heads and Optimality. *Linguistic Inquiry*. 28/3, 373–422.

Grimshaw, J., & V. Samek-Lodovici. (1995). "Optimal Subjects." *UMOP 18*.

———. (1996). "Optimal Subjects and Subjects Universals." In P. Barbosa, D. Fox, P. Hagstrom, M. McGinnis, & D. Pesetsky (eds.), *Is the Best Good Enough?* MIT Working Papers in Linguistics, Cambridge, Mass.

Hernanz, M. L., & J. M. Brucart. (1987). *La sintaxis*. Editorial Crítica.

Li, Ch. (1976). *Subject and Topic*. Academic Press, New York.

Martins, A. M. (1994). "Os Clíticos na História do Português." Ph.D. diss., University of Lisbon.

Mateus, M. H., A. M. Brito, I. Duarte, & I. Faria. (1989). *Gramática da Língua Portuguesa*. Editorial Caminho.

McCarthy, J., & A. Prince. (1994). "The Emergence of the Unmarked: Optimality in Prosodic Morphology." Ms., Rutgers University, New Brunswick, N.J., and University of Massachusetts, Amherst.

Nash, L. (1995). "Argument Scope and Case Marking in SOV and in Ergative Languages: The Case of Georgian." Ph.D. diss., Université de Paris 8.

Nespor, M., & I. Vogel. (1986). *Prosodic Phonology*. Foris Publications, Dordrecht.

Ordoñez, F. (forthcoming). "Postverbal Asymmetries in Spanish." *NLLT*.

Ordoñez, F., & E. Treviño. (1995). "Los sujetos y objetos preverbales en español." Paper presented at the 5th Colloquium on Generative Grammar, Corunna, Spain.

Pinto, M. (1997). "Licensing and Interpretation of Inverted Subjects in Italian." Ph.D. diss., Utrecht University.

Prince, A., & P. Smolensky. (1993). "Optimality Theory: Constraint Interaction in Generative Grammar." Ms., Rutgers University, New Brunswick, N.J., and University of Colorado, Boulder. To appear in MIT Press, Cambridge Mass.

Raposo, E. (1986). "On the Null Object Construction in European Portuguese." In O. Jaeggli & C. Silva-Corvalán (eds.), *Studies in Romance Linguistics*. Foris Publications, Dordrecht.

———. (1987). "Case Theory and Infl-to-Comp: The Inflected Infinitive in European Portuguese." *Linguistic Inquiry* 20, 85–110.

———. (1996). "Towards a Unification of Topic Constructions." Ms., University of California at Santa Barbara.

———. (1997). "Definite/Zero Alternations in Portuguese (Towards a unification of Topic Constructions)." Paper presented at the 27th Linguistic Symposium on Romance Languages, Irvine, Calif., 20–22 Feb. 1997.

Rizzi, L. (1982). *Issues in Italian Syntax*. Foris Publications, Dordrecht.

Samek-Lodovici, V. (1996). "Constraints on Subjects: An Optimality-theoretic Analysis." Ph.D. diss., Rutgers University, New Brunswick, N.J.

Selkirk, L. (1984). *Phonology and Syntax: The Relation between Sound and Structure*. MIT Press, Cambridge, Mass.

Vikner, S. (1997). "V°-to-I° Movement, DO-insertion, and Negation in Optimality Theory." Paper presented at NIAS, Scheveningen, Netherlands.

Zubizarreta, M. L. (1995). "Word Order, Prosody and Focus." Ms, University of Southern California, Los Angeles.

5

New Thoughts on
Stylistic Inversion

RICHARD S. KAYNE AND JEAN-YVES POLLOCK

'Stylistic Inversion' (SI), or more neutrally, nonclitic (see section 5) Subject-related Inversion, is the (unfortunate[1]) term used in the generative literature over the last twenty-five years to refer to the syntactic computation(s) responsible for the postverbal position of the subject DP in French sentences like (1a, b):

(1) a. A qui a téléphoné ton ami?
          'to whom has telephoned your friend'
     b. l'homme à qui a téléphoné ton ami
          'the man to whom has telephoned your friend'

Unlike many other Romance languages, French allows only a limited set of sentence types to take postverbal subjects; thus (2a, b, c) are sharply ungrammatical, unlike their counterparts in Italian or Spanish:

(2) a. *A téléphoné ton ami.
          'has telephoned your friend'
     b. *J'ignore si a téléphoné ton ami.
          'I don't-know if has telephoned your friend'
     c. *A téléphoné ton ami?

Defining precisely the syntactic contexts for SI was the chief goal of early generative work on SI (cf., e.g., Kayne 1972, Kayne & Pollock 1978).[2] Abstracting away from technical details, this work stated that lexical or nonlexical wh-words and phrases in the left periphery of interrogatives, relatives, exclamatives, and clefts made SI possible, as in (3a, b, c, d), as well as, because of successive cyclicity [see Kayne & Pollock, sec. 18] and (3e) below:

(3)   a.   A qui a téléphoné ton ami?
             [= (1a)]
       b.   l'homme à qui a téléphoné ton ami
             [= (1b)]
       c.   Quel beau visage a cette personne!
             'what nice face has this person'
       d.   C'est à Jean qu'a téléphoné ton ami.
             'it's to John that has phoned your friend'
       e.   A qui dis-tu qu'a téléphoné ton ami?
             'to whom say you that has telephoned your friend'

On the view that there is no covert wh-element in (2b, c),[3] these examples illustrate the fact that yes/no questions, whether embedded or root, disallow SI.

In addition to wh-contexts, a few other syntactic environments make SI possible, some of which are given in (4):

(4)   a.   Je souhaiterais que téléphone ton ami.
             'I would-wish that telephone (subjunctive) your friend'
       b.   Qu'ait téléphoné ton ami me surprend.
             'that has(subjunctive) telephoned your friend surprises me'
       c.   N'a téléphoné que ton ami.
             'neg. has telephoned than your friend' = 'only your friend has telephoned'

The complement clause of verbs like *souhaiter* in (4a) and the subject clause of (4b) allow for SI, which is to be tied to the fact that these verbs are in the subjunctive. Some attention has been paid to this instance of SI over the years (see, e.g., Deprez 1989; Kampers-Mahne 1998; Kayne & Pollock 1978, sec. 3; Pollock 1986). The *ne-que* case of (4c) has received less attention (cf. Pollock 1985, sec. 2).

We return to some of the issues raised by (3) and (4) later and attempt to integrate them with others, such as the following:

(5)   a.   *Qu'a mangé il?
             'what has eaten he'
       b.   ??Qu'a mangé quelqu'un? [4]
             'what has eaten someone'
       c.   ?*le jour où en ont téléphoné trois
             'the day when of-them have telephoned three'
       d.   *Le livre que n'ont pas lu de linguistes, c'est le mien!
             'the book that neg. have not read of linguists, it's (the) mine'
       e.   ?*Le livre qu'ont peu lu de linguistes, c'est le mien.
             'the book that have few read of linguists, it's mine

Sentence (5a) illustrates the sharp incompatibility between SI and subject clitics, (5b) a less sharp incompatibility between SI and certain kinds of indefinite subjects. Sentences (5c, d, e) illustrate the fact that the postverbal subject in SI is subject to restrictions concerning what can be 'missing' from it; (5c) shows that the clitic *en* cannot be extracted from within the postverbal subject; (5d, e) show that the postverbal subject cannot be of the *de*-NP type licensed by negation or certain quantifiers.

1. Proposal

Alongside the ungrammatical examples of (2), we have the grammatical examples of (6), with canonical French word order:

(6) a. Ton ami a téléphoné.
     b. J'ignore si ton ami a téléphoné.
     c. Ton ami a téléphoné?

The idea that SI sentences such as those of (3) and (4) show noncanonical word order is uncontroversial. The question is how best to account for it. We follow Kayne's (1994) claim that Universal Grammar (UG) allows no rightward adjunction and no right-hand Specs. Therefore, the postverbal subject in SI cannot be in a right-adjoined position, nor can it be a right-hand Spec. If so, the postverbal subject must be in some left-hand Spec position (cf. in part Deprez 1989), and the verb must end up still further to the left.

We try to demonstrate, first, that in SI the postverbal subject is actually in a high (rather than low) Spec position. Second, we argue that the verb gets to the left of the subject DP through phrasal movement (rather than by head movement).

2. Position of the Postverbal Subject

If the Spec position occupied by the postverbal subject were low, the postverbal subject would be in that respect similar to an object. In fact, to a significant (but nonetheless partial) extent, the postverbal SI subject is incompatible with a postverbal object:

(7) *A qui a montré mon article ton ami?
     'to whom has shown my article your friend'

(8) *A qui a montré ton ami mon article?

This incompatibility led Emonds (1976, p. 90)[5] to suggest that the postverbal SI subject is actually moved to the object position. Abstracting away from the question of movement to, as opposed to generation in, the object position, we note that there are several lines of argument that converge toward the conclusion that the status of (7) and (8) is not representative and that postverbal SI subjects are in fact substantially different from objects.

Of immediate relevance is the observation that whereas postverbal SI subjects are generally incompatible with a postverbal lexical object,[6] they are not incompatible with a postverbal idiomatic object

> (9)   a. Depuis quelle heure ont faim les enfants?
>   'since what time have hunger the kids'
>   b. A quelle pièce donne accès cette clé?
>   'to what room gives access this key'
>   c. Quand ont pris langue Paul et Marie?
>   'when have taken tongue P & M' = 'when did P & M discuss the issue'

This is particularly striking in that such idiomatic objects act like ordinary direct objects in dativization of the infinitival subject in causatives:

> (10)   a. Cela fera avoir faim *(à) Marie.
>   'that will-make have-infin. hunger to M'
>   b. Cela fera prendre langue *(à) Marie et Paul.
>   'that will-make take-infin. tongue to M and P'

The obligatory appearance of the preposition *à* before *Marie* in (10a) and before *Marie et Paul* in (10b) is the same as that in (11):

> (11)   Cela fera manger une glace *(à) Marie.
>   'that will-make eat-infin. an ice-cream to M'

Examples (10) and (11) contrast with (12):

> (12)   Cela fera manger (*à) Marie.

The difference between (12) and (10) and (11) with respect to *à* can be thought of in Case terms, as proposed by Rouveret and Vergnaud (1980). The Case licensing of the postinfinitival subject in (12) is due to the causative verb (and/or, in more recent terms, to a functional head associated with it). But French (as opposed to English) has the property that the embedded infinitive cannot Case-license its object. Thus in (11) the embedded object *une glace* must be Case-licensed by the causative verb itself, and so the embedded subject *Marie* needs a distinct Case-licenser, the preposition *à*. The fact that (10) behaves like (11) indicates, then, that the idiomatic objects *faim* and *langue* in (10) require the same Case-licensing that *une glace* requires in (11). This in turn makes it difficult to maintain the position that in (9) the postverbal SI subject is in object position.

Somewhat similarly, a postverbal SI subject is relatively compatible with a direct object if that object is a clitic:[7]

(13)   A qui l'a montré Jean-Jacques?
       'to whom it has shown J-J'

If the direct object is itself the wh-phrase, the resulting SI sentence is fine (in the absence of other interfering factors):

(14)   Qu'a dit Jean?
       'what has said J'

A postverbal SI subject is also compatible with a direct object if that object is a 'bare quantifier':

(15)   a. la fille à qui a tout dit Jean-Jacques
           'the girl to whom has everything told J-J'
       b. la fille à qui n'a rien laissé sa grand'mère
           'the girl to whom neg. has nothing left her grandmother'
       c. la fille à qui laissera sûrement quelque chose sa grand'mère
           'the girl to whom will-leave surely something her grandmother'

In (15a, b), the bare quantifier is *tout/rien*, which has moved leftward past the past participle. In (15c), the bare quantifier is *quelque chose*, which is not subject to comparable movement:

(16)   a. Jean a dit quelque chose.
           'J has said something.'
       b. *Jean a quelque chose dit.

Thus in (15c) it is especially clear that the postverbal SI subject (*sa grand'mère*) is not in object position [but the conclusion is also virtually as necessary in (13), (14), and (15a, b)].

We conclude, then, that the unacceptability of (7) and (8) cannot be due to any competition between the two arguments for object position, that in the general case the postverbal SI subject is not in object position,[8] and that the status of (7) and (8) must be attributed to another factor (to which we return below).

3.   Position of the Postverbal Subject *bis*

Not only is the postverbal SI subject not in object position, but also there is substantial evidence that it is not in any low position. The following considerations suggest, rather, that it is in a high, subjectlike position (past which the verb must then have moved).

To begin, 'quantitative' *en* cliticization (cf. Pollock 1986, 1998) is possible from direct objects, as in (17a), and from the associate of impersonal *il* constructions, as in (17b):

(17) a. le jour où le juge en a condamné trois
          'the day when the judge of-them has condemned three'
      b. le jour où il en est parti trois
          'the day when it-expletive of-them is gone three'

This quantitative *en* cannot be extracted from preverbal subjects:

(18) a. *Trois en ont téléphoné.
          'three of-them have telephoned'
      b. *Je ne sais pas à qui trois en ont téléphoné.
          'I neg. know not to whom three of-them have telephoned'
      c. *Trois en sont partis.
          'three of-them are gone'

Extraction of quantitative *en* from a postverbal SI subject is also deviant; the status of the following is virtually the same as that of (18) and sharply different from that of (17):[9]

(19) a. *le jour où en ont téléphoné trois
          'the day when of-them have telephoned three'
      b. *A qui en ont téléphoné trois?
          'to whom of-them have telephoned three'
      c. ?*le jour où en sont partis trois
          'the day when of-them are gone three'

With a transitive verb, we have the following:

(20) le criminel qu'ont condamné trois juges
      'the criminal that have condemned three judges'

(21) *le criminel qu'en ont condamné trois

The contrast between (17) and (18) can naturally be thought of in terms of c-command. The clitic *en* must be extracted to a position c-commanding its original position. This requirement is met in the object case in (17) but not in the preverbal subject case in (18).[10]

The deviance of (19) and (21) then suggests (with the caveat of note 9) that *en* there cannot c-command the postverbal SI subject. If *en* in these examples cannot c-command the postverbal subject, it must further be the case that neither the auxiliary nor the past participle can c-command the postverbal SI subject. Since the postverbal SI subject cannot be in a right-adjoined or right-hand Spec position, the conclusion is that the word order of (19) and (21) is available (with or without a clitic) only insofar as a phrasal constituent that contains (*en* and) auxiliary and participle can stand to the left of the SI subject (itself in a left-hand Spec position). Now this can plausibly come about only if that constituent moves leftward past the subject DP. Thus SI must involve movement of some large constituent XP past the subject, to the left.

Since *en* in (19) and (21) cannot c-command the postverbal SI subject, it is virtually certain that the clitics of (13), repeated here in (22), and (23) cannot either:

(22) A qui l'a montré Jean-Jacques?
      'to whom it has shown J- J'

(23) Que lui a dit Marie?
      'what him-dative has said M'

If the clitics *l'* in (22) and *lui* in (23) do not c-command the postverbal SI subject, they must have been preposed as part of the XP in question.

In other words, the XP preposed past the subject in SI contains the finite auxiliary (when there is one) and the preauxiliary clitics (if there are any); that is, XP looks as if it corresponds to the whole IP except for the subject itself. This is especially clear under the standard assumption that French finite verbs and auxiliaries are in the highest head position within IP. (Kayne 1994, p. 42, argues that a clitic may well be in a separate functional head from the verb, but our argument remains unaffected as long as that functional head, when present, is the highest within IP.)

A paradox now emerges since moving a constituent equal to IP less the subject of IP would amount to moving a nonmaximal projection, which is quite generally assumed not to be allowed. The conclusion that we draw is that in SI the subject must have moved out of its normal Spec-IP position to a still higher Spec (of a functional head F0). This allows taking XP movement to be, in fact, IP movement, with IP now containing an empty subject position.[11]

This 'extra' leftward movement of the subject in SI turns out to have favorable empirical consequences, to which we return after devoting the next section to additional evidence in favor of the (less specific) idea that the postverbal SI subject is in a high position.

4.   Position of the Postverbal Subject *ter*

Somewhat parallel to the facts about *en* [(17)–(21)] are the following, which involve the licensing of a determinerless *de*-NP:

(24) Jean a peu vu de linguistes.
      'J has few seen of linguists'

A quantifier like *peu* can occur between auxiliary and participle and license[12] (an object of the form) *de*-NP. In the absence of any such quantifier word, the sentence would be ill formed:

(25) *Jean a vu de linguistes.

There is a sharp subject-object contrast; that is, a quantifier word standing as in (24) cannot license *de*NP as subject:

(26)   *De linguistes ont peu vu Jean.
'of linguists have few seen J'

Postverbal SI subjects on the whole do not work like objects:

(27)   a. *le jour où ont peu téléphoné de linguistes
'the day when have few telephoned of linguists'
b. ?*Où sont peu partis de linguistes?
'where are few gone of linguists'

As in the case of *en*,[13] the deviance is not strong with unaccusatives but very strong with transitives:

(28)   a. *ce qu'ont peu dit de linguistes
'that which have few said of linguists'
b. *le jour où nous ont peu critiqués de linguistes
'the day when us have few criticized of linguists'

Sentence (24), in contrast to (26), suggests that for the licensing in question to take place the quantifier must c-command *de*-NP. If so, (27) and (28) indicate again that the postverbal SI subject cannot be c-commanded by any of the material between it and the wh-phrase, that is, that that intervening material reaches a position to the left of the (high) SI subject via phrasal (IP) movement.

We note in passing that this approach to (27) and (28) provides a natural way of characterizing the fact that if *peu* is replaced by the corresponding wh-quantifier, the resulting SI sentences are much better:

(29)   a. Combien ont téléphoné de linguistes?
'how-many have telephoned of linguists'
b. Combien sont partis de linguistes?
'how-many are left of linguists' = 'how many linguists have gone'
c. ?Combien nous ont critiqué(s) de linguistes?
'how-many us have criticized of linguists'

The reason is that although the material between the wh-phrase and subject has been moved there as part of IP movement (so that the individual subparts of that IP do not c-command the postverbal subject), the wh-phrase itself has reached its position by wh-movement and so can c-command the SI subject.[14]

Quite similar to (24) vs. (26) is the following contrast:

(30)   Jean n'a pas vu de linguistes.
'J neg. has not seen of linguists'

(31)   *De linguistes n'ont pas vu Jean.
      'of linguists neg. have . . .'

Again, it appears that *de*-NP must be c-commanded by its licenser, here the negation.[15] Consequently, the deviance of *de*-NP as postverbal SI subject, illustrated in (32), can be interpreted in the same way as that of (27) and (28):

(32)   a. *Quel livre n'ont pas lu de linguistes?
        'what book neg. have not read of linguists'
     b. ?*Le livre que ne comprennent pas de linguistes, c'est le mien.
        'the book that neg. understand not of linguists, it's mine'
     c. ?*une voûte que ne soutiennent pas de piliers
        'an arch that neg. are-holding-up not of pillars'   [Muller 1977, p. 181]
     d. ?*une fille que n'a pas aimée de garçon
        'a girl that neg. has not loved of boy' ('boy' = subject)

On the assumption, as before, that all the material between the wh-phrase (or complementizer) and the postverbal SI subject is contained in an IP that has been moved leftward past that subject, the negative licenser will not be in a position to c-command the *de*-NP.

Example (32) contrasts sharply with the following sentences, which contain *aucun* ('no') instead of *pas . . . de*:

(33)   a. Quel livre ne comprend aucun linguiste?
        'what book neg. understands no linguist'
     b. Le livre que ne comprend aucun linguiste, c'est le mien.
        'the book that neg. Understands no linguist, it's mine'
     c. une voûte que ne soutient aucun pilier
        'an arch that neg. is-holding-up no pillar'
     d. une fille que n'a aimée aucun garçon
        'a girl that neg. has loved no boy' ('no boy' = subject)

The natural interpretation is that *aucun* does not need to be licensed by a c-commanding negation. That conclusion is in turn supported by the contrast between the impossible (31) and the perfectly acceptable:

(34)   Aucun linguiste n'a vu Jean.
      'no linguist neg. has seen J'

Before returning to the leftward movement of the SI subject out of IP, we briefly note another way in which c-command bears on the position of that subject. There is widespread agreement that reflexives must be c-commanded by their antecedent, as in the reflexive clitic example:

(35)   Jean-Jacques s'est insulté.
      'J refl. is insulted' = 'J insulted himself'

If the postverbal SI subject is in a high position above IP and if IP has moved leftward past it, it is not surprising that the reflexive clitic can be carried along as part of IP and end up to the left of its subject antecedent:

(36) le jour où s'est insulté Jean-Jacques
      'the day when . . .'

The acceptability of (36) would be more surprising if the postverbal SI subject were in object position since an object in French can never be the antecedent of a reflexive clitic.[16]

5. Leftward Raising of the SI Subject out of IP

The picture that we have so far of SI is that it involves leftward IP movement past the subject DP that has itself been raised out of IP into a higher Spec-FP.

The idea that the SI subject, though in a high position, is not in ordinary subject position is supported by a variety of further considerations. Let us turn first to the fact that SI is sensitive to the person feature of the subject:[17]

(37) a. Qu'a mangé LUI?
          'what has eaten he/him' = 'What has HE eaten?'
      b. Quand ont téléphoné EUX?
          'when have telephoned they/them'

LUI and *EUX* can also surface in preverbal position:

(38) a. LUI a téléphoné.
          'he/him has telephoned.'
      b. EUX ont téléphoné.
          'they/them have telephoned.'

The first- and second-person strong pronouns are, however, excluded both in postverbal SI and in preverbal position:[18]

(39) a. *Quand ai téléphoné MOI?
          'when have telephoned I/me'
      b. *Qu'as mangé TOI?
          'what have eaten YOU'
      c. *Quand avez téléphoné VOUS?
          'when have telephoned you'
      d. *Qu'avons mangé NOUS?
          'what have eaten we/us'

(40) a. *MOI ai téléphoné hier.
          'i/me have telephoned yesterday'

b. *TOI as mangé un gâteau.
   'You have eaten a cake.'
c. *VOUS avez téléphoné hier.
   'You have telephoned yesterday.'
d. *NOUS avons mangé un gâteau.
   'We/us have eaten a cake.'

(On the last two sentences, see note 18.)

The contrast between (37) and (39) is paralleled by facts found with coordination, as in the following (brought to our attention by Dominique Sportiche):[19]

(41) le jour où ont téléphoné et Jean et elle
      'the day when have telephoned and J and she/her'

(42) a. *le jour où avons téléphoné et Jean et moi
          'the day when have telephoned and J and I/me'
      b. *le jour où avez téléphoné et Jean et toi
          '. . . and J and you'

Our proposal concerning these contrasts is based in part on the observation that (40) has an acceptable counterpart with an overt (nominative) subject clitic:

(43) a. Moi, j'ai téléphoné hier.
          'I/me I have telephoned yesterday'
      b. Toi, tu as mangé un gâteau.
          'you you have eaten a cake'
      c. Vous, vous avez téléphoné hier.
          'you you have telephoned yesterday'
      d. Nous, nous avons mangé un gâteau.
          'we/us we have eaten a cake'

The preverbal third-person strong pronouns of (38), although they do not need to cooccur with a subject clitic, can do so:

(44) a. Lui, il a téléphoné.
          'he/him he has telephoned'
      b. Eux, ils ont téléphoné.
          'they/them they have telephoned'

Example (38) is standard, somewhat "recherché," French, whereas (44) is more colloquial. The sociolects that have (38) also have SI; those that only have (44) (cf. Zribi-Hertz 1994) seem not to have SI at all, like Quebec French. Our proposal, more specifically, is that (38) contains a subject clitic, just as (44) does. The difference between them is that the subject clitic of (44) is overt, whereas that of (38) is phonetically unrealized.

The reason for the impossibility of (40), that is, for the contrast between (38) and (40), is (45):

(45)   Silent clitics in French are limited to the third person.

(This restriction in turn is to be related to the fact that various instances of *pro* in French, Italian, and English are also limited to the third person; cf. Kayne 1999a for a relevant discussion.)

The contrast between (37) and (39), along with that between (41) and (42), can now be understood in terms of the following:

(46)   SI sentences necessarily contain a silent (preverbal) subject clitic.

Since the SI examples (37) and (41) both have third-person subjects, they can without difficulty contain such a clitic. The problem with the SI examples (39) and (42) is that they have a first- or second-person DP subject. Consequently, any subject clitic they might contain would have to be first or second person [as in (43)]. But silent subject clitics, as per (45), cannot be first or second person, so (39) and (42) necessarily run afoul of (46).

Varieties of French that lack (38) do not allow silent argumental subject clitics at all. Given (46), it follows that such varieties of French will lack SI entirely, as desired. Point (46) itself is clearly related to our earlier suggestion that SI involves leftward movement of the subject out of IP to the Spec of a higher FP. What (46) implies is that that movement 'leaves behind' a silent subject clitic.

Adapting ideas about complex inversion in Kayne (1972; cf. also Kayne 1994, Pollock 1998, and Sportiche 1995 on clitic doubling in other contexts), we propose that the postverbal SI subject starts out as the DP specifier (cf. Uriagereka 1995, p. 81) of a silent subject clitic that heads a larger DP. Once that larger DP reaches Spec-IP, its DP specifier moves out into the Spec of FP. Subsequent to that, IP itself moves past Spec-FP to a still higher Spec (of another functional category (call it GP) in the Comp area, in Rizzi's (1997) sense. Abstracting away from the wh-phrase and representing the silent subject clitic as SCL, we have for (47) the partial derivation in (48):[20]

(47)   le jour où a téléphoné Jean ('the day when has telephoned J')

(48)   [$_{IP}$ Jean-SCL a téléphoné] =>
        [$_{FP}$ Jean$_i$ F0 [$_{IP}$ t$_i$-SCL a téléphoné]] =>
        [$_{GP}$ [$_{IP}$ t$_i$-SCL a téléphoné]$_j$ G0 [$_{FP}$ Jean$_i$ F0 t$_j$]]

The second consideration to support the idea that the postverbal SI subject is not in ordinary subject position (though it is in a high position, in fact above IP) comes from the counter-indefiniteness effect, originally noted by Cornulier (1974):[21]

(49) a. *Quel gâteau a mangé quelqu'un?
         'what cake has eaten someone'
      b. *Quel article critiquera quelqu'un?
         'what article will-criticize someone'

Another example is (50):

(50) *Je te dirai quand sera venu la voir un ami quelconque.
      'I you will-tell when will-be come her to-see a/some friend or other'

Kupferman (1983) indicates that an inverted subject NP must have specific
reference. Note further that the noninverted counterpart (i.e., without SI) of
(50) is fine:[22]

(51) Je te dirai quand un ami quelconque sera venu la voir.

Now our analysis of SI involves extracting the subject to Spec-FP (above
IP) and leaving behind a silent subject clitic. Furthermore, indefinites do not
like being in that kind of position in the presence of an overt subject clitic, as
illustrated in (52):

(52) *Quelqu'un, il mangera ce gâteau.
      'someone he will-eat that cake'

(53) *Un ami quelconque, il viendra la voir demain.
      'a/some friend or-other he will-come her to-see tomorrow'

Consequently, it is plausible that our analysis of SI, summed up in (48), will
provide an account of (49) and (50) by reducing their ill-formed nature to that
of (52) and (53).[23]
      The third and final consideration that we bring to bear at this point con-
cerns the fact that the postverbal SI subject cannot itself be a subject clitic:[24]

(54) a. le jour où téléphonera Jean
         'the day when will-telephone J'
      b. *le jour où téléphonera il
         '. . . he'

(55) a. Quand a téléphoné Jean?
         'when has telephoned J'
      b. *Quand a téléphoné il?

From the perspective developed so far, there is a straightforward account. The
SI examples (54a) and (55a) contain a silent subject clitic in addition to the
postverbal lexical subject. The co-occurrence of lexical subject and subject clitic
is also found with overt subject clitics:

(56)   a. Jean, il mangera ce gâteau.
          'J he will-eat that cake'
       b. Il mangera ce gâteau, Jean.

But replacing the lexical subject itself in (56) by a subject clitic is not possible:

(57)   a. *Il, il mangera ce gâteau.
       b. *Il mangera ce gâteau, il.

It is therefore plausible to attribute the unacceptability of (54b) and (55b) (which contain two subject clitics, one silent) to the same factor that excludes (57).
    Concerning what this factor might be, consider the following sharp contrast:

(58)   a. Jean ayant dit la vérité, tout va bien.
          'J having told the truth, all goes well.'
       b. *Il ayant dit la vérité, tout va bien.
          'he . . .'

The gerund form of the verb in -*ant* allows lexical subjects but not clitic subjects.[25] Let us express this fact by saying that French subject clitics must check some feature (perhaps nominative) in Spec of a finite Infl, which is lacking in (58). On the assumption that (57) contains only one finite Infl, one of the two subject clitics will remain with an unchecked feature and will be excluded. Since (54) and (55) also contain two subject clitics, they will, assuming silent subject clitics to require checking of the same feature as overt subject clitics, be excluded in the same fashion.

    In conclusion to this section, then, facts about person [(37)–(44)], indefiniteness [(49)–(53)] and subject clitics [(54)–(58)] converge in support of the analysis summarized in (46) and (48): The postverbal SI subject has moved leftward out of IP (leaving behind a silent subject clitic), subsequent to which IP itself has moved even further leftward, to a still higher Spec position.

6.   Non-wh-SI with Indicatives

The instances of SI discussed so far have all involved wh-environments such as interrogatives and relatives. There are also cases of what look like postverbal SI subjects in non-wh-environments. We suggest that these should be analyzed to a large extent in a way that is parallel to the analysis sketched above; in particular, they should also be taken as having the subject DP moving leftward out of IP (leaving behind a silent subject clitic) and having IP then move still further leftward.

    It is well known that subjunctives allow postverbal subjects, as in (59):

(59)   Il faut que parte Jean.
          'it is-necessary that leave J'

Such postverbal subjects are also very marginally possible in certain indicative contexts, for example, (60):

(60)   a. Je crois que Jean est parti.
          'I think that J is(has) left'
       b. ???Je crois qu'est parti Jean.

Let us begin with these.

Some contrasts with indicatives make them of interest despite their marginality. The simplest is that the inversion seen in (60b) is not possible in a nonembedded indicative:

(61)   *Est parti Jean.

Nor is it possible with an embedded indicative if the embedded indicative is an interrogative introduced by the complementizer *si* ('if'):

(62)   a. Je ne sais pas si Jean est parti.
          'I neg. know not if J is (has) left'
       b. *Je ne sais pas si est parti Jean.

Most surprising is the contrast between (60) and the following:

(63)   a. Il est évident que Jean est parti.
          'it is evident that . . .'
       b. *Il est évident qu'est parti Jean.

The question is how to (marginally) allow for the postverbal subject in (60b) and how best to understand the contrast with the impossible (61), (62b), and (63b).

As in our earlier discussion of the wh-cases of SI, we start from the restrictive assumption that UG disallows rightward adjunction and right-hand Specs. We then ask whether the postverbal subject in (60b) is in a high or low (left-hand) Spec position. Following the reasoning of sections 3 and 4 above, we interpret the following restrictions as indicating that the postverbal subject is not in a low objectlike position:

(64)   a. ???Je crois que sont arrivés trois linguistes.
          'I think that are (have) arrived three linguists'
       b. *Je crois qu'en sont arrivés trois.
          'I think that of-them . . .'

(65)   a. ???Je crois qu'ont émigré trop de linguistes.
          'I think that have emigrated too-many of linguists'
       b. *Je crois qu'ont trop émigré de linguistes.

(66)   *Je crois que n'ont pas émigré de linguistes.
       'I think that neg. have not emigrated of linguists'

Unlike objects [cf. (17), (24), and (30)], the postverbal subject in these embedded indicatives disallows the extraction of the clitic *en* and disallows the 'quantifier-at-a-distance' construction that involves *de*-NP.

In addition, as in (39) and (42), the postverbal subject cannot be first or second person:

(67) a. *Je croyais qu'étais parti TOI.
          'I thought that were (had) left you'
      b. *Elle croyait qu'étais arrivé MOI.
          'She thought that was (had) arrived I/me'

(68) a. *Je croyais qu'étiez partis et toi et Jean.
          'I thought that were (had) left and you and J'
      b. *Elle croyait qu'étions arrivés et moi et Jean.
          'she thought that were (had) arrived and I/me and J'

As in the wh-cases, we take this to indicate not only that the postverbal subject here is in a high position but also that it has moved out of IP to a higher Spec and has left behind a silent subject clitic (limited to the third person).

A counter-indefiniteness effect of the sort seen for the wh-cases in (49) and (50) is also found in these indicative cases:

(69) a. ???Je crois que l'appelera Jean-Jacques.
          'I think that her will-call J-J'
      b. *Je crois que l'appelera quelqu'un.
          '. . . someone'

Finally, the restriction that prohibits postverbal SI subjects from being themselves subject clitics is found with indicatives, too:

(70) *Je crois qu'est parti il.
      '. . . he'

The conclusion we draw from this set of similarities is that the postverbal subject of (60b), (64a), (65a), and (69a) is a postverbal SI subject, in the sense that it comes to be postverbal in essentially the same way as the postverbal SI subject in wh-constructions, namely, by moving leftward out of IP (leaving a silent subject clitic behind) and then having IP move past it. That (60b), (64a), (65a), and (69a) should be considered a subvariety of SI is further supported by the fact that they are limited to noncolloquial French (since colloquial French lacks silent subject clitics associated with arguments in this way [cf. the discussion following (44)].[26]

The indicative and wh-subvarieties of SI also have the property that the finite verb agrees with the postverbal subject:

(71) Je crois que sont/*qu'est partis les linguistes.
      'I think that are/is left the linguists'

(72)   Quand sont/*est partis les linguistes?
       'when . . .'

In our analysis, this is straightforward since the postverbal SI subject in both types passes through ordinary subject position prior to raising out of IP.[27]

7.   An ECM Effect

As for the question of (60b) vs. (61), (62b), and (63b), there seems to be an Exceptional Case Marking (ECM) effect at issue, as suggested especially by (60b) vs. (63b) and by the resemblance between that contrast and the following English one:

(73)   the person whom I think is intelligent
(74)   *the person whom it is obvious is intelligent

Example (73), acceptable in some varieties of English, was taken by Kayne (1980) to involve Case assignment into Comp. An updating of that proposal would have *whom* moving into the matrix in ECM fashion,[28] that is, *whom* would have its Case checked in a Spec above *think*.[29] In the relevant varieties of English, this would be possible even though *whom* also passes through the embedded subject position, as reflected by the agreement of the embedded verb. (It must be, then, that these varieties allow double Case or else allow nominative in the embedded sentence to be suspended.) The fact that (74) is not possible would be due to the fact that adjectives, at least when they have an expletive subject,[30] cannot successfully check Case:

(75)   *It is obvious John's qualities.

Returning to French, we might now think of (60b) vs. (63b) in similar terms; the former would be an instance of ECM, but the latter could not be, for the same reason that (74) could not be. The fact that (61) is impossible would then be due to the absence of any higher predicate there [but see (92) below]. What still remains to be elucidated, however, is why the indicative subtype of SI is subject to an extra Case requirement in the first place. Before attempting to answer that question, we need to look a bit more at subjunctive SI.

8.   Subjunctive SI

We noted at (59) the following example of subjunctive SI:

(76)   Il faut que parte Jean.
       'it is-necessary that leave J'

This type of SI is not marginal in the way that indicative (non-wh) SI is. It is, on the other hand, limited to noncolloquial registers, like both the indicative and the wh-types of SI. This limitation to the noncolloquial suggests, given our previous discussion (cf. the text to note 26), that subjunctive SI also involves a silent subject clitic.

Although the present subjunctive shows an orthographic distinction between third-person singular, as in (76), and third-person plural, as in (77), the pronunciation is identical:

(77)   Il faut que partent les enfants.
       'it is-necessary that leave the children'

It is thus not immediately clear whether these subjunctives have agreement. That they do (and that the lack of phonetic distinction is accidental, syntactically speaking) is suggested by the fact that the past subjunctive, although no longer used in spoken French, does show a phonetically realized agreement distinction in some cases:

(78)   a. Il aurait fallu que vînt l'enfant.
           'it would-have been-necessary that come the child'
       b. Il aurait fallu que vinssent les enfants.
           '. . . come the children'

As in the discussion of (71) and (72), this suggests that the postverbal SI subject in subjunctives has also passed through ordinary subject position.

That from ordinary subject position this ultimately postverbal subject raises leftward out of IP and, as in the other cases of SI, leaves behind a silent subject clitic is suggested by the by now familiar limitation to third-person subjects [cf. the discussion of (67) and (68)]:

(79)   *Il faut que partes TOI.
        'it is-necessary that leave you'

(80)   *Il faut que partions et moi et Jean.
        '. . . leave and I/me and J'

As in the discussion of (54), (55), and (70), the movement out of IP and the leaving behind of a silent subject clitic are further supported by the fact that the postverbal SI subject cannot itself be an overt subject clitic:

(81)   *Il faut que parte il.
        '. . . he'

If we now look at instances of subjunctive SI with an embedded transitive verb,[31] we find very clear parallels with other aspects of SI previously noted for the wh- and indicative cases. First, the clitic *en* cannot be extracted from the postverbal subject in cases like the following [cf. (19), (21), and (64)]:[32]

(82) Je doute que m'aient vu beaucoup de linguistes.
      'I doubt that me have-pl.-subjunctive seen many of linguists'

(83) *Je doute que m'en aient vu beaucoup.
      '. . . me of-them have-pl.-subjunctive seen many'

Second, negation does not license a postverbal subject *de*-NP [cf. (32) and (66)]:

(84) *Je souhaiterais que ne te critique pas de linguistes.
      'I would-wish that neg. you criticize not of linguists' - 'linguists' = subject

Nor, especially if we avoid interference from adverbial interpretations,[33] does a quantifier [cf. (27), (28), and (65b)]:

(85) a. ?Cette idée, je doute que l'aient eue beaucoup de linguistes.
          'this idea I doubt that it have-subjunc. had many of ling.'
      b. *Cette idée, je doute que l'aient beaucoup eue de linguistes.

These parallels, as in our earlier discussion, support the claim that the postverbal SI subject is not c-commanded by the position of *en* in (83), of negation in (84), or of displaced *beaucoup* in (85b). The conclusion, then, is that subjunctive SI is like wh- and indicative SI in involving leftward IP movement past the (leftward) raised subject.

9. Subjunctives vs. Indicatives

Why is indicative SI marginal in a way that subjunctive SI is not?

(86) ???Je crois qu'est parti Jean.
      'I think that is left J'

(87) Il faut que parte Jean.
      'it is-necessary that leave J'

We suggest that this contrast between indicative and subjunctive is related to the well-known fact that subjunctives are often cross-linguistically more permeable to extraction than are indicatives.[34] In French itself, this difference can be seen with quantifier extraction:

(88) a. Il faut que je leur enlève tout.
          'it is-necessary that I them take-off everything'
      b. ?Il faut tout que je leur enlève.

(89) a. Ils croient que je leur enlève tout.
          'they think that I them am-taking-off everything'
      b. *Ils croient tout que je leur enlève.

Let us adopt the usual approach to complementizers and take *que* in (86)–(89) as forming a constituent with IP.[35] The question is then whether SI (i.e., subject raising followed by IP preposing) in (87) and marginally in (86) 'applies at the IP level',—that is, applies before *que* is introduced—or not. Let us consider, in fact, the possibility that SI is actually prohibited from applying 'at the IP level'. Then subject raising out of IP (leaving an empty subject clitic behind) must apply after *que* enters the derivation. The landing site of the subject might be within the matrix IP or above it. If we assume the latter, the derivation of (87) looks like this (SCL is the silent subject clitic):

(90)   il faut que Jean-SCL parte => subject raising to Spec-F =>
       $Jean_i$ F0 $[_{IP}$ il faut que t_i-SCL parte] => IP preposing to Spec-G =>
       $[_{IP}$ il faut que t_i-SCL parte$]_j$ G0 $Jean_i$ F0 t_j

Assume, now, that this subject raising is not available out of indicatives, just as quantifier raising in (89b) is not.[36] Then (86) is not derivable in a way that would mimic the derivation of (87), a desirable result.

It remains to be understood why indicative SI is sometimes marginally possible and why it is not always possible to the same marginal degree. Let us begin with the sharp impossibility of SI in root sentences like (91):[37]

(91)   *Est parti Jean.

This recalls the proposal just made concerning the 'inapplicability' of SI 'at the IP level'. We can unify the two by adopting (92):

(92)   SI subject raising cannot target a Spec-FP immediately above IP.

To a certain extent, (92) recalls both Rizzi's (1982, p. 152) argument against short subject wh-movement in Italian and various proposals that prohibit 'vacuous' movement in general. Keeping in mind, though, that SI subject raising leaves behind a silent pronominal clitic, we see that a still closer fit may be found with the restriction in Hebrew and Irish against resumptive pronouns in the highest subject position.

Aoun (1985), Borer (1984, p. 252) and McCloskey (1990, p. 215) have assimilated that (sort of) restriction to (a generalized) binding theory,[38] and in particular to a generalized Condition B.[39] From this perspective, (92) says that the silent subject clitic left behind by SI subject raising cannot be too close to its antecedent. Let us, then, think of (92) as a special case of this generalized Condition B (GCondB). Sentence (92)/GCondB excludes (91) by prohibiting the subject-raising step that is [cf. the discussion following (23)] a necessary precursor to IP preposing. At the same time, it correctly allows the derivation in (90) since there, subject raising is 'long-distance'.[40]

We note in passing that (92) has a significant effect on the wh-subtype of SI:

(93)   Quand téléphonera Jean?
       'when will-telephone J'

If (92) holds, subject raising in (93) cannot precede wh-movement.[41] The derivation of (93) must therefore proceed as in (94):

(94)   Jean-SCL téléphonera quand => wh-movement =>
       quand$_i$ X0 [$_{IP}$ Jean-SCL téléphonera t$_i$] => subject raising =>
       Jean$_j$ F0 [$_{XP}$ quand X0 [$_{IP}$ t$_j$-SCL téléphonera t$_i$]]

The raised subject must move past the landing site of the previously moved wh-phrase.[42]

Example (94) might then continue in one of two ways. One the one hand, IP might prepose to the left of *Jean*, followed by a second movement of *quand*. On the other hand, XP might prepose to the left of *Jean*, followed or not by a second movement of *quand*. In what follows, we adopt the first sort of continuation in preference to the second.[43]

In returning to indicatives, the problem is how to allow for the marginal acceptability of (86). Our proposal is that, although (86) cannot mimic the derivation given in (90), it does have (marginal) access to a derivation with 'shorter' subject raising than in (90), one in which the embedded subject raises to an ECM-like position within the matrix, before raising to a position above the matrix IP:[44]

(95)   je crois que Jean-SCL est parti => first subject-raising step =>
       je crois Jean$_i$ que t$_i$-SCL est parti => second subj.-rais. step =>
       Jean$_i$ F0 [$_{IP}$ je crois t$_i$ que t$_i$-SCL est parti] => IP preposing =>
       [$_{IP}$ je crois t$_i$ que t$_i$-SCL est parti]$_j$ G0 [$_{FP}$ Jean$_i$ F0 t$_j$]

10. Quirky Subjects

French has impersonal passives with expletive *il*, as in (96):

(96)   Il a été procédé au réexamen de la loi.
       'it has been proceeded to-the reexamination of the law'

In SI contexts, impersonal passives can be found without *il*:

(97)   Quand a été procédé au réexamen de la loi?
       'when has been . . .' = 'when was the new law examined'

Sentences like (97) seem deprived of any lexical subject, DP, or clitic. One could envision positing that the wh-phrase of (97) somehow licenses a null expletive subject. However, this does not seem very promising, given the sharp ungrammaticality of (98); if there were a null expletive in (97), why couldn't there be one in (98), parallel to *il* in the perfect (99)?[45]

(98) *Au réexamen de quelle loi a été procédé?
      'to-the examination of what law has been proceeded'

(99) Au réexamen de quelle loi a-t-il été procédé?
      '. . . has it been . . .'

What we would like to suggest instead is that in (97) the phrase *au réexamen de la loi* first moves to Spec-IP, thus satisfying the Extended Projection Principle (EPP),[46] and then moves up via subject raising before IP (XP) preposing applies. The derivation we have in mind proceeds as in (100):[47]

(100) a été procédé au réexamen de la loi quand => Mvt to Spec-IP =>
       [au réexamen de la loi]$_i$ a été procédé t$_i$ quand => wh-movement =>
       quand$_j$ X0 [$_{IP}$ [au réexamen de la loi]$_i$ a été procédé t$_i$ t$_j$] => subject raising =>
       [au réexamen de la loi]$_i$ F0 [$_{XP}$ quand$_j$ X0 [$_{IP}$ t$_i$ a été procédé t$_i$ t$_j$]]

At this point, what happens is that IP preposes, followed by a second instance of wh-movement, as discussed for (94). This yields the desired word order:[48]

=> IP preposing => [$_{IP}$ t$_i$ a été procédé t$_i$ t$_j$]$_k$ Y0 [$_{FP}$ [au réexamen de la loi]$_i$ F0 [$_{XP}$ quand$_j$ X0 t$_k$]] => wh-movement => quand$_j$ [$_{IP}$ t$_i$ a été procédé t$_i$ t$_j$]$_k$ Y0 [$_{FP}$ [au réexamen de la loi]$_i$ F0 [$_{XP}$ t$_j$ X0 t$_k$]]

Thus, we are claiming that examples like (97) are French counterparts to Icelandic "quirky subjects,"[49] except that in French such quirky subjects are acceptable only when, as in SI, they move further up. This might follow from the fact that a phrase above IP can normally bear any case or be of any category it likes, whereas a constituent in the Spec of finite inflection must be nominative (in French, as opposed to Icelandic), or at least is prohibited from being a PP at spellout.[50]

Returning to the unacceptability of (98), we note the contrast between it and the following:

(101) Quel linguiste a écrit cet article?
       'What linguist has written this article?'

Sentence (101) is intended to indicate that ordinary subjects in French are, as Rizzi (1982) argued, readily subject to short wh-movement.[51] At the same time, the quirky subject in (98) is not. We take (101) to be compatible with GCondB by virtue of not containing any subject clitic, not even a silent one.[52] We nonetheless attribute the ill-formedness of (98) to a violation of that very condition by claiming that (98) must, contrary to the general case of interrogatives, in fact contain a (silent) pronominal clitic (in subject position). If it does, (98) will violate GCondB, just as SI does in (91).

As for why (98) must contain a silent clitic, we guess that it has to do with the presence of the preposition, the idea being that the presence of the overt preposition *à* in (97) and (98) would prohibit satisfaction of the EPP. By containing a (silent) clitic double (probably a silent counterpart of the locative/oblique clitic *y*) associated directly with no overt preposition, both (97) and (98) do satisfy the EPP. Sentence (97) is, in addition, compatible with GCondB since, as seen in (100), the subject-raising step places '[au reexamen de la loi]$_i$' to the left of the separate wh-phrase *quand*, the assumption being that the intervening *quand* creates the necessary distance between '[au reexamen de la loi]$_i$' and the silent clitic. In (98), on the other hand, GCondB is violated.[53]

There is a sharp and surprising contrast between (98) and (102):

(102)   Au réexamen de quelle loi souhaiterais-tu que soit procédé?
        'to-the reexamination of which law would-wish you that be-subjunctive
           proceeded'

The way to understand it is to bring to bear the well-formedness of the following [cf. (iii) of note 45]:

(103)   Je souhaiterais que soit procédé au réexamen de cette loi.
        'I would-wish that be-subjunctive proceeded to-the reexamination of that
           law'

Sentence (103) is an example of subjunctive SI [cf. (87)] with a quirky subject. Its derivation is much the same as that of (90), apart from the quirky subject (which we will shorten to *au réexamen*):

(104)   soit procédé au réexamen-CL=> movement to Spec-IP =>
        au réexamen-CL soit procédé (trace omitted) => further merger =>
        je souhaiterais que au réexamen-CL soit procédé => subject raising to
           (matrix) Spec-F =>
        au ré-examen$_i$ F0 [$_{IP}$ je souhaiterais que t$_i$-CL soit procédé] => IP preposing
           to Spec-G =>
        [$_{IP}$ je souhaiterais que t$_i$-CL soit procédé]$_j$ G0 au réexamen$_i$ F0 t$_j$

At this point (in a derivation with a wh-phrase in place of *cette loi*), wh-movement can apply to *au réexamen . . .* , yielding (102).

In other words, if (102) derives from a structure that corresponds to (103), (102) will create no violation of GCondB since it will involve long wh-movement of *au réexamen de quelle loi*, not short wh-movement of the sort that (98) must avail itself of. For (98) to avail itself of long wh-movement, it would have to skip the preposing-to-Spec-IP step, which would lead to an EPP violation.[54] Thus (98) vs. (102) is by and large identical to the picture drawn by Rizzi (1982, p. 152) for subject wh-movement in Italian, allowing for the fact that (102) is a case of long wh-movement of a quirky subject.[55]

11. Expletives

Our analysis of (97), (102) and (103) involves no use of a null expletive and thus converges with our earlier proposals about SI with ordinary (nonquirky) subjects (cf. especially note 31). The absence of recourse to null expletives has a very specific further advantage in that it accounts directly for the contrast between (97), (102), and (103), on the one hand, and (105)–(107), on the other:

(105) *Quand a neigé?
       'when has snowed'

(106) *Quand souhaiterais-tu que pleuve?
       'when would-wish you that rain-subjunctive'

(107) *Je souhaiterais que pleuve demain.
       'I would-wish that rain-subjunctive tomorrow'

The expletive *il* found with weather verbs cannot be absent in SI contexts, as expected, given the general absence (in French, at least) of null subject expletives.

The contrast between these weather verbs and the impersonal passive cases (with *soit procédé*) just discussed is due to the fact that in the impersonal passive cases there is a subject, albeit a quirky one, that can satisfy EPP.[56] In (105)–(107) there is no such subject, and hence an EPP violation. (The silent subject clitic is not able to satisfy EPP by itself; cf. the latter part of note 31.)

Not surprisingly, adding an overt expletive *il* to (105)–(107) yields a grammatical result:

(108) Quand a-t-il neigé?

(109) Quand souhaiterais-tu qu'il pleuve?

(110) Je souhaiterais qu'il pleuve demain.

Notable, on the other hand, is the fact that some weather verbs can fail to show an expletive in causative contexts:[57]

(111) Les scientifiques sont capables de faire pleuvoir
       'the scientists are capable of making rain-infinitive'

If there is no EPP requirement in French causatives, it is plausible to claim that (111) does contain an empty expletive (with accusative Case) and that the unavailability of empty subject expletives in finite contexts [such as (105)–

(107)] is specifically due to their being unable to satisfy the EPP (in French, at least).

12. SI 'Triggers'

In Kayne and Pollock (1978), SI was thought of in terms of 'triggers'; that is, it was said to be 'triggered' in certain contexts such as wh-contexts and sub-junctive contexts. In more current terminology, one could speak of 'licensing' contexts for SI. But the question of interest was and is this: why these con-texts, as opposed to others, or as opposed to all contexts?

The approach to SI based (in part) on (92) [whether or not (92) is best interpreted in terms of a GCondB)] has already provided the beginning of an answer to this old question. Consider this contrast:

(112)   *Est parti Jean.
        'is(has) left J'

(113)   Quand est parti Jean?
        'when . . .'

The claim in (92) accounts for this pair by requiring that the SI subject-raising operation (that precedes leftward IP/XP movement) not be 'too local'. In (112), it is because there is nothing else to the left of and above IP that could be taken to intervene between the landing site of *Jean* and the subject position. In (113), on the other hand, the interrogative wh-phrase can play that role and create more 'distance' between the landing site of *Jean* (above the interrogative phrase) and the subject position [cf. the derivation illustrated in (94)].

From this perspective, there are no real external 'triggers' or 'licensers' for SI at all.[58] Thus SI is possible whenever there happens to be something above IP that allows SI subject raising not to be 'too local' or 'vacuous'. That some-thing can be a phrase like *quand* in (113) or matrix material that is not even a phrase, as in the subjunctive cases like (114):

(114)   Il faut que parte Jean.
        'it is-necessary that leave J'

Here, as illustrated in the derivation given in (90), *Jean* raises across *il faut que*, which is not a phrase but whose presence suffices for avoiding a violation of (92). From a 'trigger' perspective, wh-phrases and subjunctives have essen-tially nothing in common; from the perspective of (92), however, their com-mon effect on SI can be made sense of.

There is a well-known contrast between (113) and apparently similar sen-tences in which the interrogative phrase is *en quel sens* (in one of its uses; cf. Cornulier 1974, p. 142):[59]

(115)   ?* En quel sens parlent les fleurs?
        'in what sense speak (the) flowers'

Possible without SI is (116):[60]

(116)   En quel sens les fleurs parlent?

Sentence (116), like the English "In what sense do flowers speak?" has an interpretation akin to that of (117):

(117)   In what sense can one say that flowers speak?

    Assume that (115) actually contains an abstract verb that corresponds to *say* [cf. Ross (1970)], and that *en quel sens* enters the derivation after that abstract verb does. Then (115) is not derivable, as desired. At the point at which the derivation reaches the embedded IP, SI subject raising cannot apply because to do so would violate (92)/GCondB; at the point just after *en quel sens* is introduced, SI subject raising cannot apply because to do so would require extracting the subject out of an indicative IP into the domain of a higher verb (here, the abstract 'say', French *dire*), but that would violate the constraint seen in the discussion of (86)–(95).[61]
    Almost certainly related to (115) is the status of the SI of *pourquoi* ('why'):[62]

(118)   a.   ?*Pourquoi parle Pierre?
                'why speaks P'
         b.   ?*Pourquoi travaillent les linguistes?
                'why work (the) linguists'

Rizzi (1990, 47)) suggests that *pourquoi* is merged outside of IP. If we interpret this to mean that there is an abstract higher verb in (118), then (118) reduces to (115). Alternatively (and this could be true for *en quel sens*, too), *pourquoi* in (118) is merged outside IP, with the property (to be explained) that SI subject raising cannot cross it.
    French allows topicalization of PPs:

(119)   A Jean, Marie ne parle jamais.
         'to J M neg. speaks never'

This topicalization provides a contrast with wh-movement, as far as SI is concerned:

(120)   *A Jean ne parle jamais Marie.

(121)   A qui ne parle jamais Marie?
         'to whom . . .'

In the derivation of (121), the wh-phrase *à qui* preposes, following which the subject *Marie* preposes to the left of *à qui*. Subsequently, *ne parle jamais* moves to the left of *Marie*, and *à qui* moves a second time [cf. (94)]. The question is why a parallel derivation with topicalization in place of wh-movement is not legitimate.[63] For it to be so, *Marie* would have to be able to raise to the left of preposed *à Jean*, just as it does across *à qui* in (121). Let us propose, then, that a preposed topic (as opposed to a preposed wh-phrase) blocks SI subject raising across it.

This difference between preposed topics and preposed wh-phrases recalls the fact that topics create islands to a greater degree than wh-phrases themselves. This is quite clear in French, in particular, since wh-islands in French are more permeable than in English.[64] For example, the following extraction from a wh-island is fully acceptable:

(122)   A qui ne sais-tu pas quoi dire?
        'to whom neg. know you not what say-infinitive'

An example of an island effect created by topicalization is (123):[65]

(123)   *Quel livre, à Jean, veut-elle donner?

The idea that (120) is excluded as the result of an island effect created by topicalization carries over to clitic left dislocation (CLLD; cf. Cinque 1990):

(124)   a. Ce livre-là, Marie l'a lu.
           'that book there M it has read'
        b. *Ce livre-là l'a lu Marie.

Sentence (124b) contrasts with interrogatives:

(125)   Quel livre a lu Marie?
        'what book has read M'

The sharp deviance of (124b), which goes well beyond the slight deviance of SI with accusative clitics in general (cf. note 7), indicates that a CLLD phrase is not a 'licenser' for SI. In our terms, this means that a CLLD phrase blocks SI subject raising; in other words, subsequent to the preposing of *ce livre-là* in (124),[66] *Marie* is unable to raise higher [unlike (125), where *Marie* can raise past *quel livre*].

Independent evidence that a CLLD phrase blocks subject raising—in this case of the interrogative subject *qui* ('who')—comes from (126):[67]

(126)   a. Ce livre-là, qui l'a lu?
           'that book there who it has read'
        b. *Qui, ce livre-là, l'a lu?

Evidence that what is at issue is a blocking effect (on SI subject raising) produced by the CLLD phrase in (124b) and by the topicalized phrase in (120), rather than simply the absence of an appropriate 'licenser', comes from examples with two phrases visibly to the left of IP, one of which is a potential 'licenser' and the other not. Consider the following:

(127)   a.   ?le jour où, ce livre-là, Marie l'a lu
             'the day when that book there M it has read'
        b.   ?le jour où, cette fille-là, Jean lui a téléphoné
             'the day when that girl there J her has telephoned'

In these relative clauses, the adjunct wh-phrase *où* ('when'; literally 'where') has moved across the CLLD phrase, with no strong blocking effect (for reasons that we will not attempt to elucidate here). Thus (127) has two phrases to the left of the relative IP, one CLLD phrase and, preceding it, one wh-phrase.

Now the wh-phrase by itself would 'license' SI:

(128)   a.   ?le jour où l'a lu Marie
             'the day when it has read M'
        b.   le jour où lui a téléphoné Jean
             'the day when her has called J'

[On the fact that (128a) is less good than (128b), see the text to note 7.] Yet SI in (127) is impossible:

(129)   a.   *le jour où, ce livre-là, l'a lu Marie
        b.   *le jour où, cette fille-là, lui a téléphoné Jean

For SI to be well formed, the subject phrase must have some phrase above it that it can raise across. However, CLLD phrases block the required subject raising, as seen in (124b). Therefore, they will block it in (129), too. The fact that in (129) there is another phrase (the wh-phrase) that by itself would have allowed the subject (*Marie* or *Jean*) to move across it [as seen in (128)] is not sufficient since for the subject in (129) to cross the wh-phrase, it would also have to cross the CLLD phrase, which it cannot do.

One might expect the combination of wh-phrase and CLLD to be compatible with SI if SI subject raising could move the subject across the wh-phrase before CLLD preposing applied. This may in fact well be what occurs in some derivations, such as that of (130), but the word order produced will not be that of (129):

(130)   a.   ?Ce livre-là, quand l'a lu Marie?
             'that book there when . . .'
        b.   Cette fille-là, quand lui a téléphoné Jean?

These contrast minimally with (131), which is essentially the same as (129):

(131)   a.   *Quand, ce livre-là, l'a lu Marie?
        b.   *Quand, cette fille-là, lui a téléphoné Jean?

If we generalize away from movement of the object clitic, and set aside the question of what allows the preposition *à* to fail to appear before *cette fille-là*,[68] as well as various questions about clitic doubling, the derivation of (130b), for example, is (132):

(132)   Jean-SCL lui a téléphoné cette fille quand => wh-movement
        quand$_i$ X0 [$_{IP}$ Jean-SCL lui a téléphoné cette fille t$_i$] =>
        subject raising (possible since CLLD preposing has not yet applied) =>
        Jean$_j$ F0 [$_{XP}$ quand$_i$ X0 [$_{IP}$ t$_j$-SCL lui a téléphoné cette fille t$_i$]]
        => IP-preposing (cf. the discussion of (94)) =>
        [$_{IP}$ t$_j$-SCL lui a téléphoné cette fille t$_i$]k Y0 [$_{FP}$ Jeanj F0 [$_{XP}$ quand$_i$ X0 t$_k$]]
            => second wh-movement =>
        quand$_i$ Z0 [$_{IP}$ t$_j$-SCL lui a téléphoné cette fille t$_i$]$_k$ Y0 [$_{FP}$ Jean$_j$ F0
        [$_{XP}$ t$_i$ X0 t$_k$]]

Only at this point does CLLD preposing apply, to yield (130b).

13. SI and Post-Subject Complements

There are cases in which the SI subject can be followed by a verbal complement:

(133)   Qu'a dit Jean à Marie?
        'what has said J to M'

Although (133) is fully acceptable, there are restrictions that severely limit the class of such sentences. The clearest no doubt has to do with direct objects, which can never follow the subject:[69]

(134)   *A qui a dit Jean tout cela?
        'to whom has said J all that'

Nor can APs that are part of a small clause complement of the verb follow the subject:

(135)   *Quand est devenu Jean célèbre?
        'when is become J famous'

With PPs, the result is sometimes fully acceptable, as in (133), sometimes less so:

(136)   ?Quand a parlé Jean à Marie?
        'when has spoken J to M'

The kind of derivation we have proposed for SI does not immediately allow for sentences like (133). What we would so far expect, in the presence of a complement like *à Marie* is the following (simplified):

(137)   Jean a dit que à Marie => wh-movement =>
         que Jean a dit à Marie => SI subject raising =>
         Jean que a dit à Marie => IP preposing =>
         a dit à Marie Jean que => second wh-movement =>
         que a dit à Marie Jean

The IP-preposing step will move IP to the left of the subject, carrying along the complement, which will consequently find itself preceding the subject:

(138)   ?Qu'a dit à Marie Jean?

This kind of sentence, which is awkward (but improves if the subject is made heavier), is also possible in some of the cases in which the order '. . . V S complement' is impossible. For example, (139) is appreciably better than (135):[70]

(139)   ?Quand est devenu célèbre Jean?

The question, then, is how to derive (133) and (136) while at the same time excluding (134) and (135).

There is reason to think that the complement *à Marie* in (133) has been topicalized (as opposed to being in situ). In particular, as pointed out by Cornulier (1974, p.157), the postsubject complement in (133) is subject to a counter-indefiniteness effect:[71]

(140)   a. ?*Qu'a avoué Pierre à quelqu'un?
             'what has confided P to someone'
         b. Qu'a avoué Pierre à Jean-Jacques?
             'what has confided P to J-J'

This recalls restrictions often found with familiar instances of topicalization:

(141)   a. ?*A quelqu'un, Pierre a tout avoué.
             'to someone P has everything confided'
         b. A Jean-Jacques, Pierre a tout avoué.

However, (120) showed that topicalization is in fact incompatible with SI, which we interpreted in terms of a blocking effect on SI subject raising because of the topicalized phrase. A way out of this apparent paradox is suggested by the surprising fact discovered by Kampers-Mahne (1998), namely that '. . . V subject complement' is not possible in subjunctive SI; that is, there is a clear contrast between (133) and (136) and the following subjunctive SI examples:

(142)   *Il faut que le dise Jean à Marie.
         'it is-necessary that it say J to M'

(143)   *Je doute qu'ait parlé Jean à Marie.
         'I doubt that has spoken J to M'

This suggests that the postsubject position of *à Marie* in (133) and (136) is somehow 'parasitic' on wh-movement, despite the fact that *à Marie* and the wh-phrase do not end up next to one another. Consider, then, the following (simplified) derivation for (133):

(144)   Jean a dit que à Marie => wh-movement with pied-piping of small clause =>
         [que à Marie] Jean a dit => SI subject raising =>
         Jean [que à Marie] a dit => IP preposing =>
         a dit Jean [que à Marie] => second wh-movement step (no pied-piping) =>
         que a dit Jean à Marie

By the pied-piping hypothesis reflected in the first step of (144), *que à Marie* is a wh-phrase, not a topicalized phrase; therefore *Jean* is allowed to move across it. On the other hand, in a subjunctive context, pied-piping would not be available, so that for *à Marie* to topicalize in such a context it would have to do so on its own, with the result that SI subject raising of *Jean* [in, e.g., (142) or (143)] would [as in (120)] be blocked by *à Marie*, as desired. From this perspective, the preference for definites seen in (140) must indicate that the pied-piped phrase *à Marie* in (144) is interpreted as a topic, despite not having been topicalized 'on its own'.

Let us return now to the contrast between (133) and (136), that is, to the fact, from the perspective of (144), that pied-piping of PP by a wh-phrase is not uniformly successful. Korzen (1983) proposed that the well-formedness in wh-based SI of 'V subject complement' was keyed to the question of whether or not the wh-phrase is closer to the verb than is the complement. In (133), the wh-phrase *que* ('what') is a direct object, and the complement is a PP. Since direct objects are closer to the verb in a familiar sense than PPs, (133) is acceptable. On the other hand, in (136) the wh-phrase is an adjunct *quand* ('when'), which is generally assumed to be less close to the verb than a PP complement; therefore (136) is less acceptable.

We take Korzen's (1983) characterization of the (133) and (136) contrast to be on the right track, and we try to give it a theoretical interpretation in terms of derivation (144). The corresponding derivation for (136) would begin with (145):

(145)   [Jean a parlé à Marie quand]

The order of constituents here reflects standard assumptions. To proceed as in (144), wh-pied-piping would have to move *à Marie quand*. But here the wh-phrase is not initial in the small clause. Let us therefore propose (146):

(146)   wh-pied-piping of the sort necessary in (144) (to avoid the blocking effect
         of pure topicalization) is available only if the wh-phrase is initial
         (highest) in the small clause.

Now (146) is, if we set aside cases of prepositional pied-piping, such as "To whom were you speaking," already familiar, in particular from Webelhuth's (1992, chap. 4) work. He notes that (apart from the 'to whom' type) the Germanic languages other than English respect something similar to (146). Let us give an English example since in some contexts English respects something like (146), too:

(147) a. I wonder whose article they're reading.
       b. *I wonder the/an article by whom they're reading.

Although it remains to be determined how to characterize the cases in English (French has some similar cases) in which (146) can be ignored,[72] we take (146) to hold for SI derivations and to prevent pied-piping from moving *à Marie quand*. Sentence (136), however, is not strongly deviant. Let us therefore take (148) to be (marginally) available as input to a derivation of type (144):

(148) [Jean a parlé quand à Marie]

Recall now that the deviance of (134) and (135) is in fact sharp. They would correspond to the following inputs to (144):

(149) a. [Jean a dit tout cela à qui]
       b. [Jean est devenu célèbre quand]

But to derive (134) and (135), one would have to move by wh-pied-piping *tout cela à qui* in (149a) and *célèbre quand* in (149b), in violation of (146). Thus we have an account of the ungrammaticality of (134) and (135).

It remains to be understood why those are more strongly deviant than (136). The answer must be that in those cases the counterpart of (148) is not available as input to wh-pied-piping:

(150) a. [Jean a dit à qui tout cela]
       b. [Jean est devenu quand célèbre]

Presumably there is, VP-internally, some flexibility in ordering such that (148) is marginally available to the PP *à Marie*,[73] whereas DPs and small clauses have no comparable flexibility.

14. SI with More Than One Verb

We have not yet given an explicit analysis of the sharp contrast:

(151) a. A qui a téléphoné Jean?
          'to whom has telephoned J'
       b. *A qui a Jean téléphoné?

Let us approach (151b) much as we did (134) and (135), starting from the derivation of (151a):

(152)   Jean a téléphoné à qui => wh-movement =>
        à qui Jean a téléphoné => SI subject raising =>
        Jean à qui a téléphoné => IP preposing =>
        a téléphoné Jean à qui => second wh-movement =>
        à qui a téléphoné Jean

The IP-preposing step in (152) brings both auxiliary and participle to the left of *Jean*. The participle could fail to be preposed as part of IP if it had previously been topicalized as part of wh-pied-piping, as is *à Marie* in (144). But by (146), pied-piping movement of *téléphoné à qui* is excluded. Nor can we have recourse to an input structure like (148), leading to (136), since in the case of (151b) that input structure would have to be (153):

(153)   [Jean a à qui téléphoné]

On the plausible assumption that whatever allows . . . *quand à Marie* in (148) does not extend to . . . *à qui téléphoné*, (153) is not available—hence no derivation at all can lead to (151b).
        Similarly, for (154) IP preposing will move along both main verb and infinitive. Pied-piping of *téléphoner à qui* is prohibited by (146), and (155) is an unavailable input structure to wh-movement, just like (153):

(154)   a. A qui voulait téléphoner Jean?
            'to whom wanted tel-infin. J'
        b. *A qui voulait Jean téléphoner?

(155)   [Jean voulait à qui téléphoner]

In (151a) and (154a), IP preposing carries along two verbs. In (156) it carries along 'main verb + complementizer *de* + infinitive':

(156)   Quelle maison envisage d'acheter Marie?
        'what house plans de buy-infin. M'

In (157), it carries along 'main verb + complementizer + embedded finite (subjunctive) sentence (less wh-phrase)':[74]

(157)   Quelle maison veut que j'achète Jean-Jacques? ('what house wants that
            I buy J-J')

The (simplified) derivation of (157) is (158):

(158)   J-J veut que j'achète quelle maison => wh-movement =>
        quelle maison J-J veut que j'achète => SI subject raising =>
        J-J quelle maison veut que j'achète => IP preposing =>
        [veut que j'achète] J-J quelle maison => 2 wh- => (157)

Now (159) shows that IP movement that is carrying along two verbs is compatible with having the subject followed by a complement:

(159)   Quel genre de cadeau veut offrir Marie à Jean-Jacques? ('what sort of gift
           wants offer-infin. M to J-J')

The derivation is as that seen in (160):

(160)   M veut offrir quel cadeau à J-J => wh-pied-piping =>
           [quel cadeau à J-J] M veut offrir => SI subject raising =>
           M [quel cadeau à J-J] veut offrir => IP preposing =>
           [veut offrir] M [quel cadeau à J-J] => wh-movement => (159)

Given the well-formedness of both (156) and (159), one might well expect to be able to combine them, that is, to have a sentence like (159), but with *envisage de* instead of *veut*. However, the result is surprisingly deviant:

(161)   ??Quel genre de cadeau envisage de donner Marie à Jean-Jacques?
           'what sort of gift plans de give-infin. M to J-J'

The same holds if we try to 'combine' (159) with (157):[75]

(162)   *?Quel genre de cadeau veut que j'offre Marie à Jean-Jacques?
           'what sort of gift wants that I give M to J-J'

Why should this be so? Consider the derivation of (161) and similarly for (162):

(163)   M envisage de donner quel cadeau à J-J => wh-pied-piping =>
           [quel cadeau à J-J] M envisage de donner => SI subj. raising =>
           M [quel cadeau à J-J] envisage de donner => IP preposing =>
           [envisage de donner] M [quel cadeau à J-J] => wh-movement => (161)

We suggest that the difference between (160), which yields the well-formed (159), and (163), which yields the relatively ill-formed (161), should be attributed to the wh-pied-piping step.

The idea that wh-pied-piping (i.e., wh-induced movement of a small clause) is what is responsible for the deviance of (161) is inspired by the observation that *envisager* ('plan') and *vouloir* ('want') differ from each other in a similar way in the case of leftward quantifier movement:[76]

(164)   Elle a tout voulu donner à Jean.
           'she has everything wanted give-infin. to J'

(165)   ?Elle a tout envisagé de donner à Jean.
           'she has everything planned de give-infin. to J'

Infinitives under verbs like *vouloir* are transparent to such extraction, whereas extraction is more difficult with verbs like *envisager*. The proposal, then, is that in a way at least partially similar to movement of *tout* ('everything'), wh-piping of a small clause is (as opposed to ordinary wh-movement) sensitive to this kind of island effect.

15.   SI and Direct Objects

In the discussion following (148), we propose an account of the fact [illustrated in (134)] that the SI subject can never be followed by a direct object. In this section we return to the question of direct objects that precede the SI subject. The basic contrast is as follows:

(166)   ?Qu'a donné à Marie Jean?
        'what has given to M J'

(167)   *A qui a donné ce livre Jean?
        'to whom has given that book J'

The SI subject can follow PP complements with some degree of awkwardness, which can be alleviated by having a heavy SI subject, but the corresponding sentence with a direct object that precedes the SI subject is substantially worse. On the other hand, we noted in (7)–(16) that there are various clear classes of exceptions; that is, (167) can be made acceptable to varying degrees by having the direct object be idiomatic, cliticized, wh-moved, or a bare quantifier. The question of why (167) itself is unacceptable nonetheless remains.

Let us begin with the derivation of (166). It might appear that (166) is a straightforward case of SI, with IP preposing carrying along the PP *à Marie*. But if that were true, it would be difficult to understand the contrast with (167). Let us propose a slightly different derivation, then, for (166):

(168)   J a donné que à M => wh-movement =>
        que J a donné à M => SI subject raising =>
        J que a donné à M => topicalization =>
        à Marie J que a donné => IP preposing =>
        a donné à Marie J que => 2nd wh-movement => (166)

In (168), IP preposing does not carry along the PP, which was instead topicalized just prior to the IP-preposing step. Since topicalization in (168) follows SI subject raising, it cannot interfere with it, so the blocking effect that holds in (120) does not come into play here.

The next question is why (166) could not also avail itself of a derivation in which the PP was carried along by IP preposing. Thinking of Koopman and Szabolcsi (in press) on Dutch and Hungarian, we propose (169):[77]

(169)   IP preposing results in a violation if IP contains a lexical argument.

Rule (169), which itself requires explanation, will force on (166) the derivation (168). Why, then, can (167) not be derived in parallel fashion? The answer, we think, is that the topicalization step of (168) is not open to direct objects in French (as opposed to English):[78]

(170)   *Ce livre Jean a donné à Marie.
        'that book J has given to M'

In other words, the unacceptability of (167) is due to the combination of (169) and (170).

There is a striking contrast between the following two examples:[79]

(171)   *?A qui voulait donner ce livre Jean-Jacques?
        'to whom wanted give-infin. that book J'

(172)   A qui envisage de donner ce livre Jean-Jacques?
        '. . . plans . . .'

Although one might try to accommodate (172) by revising (169) to include some notion of 'not too deeply embedded', we prefer to treat (172) in a parallel way to (166), that is, by having the derivation of (172) contain a topicalization step—topicalization of the infinitive phrase (*de*) *donner ce livre*—that applies prior to IP preposing and removes the direct object from the domain of (169). What we see in (166) and (172) is that although the direct object cannot topicalize by itself, it can escape (169) through topicalization of a larger constituent that contains it.

The substantial deviance of (171) suggests that the infinitival complement of *vouloir* can only very marginally be topicalized in French. If so, (171) is basically in violation of (169).This property of (171) is presumably related to *vouloir* being one of the core restructuring verbs in Rizzi's (1982, chap.1) sense. That it is that relationship rather than simply the absence of complementizer in (171) is supported by the following, which escape (169) through topicalization of an infinitive complement that lacks a (visible) complementizer:

(173)   a. A qui aurait aimé donner ce livre Jean-Jacques?
           'to whom would-have liked give-infin. that book J-J'
        b. Où vont aller acheter des fruits les gens de Paris?
           'where are-going-to go-infin. buy-infin. (some) fruit the people of P'

We note in passing that a direct object that is triggering a violation of (169) need not be adjacent to the SI subject. This is shown clearly by (174):[80]

(174)   a. ?Quel genre de divan t'a sommé d'acheter Jean-Jacques?
           'what kind of sofa you has commanded de buy-infin. J-J'
        b. *Quel genre de divan a sommé Marie d'acheter Jean-Jacques?
           = 'what kind of sofa has J-J commanded M to buy'

In (174b), IP preposing has moved *a sommé Marie d'acheter*, violating (169), despite the fact that *Marie* is internal to the moved IP.

16. Strong Focalization SI

Pollock (1985) discussed a subcase of SI, illustrated in (175):

(175)   Ne sont venus que Jean et Marie. ('neg. are come but J and M' = 'only J
          and M have come')

This subcase of SI shares various properties discussed above, for example,
compare (79) and (80):

(176)   a. Ne sont venus qu'eux.
            '. . . them/they'
         b. *Ne sommes venus que nous.
            '. . . us/we'

It differs sharply, however, in freely allowing a direct object to precede the
subject:

(177)   N'ont embrassé la jeune mariée que son père et ses frères.
          'neg. have kissed the young bride but/only her father and her brothers'

This suggests a partial reinterpretation of the ban on French direct object
topicalization. Let us propose that direct object topicalization, although quite
generally prohibited in French across an ordinary subject, is in fact available if
the crossed subject is strongly focussed.

The (simplified) relevant part of the derivation of (177) is (178):[81]

(178)   que X et Y n'ont embrassé la jeune mariée => topicalization of direct object =>
          la jeune mariée que X et Y n'ont embrassée => IP preposing => (177)

From this perspective, (177) is unusual (relative to French) in allowing direct
object topicalization,[82] but it obeys (169) straightforwardly.[83]

17. Successive Cyclicity

One of the main concerns of Kayne and Pollock (1978) is the case of SI that
involves an embedded subject but in which the 'licenser' is in the matrix:

(179)   A qui crois-tu qu'a téléphoné Jean?
          'to whom think you that has called J'

Here the wh-phrase à qui is clearly playing the role of 'licenser', as shown by
the sharp contrast with (180) [cf. (86)]:

(180)   ???Je crois qu'a téléphoné Jean.
          'I think that . . .'

A qui can play this role only if it originates in the embedded sentence:

(181)   ???A qui as-tu dit qu'est parti Jean?
        'to whom have you said that is(has) left J'

To the extent that (180) and (181) are (very) marginally acceptable, they are instances of indicative SI, with derivations like that in (95) above. Another type of derivation must evidently be available to (179).

    Transposing the successive cyclicity proposal that we made in 1978 is straightforward. The (simplified) derivation of (179) will look like this:[84]

(182)   Jean a téléphoné à qui => wh-movement =>
        à qui Jean a téléphoné => subject raising =>
        Jean à qui a téléphoné => IP preposing =>
        a téléphoné Jean à qui => 2nd wh-movement (cf. note 43) =>
        à qui a téléphoné Jean => further mergers =>
        tu crois que à qui a téléphoné Jean => second cycle wh-movement
        (plus root inversion) => (179)

18. Conclusion

Theoretical and empirical considerations converge toward an analysis of French SI (nonclitic subject-related inversion) that has the following core properties: The lexical subject moves to a high position above IP, leaving behind a phonetically unrealized subject clitic. The (remnant) IP then moves leftward past the landing site of the subject.

    The analysis covers cases of SI that involve wh-movement, as well as cases that involve subjunctives and some marginal cases with indicatives. The notion of 'trigger for SI' that seemed necessary in earlier work turns out to be superfluous from our new perspective.

    French turns out, in addition, to have no null expletives in SI sentences, contrary to appearances, but it does have quirky subjects that in part resemble those of Icelandic.

    The postverbal SI subject can sometimes be followed by a complement because of the pied-piping of the complement as a side effect of wh-movement, which accounts for a major difference between wh-SI and subjunctive SI.

    When the postverbal SI subject is preceded by a complement, the position of the complement is due to topicalization (across the subject) prior to IP preposing. Such topicalization cannot apply to a direct object, except when the subject is strongly focused.

    Multiple leftward movements are seen to interact in such a way as to provide accounts for various phenomena that were not understood in an earlier framework countenancing rightward movement.

NOTES

1. This is unfortunate because it seems to state that the computations responsible for SI are 'stylistic' in Chomsky and Lasnik's (1977, p. 431) or Rochemont's (1978) sense. Nor should SI be ascribed to the PF component of Chomsky's (1995) minimalist program. Most of the syntactic and interpretive properties of postverbal subjects to be discussed below would remain mysterious in any such approach. The terminology was originally introduced in Kayne (1972, p. 73) to reflect the fact that the 'heaviness' of the postverbal subject sometimes plays a role in the felicitousness of the construction [cf. (166)]. For perhaps relevant discussion of 'heaviness', see Kayne (1998a).

2. Cf. also Deprez (1989; 1990), Friedemann (1997), Kayne (1986), and Pollock (1986).

3. This view—see Kayne (1972, p. 77)—is not compatible with the idea that yes/no questions contain a null counterpart of a wh-phrase, as in much work making use of Rizzi's (1996) "wh-criterion," unless that null operator belongs to the same class as those wh-phrases that disallow SI; see (115)–(118).

4. Cf. Cornulier (1974, p. 185) and Kupferman (1983).

5. Cf. also Legendre (1998).

6. Even this limited statement is not always true; in particular it does not hold for the *ne . . . que*/focalization subvariety of SI that we return to below [cf. (175)–(178)].

7. Judgments are often intermediate here, for unclear reasons; cf. Kayne (1972, note 8).

8. It may be that the general case does not (always or fully) extend to instances of SI in which the verb is unaccusative; cf. note 9.

9. With unaccusatives, as in (19c), the unacceptability is not complete, perhaps indicating the marginal possibility of early *en* extraction. Since quantitative *ne* extraction in Italian is sometimes possible with intransitives like *telefonare*, some French speakers might find (19a) or (19b) only marginal. The facts with transitives are extremely sharp, on the other hand. On the different behavior of adnominal (nonquantitative) *en*, see Pollock (1998).

10. As expected, this contrast is not found in Czech, whose clitic position is higher than the preverbal subject; cf. Toman (1986).

11. This statement supports Rizzi's (1997) proposal that there are functional heads above IP that are distinct from the complementizer; cf. Pollock, Munaro, and Poletto (1999). Note that the IP movement required here would fail to be movement of a maximal projection if the subject had merely moved leftward to a second Spec position; cf. Chomsky (1995, p. 356) on IP itself.

12. This occurs in a way that we will not make precise; cf. Kayne (1975, sect. 1.5) and Obenauer (1994). Note that the passive of (24) is as bad as that of (26):

(i) **De linguistes ont peu été vus par Jean. ('of linguists have few been seen by J')

This may suggest, in the manner of Kayne (1998a), that *de linguistes* in (24) is not a constituent. Cf. also Boivin (1999).

13. Cf. note 9; also Kayne (1981b, note 61).

14. See note 42. The text idealizes the data concerning *combien* somewhat; Obenauer (1976, pp. 20ff.) reports on speakers who reject (some) cases like (29a), for example:

(i) ??Combien ont rouspété d'amis? ('how-many have grumbled of friends')

We will not be able to study these subtle differences among speakers here.

15. There is some uncertainty about which negative element is (more) crucial; cf. Kayne (1981b, note 12), Pollock (1989, pp. 414–415), and Rowlett (1998).

16. Cf. Burzio (1986, sect. 6.1), Kayne (1975, sect. 5.5), and Rizzi (1986).

17. Postverbal strong pronouns in SI must be deictic (see Kayne 1972, note 2). We use capitals for deictic strong pronouns throughout. *Elle* ('3fem.sg.'), *nous* ('1pl.'), and *vous* ('2pl./polite 2sg.') are orthographically ambiguous and can be either nominative clitics or strong (deitic) pronouns. It should be noted that strong pronouns in French show no morphological Case distinctions. As strong deictic pronouns, *EUX*, *NOUS*, and *VOUS* are incompatible with "liaison," so except for *ELLE* vs. *elle*, strong deictic pronouns can in principle be distinguished phonetically from weak nominative clitic pronouns. See also the text to note 18.

18. The liaison -*s* of *VOUS* and *NOUS* in (40c, d) must *not* be pronounced. If it is, those examples become irrelevantly acceptable, with *nous* and *vous* then the stressed variants of the weak nominative clitics.

19. Without the first *et* ('and'), (41) is less than fully acceptable, although it remains better than (42) without the first *et*, which is impossible.

20. The derivation in (48) is an instance of remnant movement in the sense of Den Besten and Webelhuth (1987; 1990); cf. Kayne (1998b, text to note 13). If SCL is overt, we derive:

(i)   le jour où il a téléphoné(,) Jean

Cf., perhaps, Cecchetto (1999) and Villalba (1999) on right dislocation; also Lanly (1962) on North African French. In the spirit of Chomsky (1977), one might consider generating *Jean* in (47) and (48) directly in Spec-FP. This would probably not change much about SI; on the other hand, it is not clear that UG should ever allow DPs to be merged above IP; cf. Kayne (1994, p. 82) on a movement approach to CLLD.

21. Probably akin to (49) and (50) is the following:

(i)   *le jour où ont téléphoné trois
        'the day when have called three'

given the impossibility of (ii), like that of (52) and (53):

(ii)   *Trois ils ont téléphoné.
        'three they have called'

Legendre (1998) has suggested that the SI subject must be focus. This does not seem correct; for example, postverbal subjects in Qu-triggered cases of SI can be discursive topics, as shown by (iii):

(iii)   a. Une nouvelle loi vient d' être votée par le parlement.
             'A new law comes from being voted by the parliament.'
         b. Et que dit/promulgue la dite loi/cette loi?
             'and what says/ promulgates the said law/that law'
         c. Et quand sera mise en application la dite loi/cette loi?
             'and when will-be put into effect the said law/that law'

In (iv) the SI subjects seem like contrastive topics:

(iv)   Je sais à qui a parlé Jean, mais je ne sais pas à qui a parlé sa femme.
       'I know to whom has spoken J but I neg. know not to whom has spoken his wife'

Probably related to (iv) is (v):

(v)   a.   A qui a parlé qui?
           'to whom has spoken who'
      b.   Sur qui est tombe quoi?
           'on whom is fallen what'

Whether the SI subject can be focus (and if so, in what sense of the term) is a separate question that we leave open.

22. Although intuitions are sometimes less sharp than Cornulier (1974) indicates and seem open to some variation, there is no doubt that his observations are basically correct, especially if indefinite generics (and some unaccusatives; cf. note 9) are set aside. *Quelqu'un* ('someone') is very hard to interpret as generic—hence the fact there is general agreement on Cornulier's original observations. When *quelque chose* ('something') is more or less acceptable in SI, as (i) would be for Pollock, we suspect that it is being reinterpreted as a shifted topic, that is, as denoting one of a previously identified set of possible occurrences:

(i)   */?Dis-moi quand se passera quelque chose de passionnant.
      'tell me when refl. take-place something of interesting'

This is more readily available when a fairly unspecific verb like *se passer* is chosen, which may account for why Pollock finds a perceptible difference between (ii) and (iii):

(ii)   *Dis-moi quand se déroulera quelque chose.
       'tell me when refl. will-unfold something'

(iii)   ?Dis-moi quand se passera quelque chose.
        'tell me when will-take-place something'

23. It remains to be understood why complex inversion, as illustrated below, seems to impose no restriction against indefinite subjects:

(i)   a.   Quel gâteau quelqu'un a-t-il mangé?
           'what cake someone has he eaten'
      b.   Quel article quelqu'un critiquera-t-il?
           'what article someone will-criticize he')

24. Somewhat similar to (55b) is the grammatical:

(i)   Quand a-t-il téléphoné?

This is an instance of subject clitic inversion, which differs from SI in a number of ways (cf. Kayne 1972), the most important of which, apart from the difference in position of the subject in (i) vs. (55), is perhaps that subject clitic inversion is limited to root sentences:

(ii)   Je sais quand a téléphoné Jean.
        'I know when has telephoned J'

(iii)   *Je sais quand a-t-il téléphoné.

It may well be, nonetheless, that there is a level of abstraction at which SI and subject clitic inversion share some significant property; cf. Pollock, Munaro, and Poletto (1999).

25. This is true despite the fact that *-ant* forms and finite verbs behave similarly in the placement of adverbs; cf. Kayne (1975, sect. 1.3) and Pollock (1989, p. 408). Note in that in the Italian counterpart of (58) a pronominal (nonclitic, noninitial) subject would have nominative Case.

26. Colloquial French does allow what is probably a silent expletive subject clitic:

(i)   Faut pas qu'il fasse ça.
       'is-necessary not that he do that')

27. Were one to claim that the postverbal SI subject is in a low position throughout the derivation, one would have to allow verb agreement in French to be determined by a lower DP (cf. Chomsky 1998, pp. 37ff.). That would create problems for past participle agreement:

(i)   *Jean a repeintes les tables.
       'J has repainted the tables'

(ii)   *Il a été repeintes plusieurs tables.
       'it has been repainted several tables'

A past participle can agree neither with a lower direct object, as seen in (i), nor with a lower 'associate' in the expletive construction illustrated in (ii). Whether the text approach can be generalized to English expletive constructions, which appear to allow agreement with a lower DP, is left open here. The question is whether in (iii) *five tables* is not at some point (in a derivation akin to that of SI) actually above the agreeing verb (prior to some version of IP movement):

(iii)   There are five tables in the garage.

The absence of downward verb agreement would be expected if verb agreement (of all types) is akin to an antecedent-pronoun relation (cf. Fauconnier 1974) and if antecedent pronoun relations of this sort are reducible to movement of the antecedent, away from the pronoun double, as in Kayne (1997). From this perspective, verb agreement, as opposed to clitic doubling [cf. the discussion following (46)], would not be a primitive of UG.

28. Cf. Postal (1974).

29. Cf. Chomsky (1995).

30. Adjectives with a thematic subject act differently; thus (i) is closer in status to (73) than to (74):

(i)   (?)the person whom I'm sure is intelligent

Similar, now, is the fact that (ii) seems closer to (60b) than to (63b):

(ii)   ???Je suis sûr qu'est parti Jean. ('I am sure that is (has) left J')

Note in this regard that adjectives in other Germanic languages differ sharply from nouns in those languages, in that adjectives can have nonprepositional objects, with visibly oblique Case if Case is morphologically expressed; cf. Holmberg and Platzack (1995, p. 150). It remains to be understood why, alongside (i), there are in English no examples like (iii):

(iii)   *I'm sure John to be intelligent.

That (iii) is actually not a simple fact about adjectives is suggested by the apparently parallel contrast (cf. Kayne 1980, sect. 1.3):

(iv)   (?)John, whom I assure you is intelligent, . . .

(v)   *I assure you John to be intelligent.

31. Cf. the discussion of (7)–(16), especially note 7. For many speakers, the unaccusative (and similarly for verbs like *téléphoner*) counterparts of (84) and (85b), although deviant, are less so, especially the negation example in (i), than in the transitive cases:

(i)   ?Je doute que ne soient pas entrés de linguistes dans cette pièce depuis ce matin.
       'I doubt that neg. be (subjunctive) not entered of linguists into this room since this morning'

(ii)   ?Il aurait été souhaitable que soient beaucoup partis de linguistes.
       'it would-have been desirable that be (subjunctive) many gone of linguists'

For some of these speakers, (i) and (ii) are fully acceptable. At the same time, for such speakers, the unaccusative counterpart of (83) is less acceptable than (i) and (ii):

(iii)   ??Je doute qu'en soient entrés vingt-cinq.
        'I doubt that of-them be-subjunctive entered twenty-five'

The deviance is sharper still if the numeral/quantifier is not pronounced; thus (v) contrasts with (iv), even for the speakers in question:

(iv)   Elle en a vu.
       'she of-them has seen' = 'she has seen some'
(v)   *?Je doute qu'en soient entré(s).
       'I doubt that of-them be entered'

How best to account for these gradations [(iii) and (v) would be '?' and '??' for those who accept (i) and (ii)] is left open. It is important to keep in mind that even taking into account the graded judgments of this note, the subjunctive SI facts of (i)–(iii) and (v) are substantially different from those concerning the expletive *il*, which allows all of the following, for all speakers—with the caveat that speakers who do not fully accept displaced quantifiers in general will not fully accept (vii):

(vi)   Il n'est pas entré de linguistes dans cette pièce.
       'it neg. is not entered of linguists in this room'

(vii)   Il est beaucoup parti de linguistes.
        'it is many left of ling.'

(viii) Il en est venu vingt-cinq.
        'it of-them is come 25'

(ix)   Il en est venu.

In addition, the expletive *il* construction does not show agreement with the postverbal DP, as opposed to SI. It further differs from SI in showing a definiteness effect, that is, a preference for the postverbal DP to be indefinite, whereas SI shows the opposite preference. We conclude, contrary to Kayne and Pollock (1978, p. 611), that no instance of SI is an expletive *il* sentence with *il* unpronounced. (The silent subject clitic that SI sentences do contain differs from the expletive *il* in always being doubled by a DP, which can marginally itself be unpronounced, in the special case of (v), with an abstract quantifier).

32. On the so-called adnominal *en* that in part behaves differently, cf. Pollock (1998).

33. Less bad than (85b) is this:

(i)   ??Je doute que m'aient beaucoup vu de linguistes.
       'I doubt that me have many seen of linguistes'

For relevant discussion of the interpretation of displaced *beaucoup*, cf. Obenauer (1994).

34. Sometimes the conditional (and future) act like the subjunctive more than like the present and past indicative; cf. Poletto (2000).

35. If Kayne (1998a; 1999b) is on the right track about complementizers, the text proposal that follows will need to be recast.

36. These two operations differ from wh-movement, to which indicatives are permeable, in not involving 'Comp'; cf. Chomsky (1973) and Kayne (1981a, sect. 2).

37. Sentence (91) is to be read here without strong contrastive focus on the postverbal subject, which would allow it to fall under the *ne . . . que* subtype of SI, to be discussed below.

38. For a different approach, cf. Shlonsky (1992).

39. Cf. also Kayne (1997). Short subject wh-movement in French (cf. Rizzi 1982, p. 152) will be allowed as long as it need not involve a (silent) subject clitic. The Italian ban on short wh-movement of the subject may be (virtually) identical to the Hebrew facts if Italian null subject sentences necessarily contain a pronominal subject—*pro* in the third person, a verbal suffix in the first and second, if Kayne (1999a) is correct. Consider subject CLLD (cf. note 20) in French:

(i)   Jean, il est parti.
       'J he is gone'

It may be that French overt subject clitics are to both French silent subject clitics and Hebrew subject pronouns as English reflexives with *-self* are to English simple pronouns. This is true for Italian null subject CLLD, as in (ii), and in all likelihood for Italian sentences with postverbal subjects, on the assumptions of the preceding paragraph:

(ii)   Gianni, è partito.

That is, the Italian null subject (or agreement suffix) will have the status of overt French subject clitics. English topicalization may be relevant, too, if (iv) cannot be pronounced with the same intonation as (iii):

(iii)   JOHN, Mary has always liked.

(iv)   MARY has always liked John.

Cf. Nelson (1997) on English exclamatives. As for (38) above, on the assumption that it contains a silent subject clitic (as we have argued), it must be either the pronominal status of *lui* or *eux* and/or the strong contrastive stress (cf. the *ne . . . que* case to be discussed below) that make it compatible with (92), in a way that needs to be made precise.

40. Subjunctive SI is possible in 'topic sentences', for example, (i) (cf. Pollock 1986):

(i)   Que partent ces linguistes, ça vous laisse indifférent?
      'that leave-subjunctive those linguists, that you leaves indiff.'

It might be that subject raising moves *ces linguistes* in (i) to a position just above *que*, as seems called for in any event in (ii):

(ii)   Que partent ces linguistes!
       'that leave those linguists' = 'may/let those linguists leave'

On the other hand, subject raising in (i) might take place before the preposing of *que partent ces linguistes*, that is, at a point in the derivation that looks like (iii):

(iii)   Ça vous laisse indifférent que ces linguistes partent?

If this is so, subject raising might, in the derivation of (i), move *ces linguistes* to a position above the matrix IP.

41. This is true if we assume that there cannot be any unfilled projections between FP and IP.

42. This is also the case when the wh-phrase corresponds to part of the subject:

(i)   combien de linguistes-SCL ont téléphoné => wh-movement =>
      combien$_i$ X0 [$_{IP}$ t$_i$ de linguistes-SCL ont téléphoné] => subject raising =>
      de linguistes$_j$ F0 [$_{XP}$ combien$_i$ X0 [$_{IP}$ t$_i$ t$_j$-SCL ont téléphoné]]

IP preposing followed by a second movement of *combien* will yield (cf. note 43) (ii):

(ii)   Combien ont téléphoné de linguistes?
       'how-many have called of ling'

43. We are thinking in particular of (146) below. Having (the option of) two wh-movements in one 'simple' sentence is motivated by Pollock, Munaro, and Poletto (1999).

44. Note that subjunctive SI does not show the ECM-like effect [illustrated by (86) vs. (63b)] found with indicatives; that is, (i) is possible in addition to (87) [cf. also examples (i) and (ii) of note 40]:

(i)   Il est souhaitable que parte Jean.
       'it is desirable that leave J'

Whether subjunctives themselves have access to an ECM-like derivation, in addition to (90), is left open. The two-step subject-raising derivation illustrated in (95) will also (less the IP preposing step) hold for (73) (cf. also Pollock 1985). In addition it probably (again without IP preposing) holds for (ii):

(ii)   ?the people who John think should be invited

For this construction, in which *think* agrees with *who*, cf Kayne (1995) and Kimball and Aissen (1971). As for the impossibility of (62b), it must be that *si* ('if') blocks subject-raising. This is as if *que* (as opposed to *si*) were not present at the first subject-raising step, a possibility probably compatible with Kayne (1998a; 1999b).

45. Cf. also the objections to null expletives raised in note 31. In addition, note the similarity between (60b) vs. (63b) and (i) vs. (ii):

(i)   ???Je crois que sera procédé au réexamen de la loi.
       'I think that will-be proceeded to-the reexamination of the law'

(ii)   *Il est évident que sera procédé au réexamen de la loi.
        'it is obvious that . . .'

Furthermore, much as (87) is substantially better than (86), so is (iii) substantially better than (i):

(iii)   Je veux que soit procédé au réexamen de la loi.
         'I want that . . .'

Thus there are quite a few reasons for taking the *procédé* cases to be a somewhat special subvariety of SI. Cf. also below.

46. This also occurs for *à la guerre* and *de ces amendements* in examples like (i) and (ii):

(i)   Quand sera mis fin à la guerre?
       'when will-be put end to the war'

(ii)   Quand sera tenu compte de ces amendements?
        'when will-be taken account of these amendements'

In these sentences, *fin* and *compte* are not subjects but rather (idiomatic) objects, much as *advantage* in English examples like (iii):

(iii)   John has been taken advantage of.

47. If Kayne (1998a, 1999b) is on the right track about prepositions, this derivation will need to be partly recast.

48. It should be noted that parallel derivations with certain other PPs yield ungrammatical sentences:

(i) a. *Quand sera voté contre/pour Clinton au Senat?
         'when will-be voted against/for C in the S'
     b. *Quand sera nettoyé dans la maison?
         ' . . . cleaned in the house'
     c. *Quand a été tiré sur le bateau?
         'when has been shot on the boat'

It may be that Case theory restricts the first step of (100) to DPs associated with the prepositions *à* and *de*, that is, to DPs with prepositions that have often been argued in the literature to be genuine "(oblique) Case-markers." Furthermore, theta theory may restrict such oblique subjects to DPs that can be (re)interpreted as receiving an internal theta-role from a complex predicate: *procéder au réexamen de la loi = réexaminer la loi; mettre fin à la guerre = finir la guerre*; and so on. This would yield an account of (ii) if *renvoyé à cet article* could not be so reanalyzed:

(ii) *Depuis quand est renvoyé à cet article dans LI?
      'since when is referred to this article in LI'

49. Cf. Zaenen, Maling, and Thrainsson (1985); also Belletti and Rizzi (1988) on *piacere* ('please-infin.').

50. In (i), 'under the bed' may well be associated with or preceded by an unpronounced noun akin to 'place':

(i) I consider under the bed a good hiding place.

Similarly for (ii):

(ii) John came out from under the bed.

The presence of this abstract element—. . . 'from PLACE under the bed'—might account for the deviance of (iii):

(iii) *Under which bed did he just come out from?

Compare the following:

(iv) *Under which bed did he just come out from someplace?

(v) *Someplace under which bed did he just come out from?

51. A separate question is whether French ever has recourse to a true in situ wh-strategy. It certainly appears to:

(i) Tu as fait quoi?
     'You have done what?'

We suspect, however, that (i) does not really have *quoi* in situ. Cf. Pollock, Munaro, and Poletto (1999, sect. 7). On yes-no questions from a similar perspective, cf. Sportiche (1995, p. 388).

52. We are setting aside here the question of why UG imposes on SI the presence of a (silent) subject clitic.

53. There is for some speakers a weak contrast between (98) and (i):

(i)   ??Au réexamen de la loi sera procédé demain.
      'to-the examination of the law will-be proceeded tomorrow'

The status of (i) is hard to assess, in part because such sentences all have a very literary ring to them (i.e., they sound dated). The question is why (i) does not violate GCondB more strongly, for those speakers. Perhaps (i) is a (very) marginal case of the PP that is actually able to remain in subject position.

54. That EPP violation could be neutralized by having the expletive *il* in subject position, as in (99); thus long wh-movement of *au réexamen de quelle loi* is in fact available in (99).

55. And also allowing for the fact that French does not allow wh-movement to apply to a structure like (87), yielding:

(i)   *Qui faut-il que parte?
      'who is-necessary it that leave'

The contrast between (i) and (102) is probably related to the fact that (102) lacks a silent subject clitic (as opposed to a silent locative/oblique clitic), but the exact reason for the impossibility of (i) needs to be made more precise.

56. This has the restrictions mentioned in note 48 above. Similarly, (i) is like (105)–(107) despite having a PP complement:

(i)   *Quand s'agira de lui?

Well-formed, with an overt expletive, is (ii):

(ii) Quand s'agira-t-il de lui?
      'when reflexive will-act it- explet. of him' = 'when will he be at issue'

57. Sentence (111) seems similar to (i), which contrasts with English:

(i)   Ça fait rire.
      'that makes laugh-infin.'

(ii) That makes *(one) laugh.

In (i), there is presumably a silent generic subject, which like the expletive of (111) cannot appear in finite contexts:

(iii) *Quand rit?
      'when laughs'

(iv) *Je souhaiterais que rie.
      'I would-wish that laugh-subjunc.'

On the other hand, (111) contrasts with (v):

(v)   *Les scientifiques sont capables de faire faire froid.
       '. . . of making do(be) cold'

This is probably related to (vi) vs. (vii):

(vi)   Ça pleut./Ça neige.
       'that rains/that snows'

(vii) *Ça fait froid.

58. A separate question is whether the silent subject clitic that we have postu-
lated should be taken to be an 'internal trigger'. That is, could it be that DPs in French
are optionally introduced in conjunction with a doubling clitic and that, when such a
clitic is present and silent and in a nominative subject position, SI subject raising must
take place? As for the question of what would compel such movement (and somewhat
similarly in the case of object clitic doubling), see perhaps Moro (2000).

59. When argumental, *en quel sens* is compatible with SI, as in (i):

(i)   En quel sens a tourné la voiture?
       'in what direction has turned the car'

60. In standard French, sentences such as (116) are, as with most wh-phrases,
not possible; cf. Pollock, Munaro, and Poletto (1999) for relevant discussion.

61. The fact that (115) is less than a full * may be linked to the marginal availability of (86) and (95).

62. The unacceptability of (118) is somewhat less sharp than that of (62b), indicating that *si* ('if') is not a wh-phrase at all (cf. Kayne 1991, sect. 2); it also indicates
that if there is an abstract wh-phrase in (62b), it must be so high that the embedded
subject cannot cross it.

63. There are acceptable sentences like (i):

(i)   A Jean correspond Pierre.
       'to J corresponds P'

These differ from (120) is not having a noninverted counterpart, that is, (ii) contrasts
with (119):

(ii)   *A Jean Pierre correspond.

Conceivably, (i) has an in situ quirky subject; cf. note 53. Note that the contrast between (120) and (121) suggests that Chomsky's (1977) abstract wh-phrase analysis of
English topicalization, whether or not correct for English, should not be transposed to
French (as suggested also by the fact that French by and large disallows topicalization
(but not wh-movement) of a direct object).

64. Cf. Godard (1988) and Sportiche (1981).

65. Contrasts with (i):

(i)   J'aurais, à Jean, donné un livre de linguistique.
       'I would-have to J given a book of linguistics'

What has moved past *à Jean* is a rather different constituent, probably a remnant IP. The island effect induced by topicalization may be weaker when that which is crossing the topic is a PP; cf. Rizzi (1997, p. 306). Sentence (123) constitutes a closer match with (nonprepositional) SI subject raising.

66. On CLLD as preposing, cf. Dobrovie-Sorin (1990, p. 394) and Kayne (1994, p. 82).

67. On (126b), cf. also Rizzi (1997, p. 306).

68. Some French speakers allow (i):

    (i)   A cette fille-là, quand lui a téléphoné Jean?

69. This is to be kept separate from the question of whether the subject can immediately follow a direct object, where things are appreciably less black and white; cf. (9) and (15c), which are completely impossible with the order verb-subject-object:

    (i)   *Depuis quelle heure ont les enfants faim?
          'Since when have the children hunger'?

    (ii) *la fille à qui laissera sa grand'mère quelque chose
          'the girl to whom will-let her grandmother something'

Cf. also below.

70. This contrast is unexpected from the Emonds (1976) and Legendre (1998) perspective mentioned in the discussion of (7) and (8), especially since in non-SI contexts the more normal order is 'V-DP-AP':

    (i)   Cela a rendu Jean célèbre.
          'that has made J famous'

   (ii) ?Cela a rendu célèbre Jean.

71. The subject clitic inversion construction mentioned in note 24 does not show any comparable restriction:

    (i)   Qu'a-t-il avoué à quelqu'un?
          'what has he confided to someone'

72. For example, in (literary) relatives:

    (i)   the linguist a statue of whom is standing in the parlor

For relevant discussion, cf. Cinque (1982), Kayne (1983, pp. 42–79), and Obenauer (1994).

73. Perhaps this is related to the proposals concerning prepositions made in Kayne (1998a, 1999b).

74. It remains to be understood why the counterpart of (157) with an embedded indicative is less good (though not impossible):

    (i)   ?Quelle maison croit que tu achèteras Jean-Jacques?
          'what house believes that you will- buy J-J'

75. Not surprisingly, given note 74, the indicative counterpart of (162) is strongly unacceptable:

(i)   *Quel genre de cadeau croit que tu offriras Marie à Jean-Jacques?

76. Cf., for example, Baker (1996, pp. 150–151), Kayne (1975, chap. 1), and Pollock (1978).

77. The correct notion of 'lexical' will want to distinguish between (i) and (ii):

(i)   *A qui en a offert trois Jean-Jacques?
      'to whom of-them has offered three J-J'

(ii) (?)A qui en a offert Jean-Jacques?

On the presence of an abstract quantifier/numeral in (ii), cf. Kayne (1975, sect. 2.9) and Pollock (1998, p. 315). The idiomatic objects of (9) and the bare quantifier objects of (15) must not count as lexical. If *tous* ('all') did count as lexical in sentences like (iii), we could correctly account for the following (cf. Deprez 1990, p. 56):

(iii) a. le jour où tes amis ont (tous) téléphoné
          'the day when your friends have all telephoned'
       b. le jour où ont (*tous) téléphoné tes amis

There is probably a link here with . . . *l'un* . . . *l'autre* . . . constructions (cf. Kayne 1975, sect. 1.9) and with gapping (cf. Johnson 1994), which is beyond the scope of this chapter. A problem that may or may not be related to the question of (iii) is raised by (iv), in which *lui* and *Jean* cannot be coferential:

(iv) le jour où lui ont téléphoné les amis de Jean
      'the day when him have phoned the friends of J'

Although this might look like a Condition C effect (which would be unexpected if *lui* is preposed as part of IP), it also appears in (v), where Condition C is less plausible:

(v)   le jour où ont voulu lui téléphoner les amis de J
      'the day when have wanted him(dative) phone the friends of J'

Nor is condition C likely to be at issue in (vi)—where *le* still seems noncoreferential with *Al Capone*—especially given (172):

(vi) le jour où ont envisagé de le descendre tous les voyous qu'avait engagés
          Al Capone
      'the day when have planned de him shoot-down all the gangsters that has
         hired Al Capone (subject)'

78. Cf. note 40 and Cinque (1990, 71).
79. Similar to (171a) is this:

(i)   *Que veuillent écrire un livre beaucoup de linguistes, ca . . .
      'that want-subjunctive write-infin. a book many of linguists, that . . .'

The contrast between (i) and (ii), which is like (166), supports the idea that subjunctive SI and wh-SI are largely the same:

(ii)   ?Que veuillent parler à Marie beaucoup de linguistes, ça . . .
        'that want-subjunctive speak-infin. to M . . .'

It remains to be understood why the counter-indefiniteness effect of (49) is weak with subjunctives; that is, the following is fairly acceptable:

(iii)   Je souhaiterais que te critique quelqu'un.
         'I would- wish that you(object) criticize someone(subject)'

80. This contrast is found in Italian, too:

(i)   ?L'ha costretta ad andar via Gianni.
       'her has forced to go away G'

(ii)   *Ha costretto Maria ad andar via Gianni.

This suggests that Italian is also subject to (169) and that Italian has IP preposing of the sort we have been discussing for French; cf. Belletti (1998).

81. Example (178) seems to imply that *ne* need not c-command *que*, in which case the ungrammaticality of (i) must be due to another factor:

(i)   *Que Jean n'est venu.

On the fact that the second line of (178) does not itself correspond to a grammatical sentence, see Barbaud (1976) and/or Pollock, Munaro, and Poletto (1999).

82. See Ordóñez (1998) on Spanish scrambling.

83. Another question about (175) concerns IP preposing and subject raising. As indicated in (178), we take IP preposing to apply here just as in all other cases of SI. But we have argued, at the end of section 3, following example (23), that for IP preposing to apply the subject must have raised out of Spec-IP to a higher Spec position. We have in addition proposed in (92) that this higher Spec cannot be that of the projection immediately above IP. How is (175) compatible with this last requirement? A detailed answer would take us too far afield, but it seems likely that it is the *que* itself that plays an essential role, which is similar to the silent strong-focalizing head in (i):

(i)   Ont embrassé la jeune mariée son père, ses frères et ses soeurs.

In particular, it may be that (92) applies only to F0 and that the presence of a head like *que* makes (92) irrelevant to (175). On the fact that English *only* and similar heads induce IP preposing themselves, see Kayne (1998b).

84. Note that SI subject raising on the lower cycle is compatible with (92) by virtue of the previous application of wh-movement. Having subject raising wait until after the wh-phrase reaches the matrix is ruled out [modulo the '???' of (181)] by the indicative island effect discussed above; see the paragraph following (90). The counterpart of (179) with an embedded subjunctive will have this option, however; see the discussion of (102).

REFERENCES

Aoun, J. (1985). *A Grammar of Anaphora*. MIT Press, Cambridge, Mass.

Baker, M. C. (1996). *The Polysynthesis Parameter*. Oxford University Press, New York.

Barbaud, P. (1976). "Constructions superlatives et structures apparentées." *Linguistic Analysis* 2, 125–174.

Belletti, A. (1998). "'Inversion' as Focalization." Ms., University of Siena.

Belletti, A., & L. Rizzi. (1988). "Psych-Verbs and theta-Theory." *Natural Language and Linguistic Theory* 6, 291–352.

Boivin, M-C. (1999, April). "Subject/object Asymmetries without the ECP: The Case of French *Beaucoup*." Paper presented at LSRL29, University of Michigan, Ann Arbor.

Borer, H. (1984). "Restrictive Relatives in Modern Hebrew." *Natural Language and Linguistic Theory* 2, 219–260.

Burzio, L. (1986). *Italian Syntax. A Government-Binding Approach*. Reidel, Dordrecht.

Cecchetto, C. (1999). "A Comparative Analysis of Left and Right Dislocation in Romance." *Studia Linguistica* 53, 40–67.

Chomsky, N. (1973). "Conditions on Transformations." In S. R. Anderson & P. Kiparsky (eds.), *A Festschrift for Morris Halle*. Holt, Rinehart & Winston, New York, 232–286.

———. (1977). "On Wh-movement." In P. W. Culicover, T. Wasow, & A. Akmajian (eds.), *Formal syntax*. Academic Press, New York, 71–132.

———. (1995). *The Minimalist Program*. MIT Press, Cambridge, Mass.

———. (1998). "Minimalist Inquiries: The Framework." *MIT Occasional Papers in Linguistics* 15, MITWPL, Cambridge, Mass.

Chomsky, N., & H. Lasnik. (1977). "Filters and Control." *Linguistic Inquiry* 8, 425–504.

Cinque, G. (1982). "On the Theory of Relative Clauses and Markedness." *The Linguistic Review* 1, 247–294.

———. (1990). *Types of A'-Dependencies*. MIT Press, Cambridge, Mass.

Cornulier, B. de. (1974). "*Pourquoi* et l'inversion du sujet non clitique." In C. Rohrer & N. Ruwet (eds.), *Actes du Colloque Franco-Allemand de Grammaire Transformationnelle*, vol. 1. Niemeyer, Tubingen, 139–163.

Den Besten, H., & G. Webelhuth. (1987). "Remnant Topicalization and the Constituent Structure of VP in the Germanic SOV Languages." Abstract, *GLOW Newsletter* 18, 15–16.

———. (1990). "Stranding." In G. Grewendorf & W. Sternefeld (eds.), *Scrambling and Barriers*. Academic Press, Amsterdam, 77–92.

Deprez, V. (1989). "Stylistic Inversion and Verb Movement." In J. Powers & K. de Jong (eds.), *Proceedings of the Fifth Eastern States Conference on Linguistics*. Ohio State University, Columbus, 71–82.

———. (1990). "Two Ways of Moving the Verb in French." In L. Cheng & H. Demirdache (eds.), *MIT Working Papers in Linguistics, Vol. 13: Papers on wh-movement*. MIT Press, Cambridge, Mass., 47–85.

Dobrovie-Sorin, C. (1990). "Clitic Doubling, wh-Movement, and Quantification in Romanian." *Linguistic Inquiry* 21, 351–397.

Emonds, J. E. (1976). *A Transformational Approach to English Syntax. Root, Structure-Preserving and Local Transformations*. Academic Press, New York.

Fauconnier, G. (1974). *La coréférence: Syntaxe ou sémantique?* Editions du Seuil, Paris.

Freidemann, M.-A. (1997). *Sujets syntaxiques, positions, inversions, et pro*. Peter Lang, Berlin.

Godard, D. (1988). *La syntaxe des relatives en français*. Editions du CNRS, Paris.

Holmberg, A., & C. Platzack. (1995). *The Role of Inflection in Scandinavian Syntax*. Oxford University Press, New York.

Johnson, K. (1994). "Bridging the Gap." Ms., University of Massachusetts, Amherst.

Kampers-Mahne, B. (1998). "*Je veux que parte Paul*, a neglected construction." In A. Schegler, B. Tranel, & M. Uribe-Extebarria (eds.), *Romance Linguistics, Theoretical Perspectives*. John Benjamins, Amsterdam, 129–141.

Kayne, R. S. (1972). "Subject Inversion in French Interrogatives." In J. Casagrande & B. Saciuk (eds.), *Generative Studies in Romance Languages*. Newbury House, Rowley, Mass., 70– 126.

———. (1975). *French Syntax. The Transformational Cycle*. MIT Press, Cambridge, Mass.

———. (1980). "Extensions of Binding and Case-marking." *Linguistic Inquiry* 11, 75–96 (reprinted in Kayne 1984).

———. (1981b). "ECP extensions." *Linguistic Inquiry* 12, 93–133 (reprinted in Kayne 1984).

———. (1981a). "Binding, Quantifiers, Clitics and Control." In F. Heny (ed.), *Binding and filtering*. Croom Helm, London, 191–211 (reprinted in Kayne 1984).

———. (1983). "Connectedness." *Linguistic Inquiry* 14, 223–249 (reprinted in Kayne 1984).

———. (1984). *Connectedness and Binary Branching*. Foris, Dordrecht.

———. (1986). "Connexité et inversion du sujet." In M. Ronat & D. Couquaux (eds.), *La grammaire modulaire*. Editions de Minuit, Paris, 127–147.

———. (1991). "Romance Clitics, Verb Movement and PRO." *Linguistic Inquiry* 22, 647–686.

———. (1994). *The Antisymmetry of Syntax*. MIT Press, Cambridge, Mass.

———. (1995). "Agreement and Verb Morphology in Three Varieties of English." In H. Haider, S. Olsen, & S. Vikner (eds.), *Studies in Comparative Germanic Syntax*. Kluwer, Dordrecht, 159–165.

———. (1997). "Movement and Binding Theory." Paper presented at MIT, Cambridge, Mass., and University of Massachusetts, Amherst.

———. (1998a). "A Note on Prepositions and Complementizers." Article posted on The Chomsky Internet Celebration (in Kayne 2000).

———. (1998b). "Overt vs. Covert Movement." *Syntax* 1, 128–191.

———. (1999a) "A Note on Clitic Doubling in French." Ms., New York University (in Kayne 2000).

———. (1999b). "Prepositional Complementizers as Attractors." *Probus* 11, 39–73.

———. (2000). *Parameters and Universals*. Oxford University Press, New York.

Kayne, R. S., & J.-Y. Pollock. (1978). "Stylistic Inversion, Successive Cyclicity and Move NP in French." *Linguistic Inquiry* 9, 595–621.

Kimball, J., & J. Aissen. (1971). "I Think, You Think, He Think." *Linguistic Inquiry* 2, 242–246.

Koopman, H., & A. Szabolcsi. (in press). *The Hungarian Verbal Complex: Incorporation as XP-movement*. MIT Press, Cambridge, Mass.

Korzen, H. (1983). "Réflexions sur l'inversion dans les propositions interrogatives en francais." In M. Herslund, O. Mordrup, & F. Sorensen (eds.), *Analyses grammaticales du français. Etudes publiées à l'occasion du 50e anniversaire de Carl Vikner, Revue Romane, Numéro spécial* 24, 50–85.

Kupferman, L. (1983)."Syntaxe et conditions pragmatiques" (A propos de "Approaches to island phenomena" de A. Grosu). *Linguisticae Investigationes* 7/2, 385–400.

Lanly, A. (1962). *Le français d'Afrique du Nord, Etude linguistique*. Presses Universitaires de France, Paris.

Legendre, G. (1998). "Focus in French Stylistic Inversion." Paper presented at conference on Inversion in Romance, University of Amsterdam/HIL.

McCloskey, J. (1990). "Resumptive Pronouns, A-bar Binding, and Levels of Representation in Irish." In R. Hendrick (ed.), *The Syntax of the Modern Celtic Languages (Syntax and Semantics* 23). Academic Press, San Diego, 199–248.

Moro, A. (2000). *Dynamic Antisymmetry*. MIT Press, Cambridge, Mass.

Muller, C. (1977). "A propos de 'de' partitif." *Lingvisticae Investigationes* 1, 167–195.

Nelson, N. (1997). "The Structure of Exclamatives: An Extension of Kayne's (1997) Analysis of Sentential Negation." Ms., Rutgers University, New Brunswick, N.J.

———. (1994). "Aspects de la syntaxe A-barre. Effets d'intervention et mouvements des quantifieurs." Thèse de doctorat d'etat, Université de Paris VIII.

Ordonez, F. (1998). "Post-Verbal Asymmetries in Spanish." *Natural Language and Linguistic Theory* 16, 313–346.

Poletto, C. (2000). *The Higher Functional Field in the Northern Italian Dialects: Evidence from Northern Italian Dialects*. Oxford University Press, New York.

Pollock, J.-Y. (1978). "Trace Theory and French Syntax." In S. J. Keyser (ed.), *Recent Transformational Studies in European Languages*. MIT Press, Cambridge, Mass., 65–112.

———. (1985). "On Case and the Syntax of Infinitives in French." In J. Gueron, H.-G. Obenauer, & J.-Y. Pollock (eds.), *Grammatical Representation*. Foris, Dordrecht, 293–326.

———. (1986). "Sur la syntaxe de *en* et le paramètre du sujet nul." In M. Ronat & D. Couquaux (eds.), *La grammaire modulaire*. Editions de Minuit, Paris, 211–246.

———. (1989). "Verb Movement, Universal Grammar, and the Structure of IP." *Linguistic Inquiry* 20, 365–424.

———. (1998). "On the Syntax of Subnominal Clitics: Cliticization and Ellipsis." *Syntax* 1, 300–330.

Pollock, J.-Y., N. Munaro, & C. Poletto. (1999). "Eppur si muove! On Comparing French, Portuguese and Bellunese wh-Movement." Ms., CNRS, Lyon, and University of Padua.

Postal, P. M. (1974). *On Raising: One Rule of English Grammar and Its Theoretical Implications*. MIT Press, Cambridge, Mass.

Rizzi, L. (1982). *Issues in Italian syntax*. Foris, Dordrecht.

———. (1986), "On Chain Formation." In H. Borer (ed.), *Syntax and Semantics. Vol. 19. The Syntax of Pronominal Clitics*. Academic Press, Orlando, Fla., 65–95.

———. (1990). *Relativized Minimality*. MIT Press, Cambridge, Mass.

———. (1996). "Residual verb second and the wh-criterion." In A. Belletti & L. Rizzi (eds.), *Parameters and Functional Heads: Essays in Comparative Syntax*. Oxford University Press, New York, 63–90.

———. (1997). "The Fine Structure of the Left Periphery." In L. Haegeman (ed.), *Elements of Grammar: Handbook of Generative Syntax*. Kluwer, Dordrecht, 281–337.

Rochemont, M. (1978). "A Theory of Stylistic Rules in English." Ph.D. diss., University of Massachusetts, Amherst.

Ross, J. R. (1970). "On Declarative Sentences." In R. A. Jacobs & P. S. Rosenbaum (eds.), *Readings in English Transformational Grammar*. Ginn, Waltham, Mass., 222–272.

Rouveret, A., & J. R. Vergnaud (1980). "Specifying Reference to the Subject: French Causatives and Conditions on Representations." *Linguistic Inquiry* 11, 97–202.

Rowlett, P. (1998). *Sentential Negation in French*. Oxford University Press, New York.

Shlonsky, U. (1992). "Resumptive Pronouns as a Last Resort." *Linguistic Inquiry* 23, 443–468.

Sportiche, D. (1981). "Bounding Nodes in French." *Linguistic Review* 1, 219–246.

———. (1995). "Sketch of a Reductionist Approach to Syntactic Variation and Dependencies." In H. Campos & P. Kempchinsky (eds.), *Evolution and Revolution in Linguistic Theory*. Georgetown University Press, Washington, D.C., 356–398.

Toman, J. (1986). "Cliticization from NPs in Czech and Comparable Phenomena in French and Italian." In H. Borer (ed.), *The Syntax of Pronominal Clitics* (*Syntax and Semantics 19*). Academic Press, Orlando, Fla., 123–145.

Uriagereka, J. (1995). "Aspects of the Syntax of Clitic Placement in Western Romance." *Linguistic Inquiry* 26, 79–123.

Villalba, X. (1999). "Right Dislocation Is not Right Dislocation." In O. Fullana & F. Roca (eds.), *Studies on the Syntax of Central Romance Languages. Proceedings of the III Symposium on the Syntax of Central Romance Languages*. Universitat de Girona, 227–241.

Webelhuth, G. (1992). *Principles and Parameters of Syntactic Saturation*. Oxford University Press, New York.

Zaenen, A., J. Maling, and H. Thrainsson. (1985). "Case and Grammatical Functions: The Icelandic Passive." *Natural Language and Linguistic Theory* 3, 441–483.

Zribi-Hertz, A. (1994). "The Syntax of Nominative Clitics in Standard and Advanced French." In G. Cinque, J. Koster, J.-Y. Pollock, L. Rizzi, & R. Zanuttini (eds.), *Paths towards Universal Grammar: Studies in Honor of Richard S. Kayne*. Georgetown University Press, Washington, D.C., 453–472.

6

Subject Extraction, the Distribution of Expletives, and Stylistic Inversion

KNUT TARALD TARALDSEN

The main purpose of this chapter is to argue that subject/verb inversion is more pervasive in the syntax of modern French than is generally recognized. In particular, I argue that in all cases where wh-movement extracts a subject from an embedded clause, the subject is in a position lower than the usual preverbal subject position. An analysis based on this assumption is shown to provide an account of the French *que/qui* alternation that is superior to previous accounts. Arguments to this effect are provided throughout sections 1 and 2.

The analysis turns on certain hypotheses about the interaction of expletive clitics and the properties of certain functional heads in French. These hypotheses, in turn, have consequences for the analysis of Stylistic Inversion, which is discussed in section 3.

1. Motivating an Alternative Account of the *qui/que* Alternation

1.1. The Standard Analysis

According to Rizzi (1990), *qui* is an agreeing form of C, replacing *que* in (2) to provide a "formal licenser" for a trace in Spec-IP:

(1) Quel livre crois-tu que /*qui les filles vont acheter?
     which book think-you that the girls will buy

(2) Quelles filles crois-tu *que/qui vont acheter ce livre-là?
     which girls think-you that will buy that book

With *que*, a nonagreeing complementizer in C, the trace in Spec-IP in (1) would not be formally licensed and would therefore violate this version of the Empty Category Phrase (ECP). In (2), however, the trace of the wh-phrase is formally licensed by the V. So, *qui* need not occur, and in fact cannot since, according to Rizzi, Spec-CP with an agreeing complementizer is an A-position, and thus Spec-IP, also an A-position, which is intervening between the wh-phrase and its trace, would cause a violation of Relativized Minimality with C = *qui*.

1.2. Some Problems

Rizzi's (1990) analysis, essentially rephrasing Pesetsky (1982), leads to some expectations that are not fulfilled. It is striking, for instance, that *qui* does not actually show any morphophonemic reflexes of the person/number features it would acquire through agreement. Of course, this could be accidental. After all, within the West Germanic group of languages, in which a particularly good case can be made for an agreeing C, there is a great deal of dialect variation in the morphophonemic realization, ranging from a full paradigm of six distinct forms (West Flemish) to a single invariant form (e.g., standard Dutch). Yet, it remains striking that not a single dialect of French (or any other Romance language) has any morphophonemic reflex of agreement in its complementizer system.

Qui also has a syntactic property, which is not shared by agreeing complementizers in West Germanic. It cannot occur unless the subject of the clause has been wh-moved. Rizzi (1990) accounts for the contrast of (1) and (2) in terms of Relativized Minimality. Taking Spec-CP as an A-position whenever C holds agreement features, he points out that (1), with *qui* instead of *que*, would be well formed only if the object could move to an A-position across an intervening closer A-position (the subject). But that raises the question of why West Germanic counterparts of (1) are perfectly fine with agreement in C,[1] and the assumption about Spec of agreeing C being an A-position would seem to stand in the way of an improper movement account of (3):

(3)   *Les filles semblent qui vont acheter ce livre-là
      the girls seem that will buy that book

On the conceptual side, there is the question of why a trace in Spec-IP (-AgrSP) should be allowed just in case C agrees with it (through its agreement with Spec-CP). In Rizzi's (1990) analysis, agreeing C shares with the lexical heads the property of being formal licensers. But why should this be? To the extent that a subject trace governed by agreeing C is formally licensed just because the two are coindexed (assuming agreement to be represented by coindexing), we bring back a conceptual problem that Rizzi's formulation of the ECP was designed to eliminate, the one concerning the disjunction between lexical government and antecedent government in the classical statement of the ECP. Rizzi's analysis eliminates the disjunction from the statement of his Identification Requirement, but it is now seen to return in disguise in the formulation of Formal Licensing, as a direct consequence of Rizzi's analysis of *qui*.

1.3.   A Similar Paradigm Unaccounted for by Rizzi's Analysis

It is also striking that Rizzi's (1990) account of the *que/qui* alternation fails to extend to partially similar phenomena in other languages. In Norwegian, for example, the distribution of *som* in embedded win-interrogatives appears to mirror the distribution of *qui*; that is, the contrast between (4) and (5) seems similar to (1) and (2) in French:

(4)   Vi vet ikke hvem *(som) oppfant ostehøvelen
      we know not who that invented the cheese slicer

(5)   Vi vet ikke hvem (*som) de her ansatt
      we know not what that they have hired

Taking *som* as an agreeing C, Rizzi's analysis at first glance seems to carry over:

(6)   ... [$_{CP}$ **hvem**$_j$ [$_{Cj}$ som] [$_{AgrSP}$ t$_j$ AgrS ...
          A   Agr   A

(7)   [$_{CP}$ **hvem**$_j$ [$_{Cj}$ som] [$_{AgrSP}$ de her ansatt t$_j$ ...
         A   Agr   A

    In (4), analyzed as in (6), *som* must be present to provide a formal licenser for the subject trace, but in (5), analyzed as in (7), the presence of *som* is not called for and, in addition, causes a violation of Relativized Minimality, as indicated. The problem is that *som* behaves differently in relatives. Here, *som* is still obligatory in conjunction with subject extraction, but it is also possible, though not obligatory, with extraction of nonsubjects:

(8)   den mannen *(som) oppfant ostehøvelen
      the man that invented the cheese slicer

(9)   den mannen (som) de ansatte
      the man that they hired

Analyzed as in (10), with *som* an agreeing C, (9) should disallow *som* for the same reason as (5):

(10)   [$_{DP}$ den [$_{CP}$ mannen$_j$ [$_C$ som$_i$] [$_{AgrSP}$ de ansatte t$_j$]]]

1.4.   Danish *der*

At the same time, an alternative analysis of *som* is suggested by the distribution of *der* 'there' in Danish interrogatives and relatives. In Danish, *der* is obligatory after the wh-phrase in embedded interrogatives with an extracted subject:

(11)   Vi ved ikke hvem *(der) opfant ostehøvelen
       we know not who there invented the cheese slicer

It also alternates with *som* in relatives with subject extraction:

(12)   den mand *(der) opfant ostehøvelen
       the man there invented the cheese slicer

(13)   den mand *(som) opfant ostehøvelen
       the man that invented the cheese slicer

Unlike *som*, however, *der* never appears when a nonsubject is extracted, even in relatives:

(14)   den mand (som) de ansatte
       the man that they hired

(15)   den mand (*der) de ansatte
       the man there they hired

(16)   Vi ved ikke hvem (*der) de ansatte
       we know not who there they hired

Thus, the distributional properties of *der* are exactly like those of *qui;* on the other hand, *der* is rather clearly an expletive subject, not an element in C. Thus, *der* is necessarily analyzed as an expletive rather than as a complementizer in (17), and the simplest analysis will hold that it is always an expletive subject:

(17)   Der er ankommet en mand fra Skåne
       there is arrived a man from Scania

In fact, not only considerations of simplicity but also a comparative observation supports this contention: Norwegian differs from Danish by not allowing *der* in (11) and (12), and this follows straightforwardly from the fact that Norwegian does not allow *der* in (17) either (the Norwegian expletive being *det* 'it'), provided *der* must be an expletive subject in (11) and (12).

Moreover, *der* co-occurs with the complementizer *at* 'that' in slightly colloquial Danish and must then follow it, as seen in (18) and (19), exactly as predicted if *der* is an expletive subject:

(18)   ?Hvem tror de **at der** opfant ostehøvelen?
       who think they that invented the cheese slicer

(19)   *Hvem tror de **der at** opfant ostehøvelen?
       who think they there that invented the cheese slicer

Finally, the ungrammaticality of (15) and (16) follows directly: With *der* in the subject position, there is no room for another preverbal subject.

On the basis of these observations, one is led to conclude that a sentence like (11) should be analyzed as in (20), where the wh-phrase has been extracted from a position lower than the usual subject position:

(20) ... [$_{CP}$ **hvem**$_j$ C [$_{AgrSP}$ der Agrs ... t$_j$ ...

But this conclusion raises the question of why (21) is ungrammatical:

(21)   *Der opfant en normand ostehøvelen
       there invented a Norwegian the cheese slicer

In general, the subject cannot surface in the low position with transitive verbs in Danish. I suggest that (21) is ungrammatical because Danish I has a number feature that fails to be licensed by Spec-IP when Spec-IP contains *der*, a locative pronoun incapable of controlling agreement, much like the oblique subject in an Icelandic sentence like (22):

(22)   Okkur líkar/ *líkum ekki bokin
       we-DAT like-3sg/*-1pl not book-the-NOM
       "We don't like the book."

As for (17), one may assume that the number feature of I is licensed by a number feature that is raising from the DP in Spec-AgrO, an option for which object agreement in Icelandic sentences like (23) provides independent evidence:

(23)   Okkur líka ekki bækurnar.
       we-DAT like-3pl not books-the-NOM
       "We don't like the books."

It is crucial that the low subject of (21) cannot be in Spec-AgrO, and its number feature, therefore, cannot be used to license the number feature of I.[2] On the other hand, our analysis presupposes that there is an alternative way of licensing the number feature of I when the low subject in a structure like (20) undergoes movement to Spec-CP. I assume that in fact the number feature of I may raise to C to be licensed by the subject raised to Spec-CP, as indicated in (24):

(24)   ... [$_{CP}$ [$_{DP}$ **hvem**] **AgrS + C** [$_{AgrSP}$ der t$_{AgrS}$ ...

Thus, my analysis converges with Kayne's (1989) account of the substandard agreement in (25), analyzed by him as in (26):

(25)   the people who Clark **think** are in the garden

(26)   ... [$_{CP}$ [$_{DP}$ who] Agr$_S$+C [$_{AgrSP}$ Clark t$_{AgrS}$ ...

On Kayne's (1989) analysis, raising AgrS (or its number feature) to C, as indicated in (26), enables the matrix verb (*think*) to agree with the embedded subject, the wh-phrase *who* (analyzed as a plural DP, in agreement with *people*, the "head" of the relative construction) once the latter has raised to the Spec of the matrix CP. According to our proposal for *der* in Danish relatives and inter-rogatives, raising AgrS (or its number feature) to C also allows agreement to be checked by a DP, which never visits the relevant Spec-AgrSP but raises to Spec-CP from a lower position.

1.5.   More on *som*

Going back to the problem of accounting for the distribution of Norwegian *som*, one can now provide a solution by taking *som* to be a variant of the pronoun *det* 'it'. In particular, like Norwegian *det*, but unlike *der* 'there', *som* can be both an expletive and an argument. In relative clauses, the DP/NP in Spec-CP is not an operator and can be doubled by argument *som*, much as in Romance clitic left dislocation. In (9) (repeated below), where *som* cannot be an exple-tive related to the subject position, it must in fact be a doubling argument:

(9)   den mannen (som) de ansatte
       the man that they hired

In (8) on the other hand, *som* can be either an expletive or an argument:

(8)   den mannen *(som) oppfant ostehøvelen
       the man that invented the cheese slicer

Interrogatives have operators in Spec-CP, and operators cannot be doubled by pronouns. Hence, the *som* in (4) can only be an expletive, and (5), where *som* cannot be an expletive, is ungrammatical with *som*:

(4)   Vi vet ikke hvem *(som) oppfant ostehøvelen
       we know not who that invented the cheese slicer

(5)   Vi vet ikke hvem (*som) de her ansatt
       we know not what that they have hired

Notice finally that although *som* and *der* alternate freely in relative clauses like (12) and (13) in Danish, *som* cannot substitute for *der* in interrogatives like (11); that is, (4) is ungrammatical in Danish. This follows from the assump-tion that *som* must be an expletive in interrogatives (although not in relatives) and that *som* is a variant of the pronoun *det* 'it', in conjunction with the fact that Danish, unlike Norwegian, does not use *det* as an expletive.

Thus, we have reached two conclusions: We have seen that Rizzi's (1990) account of the *que/qui* alternation does not easily extend to rather similar alter-nations in other languages, and we have also found that analyzing these alterna-tions as involving subject extraction from a low position, co-occurring with an expletive in the high subject position, seems to provide interesting accounts. With this in mind, we now return to the French *que/qui* alternation through a discus-sion of a partially similar alternation in another Romance language.

2. Reanalyzing the *que*/*qui* Alternation

2.1. The *cha*/*chi* Alternation

In Vallader, a Rheto-Romance variety spoken in the Engiadina, we find a similar alternation between *cha* (= *que*) and *chi* (= *qui*) in sentences like (27) and (28):

(27)   Qual cudesch crajast cha/*chi las mattes cumpraran?
        which book think-you that the girls will buy
(28)   Qualas mattes crajast chi/*cha cumpraran quel cudesh?
        which girls think-you that will-buy that book

In the absence of further information, one might well attempt to apply Rizzi's (1990) analysis here, too. But Vallader also has *chi* introducing sentences from which nothing has been extracted, provided the subject is not preverbal, as well as a "free" expletive subject *i*, strongly suggesting that the *chi* of (29) is simply *cha* (with its final vowel elided) followed by expletive *i*:[3]

(29)   ... la spranza chi/*cha turnaran quels temps docts
        the hope that will-return those times learned

(30)   I turnaran quei temps docts
        it will-return those times learned

This suggestion is reinforced by the observation that *i* and *chi* share the idiosyncratic morphophonemic property of adding a –*d* before vowels:[4]

(31)   ... il vast territori ... pro'l qual i**d** appartaignava eir Iowa
        the vast territory to which it belonged also Iowa

(32)   El disch chi**d** es turnà Peider
        he says that-it is returned Peter

This idiosyncracy is also shared by the *chi* of (28):

(33)   Qualas mattas crajast chi**d** han cumprà quel cudesch?
        which girls think-you that-it have bought that book

So, Vallader probably wh-moves subjects from a position lower than Spec-IP, just as Italian does.[5] According to Rizzi (1982), an Italian sentence such as (34) would have an analysis like that in (35), with a covert expletive (*pro*) in Spec-IP:[6]

(34)   Quali ragazze credi che compreranno quel libro?
        which girls think-you that will-buy that book

(35)   quali ragazze ... [$_{CP}$ che [$_{IP}$ pro compreranno+I [$_{VP}$ t V quel libro ...

The corresponding Vallader example in (28) should be analyzed the same way, except that Vallader, not a null subject language, requires an overt expletive in Spec-IP:

(36)   qualas mattas . . . [$_{CP}$ cha [$_{IP}$ i cumpraran + I [$_{VP}$ t V quel cudesch . . .

As in Italian, the subject trace causes no that-trace problem because it is not in Spec-IP.

2.2.   French *qui = qu(e) i*

Rethinking the French *quel/qui* alternation along similar lines, we would take *qui* as *qu(e) i*, with expletive *i* in Spec-IP:[7]

(37)   Quelles filles . . . [$_{CP}$ que [$_{IP}$ i vont+I [$_{VP}$ t V acheter . . .

The expletive *i* is different from the usual French expletive *il* in three respects: It never has a final *–l* (in any register), it does not control subject-verb agreement (always 3sg with *il*), and it does not require an indefinite associate (cf. **Quelles filles est-ce qu'il est arrivé?* vs. *Qu'est-ce qu'il est arrivé?*).

An immediate advantage of this analysis is that the ungrammaticality of *qui* in (1) becomes straightforward, provided a preverbal subject is in Spec-IP rather than in the low position held by the wh-trace in (15), leaving no room for the expletive *i*.[8]

This approach is also, in a sense, immanent in Kayne and Pollock's (1978) analysis of (38) as having a null expletive that fails to control verbal agreement or induce an indefiniteness requirement on its associate:

(38)   Où crois-tu que vont se cacher les chats?
       where think-you that will themselves hide the cats

(39)   où . . . [$_{CP}$ que [$_{IP}$ pro vont+I [$_{VP}$ V se cacher les chats . . .

The structure in (39) is licensed by wh-movement out of the embedded clause. In (39), the relevant wh-phrase is *où* 'where', an adverbial complement. If the wh-phrase is the subject of the embedded clause, it should still be possible to have (the trace of) the subject in the low subject position, to the extent that this depends only on having a wh-phrase that is passing through the embedded Spec-CP. Yet, the structure in (40) must be ill formed since otherwise (2) (repeated below) would be expected to be possible with *que*:

(2)   Quelles filles crois-tu *que/qui vont acheter ce livre-là?
      which girls think-you that will buy that book

(40)   quelles filles . . . [$_{CP}$ que [$_{IP}$ pro vont+I [$_{VP}$ V acheter ce livre-là t . . .

In particular, there should be no *that-trace effect.

Kayne (1980) suggests that the null expletive fails to be licensed in structures like (40). But then, the natural expectation should be that an overt expletive with the same properties as the covert expletive of (39) would show up in connection with subject extraction in French, especially since Vallader shows that subject extraction from a "low" position does not depend on the expletive being null. In the analysis of *qui* as *qu*(*e*) *i*, this expectation is fulfilled since *i* is an overt expletive, which, like the *pro* of (39) but unlike *il*, does not control verbal agreement or require an indefinite associate.[9]

2.3.   Another Manifestation of French Expletive **i**

Unlike Vallader, standard French does not seem to have an expletive *i* in isolation from *que*:

(41)   *Elle dit qui sont arrivées ses copines
      she says that **i** are arrived her girl-friends

(42)   *I sont arrivées ses copines
      i are arrived her girl-friends

But in "complex subject inversion" environments, colloquial styles of French allow an invariant (*t*)*i*:

(43)   Pourquoi tu dois-**ti** partir?
      why you must-**ti** leave

Putting aside the status of the initial –*t*,[10] one can profitably look at this *i* as another manifestation of the expletive *i* that follows *que* in (2). In particular, it is invariably *i*; it does not control verbal agreement or induce an indefiniteness requirement on its associate.[11]

The classical analysis of complex inversion (Kayne 1983, chap. 10; Rizzi & Roberts 1989) would parse the standard French sentence (44) as (45):

(44)   Pourquoi tes copines doivent-elles partir?

(45) $[_{CP}$ pourquoi $[_{CP}$ tes copines $[_C$ doivent$]$ $[_{IP}$ elles . . .

The standard analysis of complex inversion applies to the "*ti* construction" as well, once the morphological differences between *i* and the expletive *il* are taken into consideration, so that the (*t*)*i* of (43) is licensed in the following context, with C filled by the finite V:

(46)   . . . SUBJ C $[_{IP}$ i I . . . t$_{SUBJ}$ . . .

In particular, the *ti* construction, just like the standard construction, is confined to main clauses, a property generally attributed to V-to-C movement.[12]

Unlike the standard construction, however, the *ti* construction allows the preverbal subject to be a pronoun, and *(t)i*, unlike standard subject clitics, does not appear unless there is an additional subject:

(47) *Pourquoi **tu** dois-**il** / **tu** partir?
       why you must-he/you leave

(48) *Pourquoi **elle** doit-**il** / **elle** partir?
       why she must-he/she leave

(43) Pourquoi **tu** dois-**ti** partir?
       why you must-ti leave

(49) Pourquoi **elle** doit-**(t)i** partir?
       why she must-ti leave

(50) Dans quel pays habite-t-**il**?
       in which country lives-he

(51) *Dans quel pays habite-**ti**?
       in which country lives-ti

Both contrasts follow from *(t)i* having a more impoverished morphology than the other subject clitics. In particular, it lacks gender and number specifications. If arguments must be endowed with such features, (51) is a straightforward violation of the Θ-criterion.[13]

The ill-formedness of (47) and (48) has been taken to reflect a general prohibition against spelling out a morphological feature in more than one position in a chain (Kayne 1983). In (47) and (48) gender and number features are spelled out both by the preverbal subject pronoun and by the postverbal subject clitic—hence twice within the same chain since the subject pronoun and the subject clitic are associated with the same Θ-role.[14] In (43)–(49), on the other hand, the gender and number of the chain are specified only by the preverbal subject pronoun since *(t)i* lacks these features.

2.4.   The Distribution of French Expletive *i*

According to Rizzi (1990), the wh-moved subject in (2) moves through the embedded Spec-CP:

(52) quelles filles . . . [$_{CP}$ t que [$_{IP}$ i vont+I [$_{VP}$ t $_V$ acheter . . .

If so, the *i* in (2) occurs in the same environment (46) that licenses the *(t)i* of colloquial complex inversion, modulo C = *que* vs. C = V (but see note 12). Why should this be the only context that licenses the French expletive *i*? And why should French differ from Vallader?

In section 2.3, I found reasons to maintain that the French expletive *i* does not have (specified) gender and number features. In particular, the contrasts between i and other subject clitics exhibited by (47)–(51) follow from that hypothesis. I now argue that the limited distribution of the French expletive i follows in toto from its impoverished morphology. If i has no number feature and finite I has an uninterpretable number feature that must be checked before Spell-Out, the sentences like (41) and (42) (repeated below) have no convergent derivation:

(41)   *Elle dit qui sont arrivées ses copines

(42)   * I sont arrivées ses copines

In structures subsumed under (46), however, the number feature may raise from I to C, where it is checked pre-Spell-Out by the raised subject DP, as is implicit in standard accounts of complex inversion.[15]

    This raises the question of why the number feature of I couldn't be checked by raising the number feature of the subject DP before Spell-Out. Chomsky (1995) stipulates that pure feature movement is possible only after Spell-Out, but the analysis just proposed for structures conforming to (24) would be incompatible with that belief. Rather, the analysis presupposes that the dichotomy "weak" vs. "strong" is reinterpreted according to a suggestion in Taraldsen (1996; see also Chomsky 1998), who proposes to identify covert movement with pre-Spell-Out pure feature movement, eliminating LF movement: A strong feature is one that cannot raise without pied-piping its host category. From this point of view, our claim really is that D has a strong number feature in this new sense in French, but not in Vallader, whereas I in both languages has an uninterpretable number feature that can raise without pied-piping its host.[16] To account for the obligatory presence of i in (46), we also have to assume that I has an Extended Projection Principle (EPP) feature that does not raise to C. Example (53) displays the movements and checking relations relevant to licensing structures of the form (46) in French:[17]

(53)   *Checking*:
            number   EPP
            ——>   ——>
            ... SUBJ C [$_{IP}$ i I ... t$_{SUBJ}$
                    |_____|
            raising of I's number feature

    In this perspective, the limited distribution of the French expletive follows from its being a "pure expletive," in Chomsky's (1995, chap. 4) sense, in a language in which a number feature cannot raise from D without pied-piping the DP. This might make it tempting to account for the contrast between French and Vallader i by identifying French i with y 'there' vs. Vallader $i(d)$ = 'it', an expletive endowed with a number feature. This temptation should probably be resisted, however. If Vallader $i(d)$ had a number feature, like it, it would presumably be singular. But the number feature of I in Vallader sentences with expletive *i(d)* is not always singular; rather it corresponds to the number of the associate of the expletive, as in the case of "pure expletives," as we already saw in (29) and (30) (repeated below), where the verb occurs in a plural form, agreeing with the postverbal subject:

(29)   . . . la spranza chi/*cha turnaran quels temps docts
        the hope that will-return-pl those times learned

(30)   I turnaran quei temps docts
        it will-return-pl those times learned

Thus, Vallader *i(d)* does not have a specified number feature either. To account for the contrast between French and Vallader, we therefore need the assumption that in Vallader the number feature of a postverbal subject DP can raise to I without pied-piping the DP.[18]

In Vallader, there is no counterpart to French *y*, that is, no other numberless form to which *i(d)* might be assimilated. Rather, we take it that *i(d)* descends from Latin *id* 'it' but has lost its gender/number features in the transition from the Latin three-gender system to the Romance two-gender system. More specifically, we suggest that the Latin neuter pronoun lost its gender feature altogether by refusing to become masculine, and because the number feature is dependent on gender, it was lost also. If this suggestion is correct, there is now no reason not to consider the French expletive *i* a result of the same development.

3.   French Stylistic Inversion

3.1.   Problems with the Classical Analysis

The claim that French does not allow a number feature to raise from a postverbal subject DP without pied-piping the DP appears to be contradicted by the existence of sentences with Stylistic Inversion, for example, (38) (repeated below):

(38)   Où crois-tu que vont se cacher les chats?
        where think-you that will themselves hide the cats

According to the classical analysis of Stylistic Inversion (Kayne & Pollock 1978), (38) would have a structure like (39) (repeated below), in which *pro* would be a "true expletive," like *i*, and the number feature of I would be checked by covert raising of the associate (*les chats*) or its number feature:

(39)   où . . . [$_{CP}$ que [$_{IP}$ pro vont+I [$_{VP}$ V se cacher les chats . . .

The classical analysis, however, encounters certain difficulties that lead us to think that it should be discarded for independent reasons. Most notably, it fails to explain why a null expletive should be possible in structures where a wh-phrase has been raised to the immediately higher Spec-CP (possibly as a step in successive cyclic win-movement) but not elsewhere.[19] Kayne (1980) suggests that the raised wh-phrase triggers covert movement of the expletive's associate, which in turn licenses *pro*. In French, according to this analysis, the null expletive would otherwise be illicit since French is not a null subject language. But how can post-Spell-Out movement be relevant to whether an expletive is pronounced or not, a PF property? In the approach taken in section 2.4., where covert movement is replaced by pre-Spell-Out feature movement, this problem does not necessarily arise, as pointed out by P. Svenonius (p.c.), but there would instead be another problem: Why should formal features of the postverbal DP be able to rise to I without pied-piping the DP only in Stylistic Inversion contexts? Moreover, if Kayne (1995) is correct, we need to be able to account for the fact that the whole VP (excluding a V-movement account) precedes the postverbal subject in sentences like (3) without appealing to rightward movement of the subject.

3.2. Stylistic Inversion as Remnant VP Raising

I now assume that Stylistic Inversion as required by Kayne's (1995) theory is in fact the case: The subject moves out of the VP to a relatively low Spec-position, and the VP subsequently crosses over it to a higher Spec-position.[20] In particular, one may assume that VP raising can be scrambling to a position lower than I:

(54)   ... Spec I ... [$_{VP}$ t ...] ... Subj ... t$_{VP}$ ...

In that case, Spec-IP must be filled by an expletive that can be covert in a null subject language like Italian but not in French or Vallader. Whereas Vallader can always use $i(d)$, since the uninterpretable number feature of I can be checked by pure feature movement from the postverbal subject in Vallader, French can resort to i only if the subject raises to Spec-CP before Spell-Out. Thus, (54) represents a legitimate stage in the derivation of the structures subsumed under (46) and only those structures. Sentences like (38) must be analyzed as in (55), with the VP raised to Spec-IP:

(55)   [$_{CP}$ que [$_{IP}$ [$_{VP}$ t$_{Subj}$ vont se cacher] I ... les chats ... t$_{VP}$ ...

In (55), the number feature of I is checked by the number feature of the subject trace in Spec-VP: In Kayne's (1995) theory, the Spec of Spec-XP is in the checking domain of X.[21] Since the trace is a copy of the subject, the appearance of agreement with the low subject is created. Alternatively, Spec-VP licenses a number feature on the head of VP, and this number feature projects to VP and licenses the number feature of I in (55). Again, I will appear to agree with the low subject.

When the VP is scrambled, as in (54), the chain that links the low subject to its trace in Spec-VP is recoverable by reconstruction because scrambling generally allows for reconstruction. Movement to Spec-IP, an A-position, should not reconstruct, however.[22] Therefore, structures like (55) end up by violating the Θ-criterion unless the low subject eventually raises to a position c-commanding the trace inside the VP in Spec-IP, if we adopt the traditional assumption that the head of a chain must c-command all other members of the chain at LF. Like Kayne, we may assume that the subject raises (covertly) just in case a win-phrase has been raised to the immediately higher Spec-CP.[23] But unlike Kayne, we succeed in accounting for the restrictions on Stylistic Inversion without having LF movement sanction a PF property.

3.3.   Some Refinements

Even though we have so far analyzed French Stylistic Inversion as VP movement to Spec-IP, it is clear that what raises must be an extended projection of the V, including a number of functional heads above the bare VP. In particular, the constituent raised to Spec-IP must contain the position(s) that clitic pronouns move to and, therefore, also all functional heads that occur between the clitic position and the VP:[24]

(56)   Pourquoi se sont cachés les chats?
       why themselves are hidden the cats

(57)   *Pourquoi sont cachés les chats se?
       why are hidden the cats themselves

Hence, a French finite clause must in general occur as shown in (58), where either a DP (in Spec-FP) or the complement of F raises overtly to Spec-IP (unless an expletive is inserted):

(58) $[_{IP}$ Spec I $[_{FP}$ Spec F $[$ $_{XP}$ ... Cl ... VP

Taking the second option after the subject DP has moved to Spec-FP gives rise to Stylistic Inversion.[25]

In (58), I and a functional head F in the complement of F must both bear agreement features, F' licensing the corresponding features of the V. The existence of F follows from the standard minimalist assumption (see Chomsky 1995, chap. 4) that the agreement features of the V must be checked against the features of a functional head to which V adjoins, as well as the fact that if the XP that contains the V raises to Spec-IP, V cannot adjoin to I (or F). Taking F' to be X, the head of the complement of F, we may exploit this property to find a way around an outstanding problem for the analysis above:

(59)   Quand crois-tu que sera procédé à un réexamen de la question?
       when think-you that will-be proceeded to a reexamination of the case

The distribution of impersonal sentences without the expletive il, like the embedded clause in (59), is subject to the same limitations as are sentences with

Stylistic Inversion (cf. Kayne & Pollock 1978).[26] Our analysis of Stylistic Inversion should therefore extend to (59), but (59) seems to lack both a (visible) subject DP that could raise to Spec-FP and a trace of that subject in Spec-XP that would license the number feature of I after the raising of XP to Spec-IP. We might now say that the number feature of I in Stylistic Inversion contexts is not licensed by the Spec-XP, but rather by the number feature of X that is projected onto XP (the second of the two possibilities mentioned above), and we allow X, but still not I, to be singular by default. Assuming that F attracts PP [*à un réexamen de la question* in the case of (59)], as well as DP, to Spec-FP, we see that the similarity with the Stylistic Inversion paradigm will be accounted for.

Thus, we end up with an analysis according to which a finite clause contains two functional heads, I and F, associated with EPP features, whose exact nature must be further investigated. Similarly, the two distinct functional heads, I and X, carry number features. Unlike X, however, I does not allow default licensing of its number feature. Like all uninterpretable features, the number feature of I must therefore be checked before Spell-Out; that is, Spec-IP must be filled by a YP that bears a number feature, DP or XP, or the number feature of I raises to C and is checked by an appropriate phrase in Spec-CP, as indicated in (53). Given the ungrammaticality of Stylistic Inversion with transitive verbs in French, a property illustrated by (60), it is perhaps possible to identify the functional head X with AgrO:

(60)   *Où crois-tu que vont cacher leurs jouets les chats?
        where think-you that will hide their toys the cats

If AgrO, like I, can Case-license a nominative DP that is checking its number feature, as suggested by Icelandic sentences with oblique subjects like (61), the ungrammaticality of (60) could be attributed to the failure of the postverbal subject to have its Case licensed: It is neither in Spec-IP nor in Spec-AgrOP:[27]

(61)   Okkur líka hestarnir.
        we-dative like-3pl horses-the
        "We like the horses."

3.4.   The *Que*-trace Effect

In section 2.2, we saw that Kayne and Pollock's (1978) analysis of Stylistic Inversion raises the question of why the position of the postverbal subject of a sentence like (38) (repeated below) cannot be filled by a wh-trace so that (62) would be analyzable as (63), which does not violate the ECP/*that-trace filter:

(38)   Où crois-tu que vont se cacher les chats?
        where think-you that will themselves hide the cats

(62)   *Quels chats crois-tu que vont se cacher?
        which cats think-you that will themselves hide

(63)   quels chats . . . [$_{CP}$ que [$_{IP}$ pro vont+I [$_{VP}$ V se cacher t . . .

The analysis of Stylistic Inversion in sections 3.2. and 3.3. raises a similar question: Why cannot (62) receive the analysis in (64)?

(64)   quels chats . . . [$_{CP}$ que [$_{IP}$ [$_{VP}$ t$_{SUBJ}$ vont se cacher] I . . . t . . . t$_{VP}$

Again, we assume that the ECP/*that-trace filter would not be violated.

If (64) is to come out well formed at LF, the subject trace inside the raised VP must have an antecedent in a c-commanding A-position. Since the wh-phrase itself is not likely to be in an A-position or to have left behind traces in A-positions that c-command the embedded IP, the trace in the low subject position must move covertly to an IP-external A-position, a movement triggered by the presence of (the trace of) a wh-phrase in Spec-CP. If it cannot, (64) has no well-formed LF representation.

For the required movement to take place in (64), (a trace of) the wh-phrase must attract the low subject in the same way as in the grammatical instances of Stylistic Inversion discussed above. But if attraction ought to culminate in "quantifier absorption," as suggested by Kayne (1980), one would not expect to see its effects in (64), where the low subject is not interpretable as a separate quantifier to be absorbed but rather as the variable to be bound by the wh-quantifier.

More generally, whatever turns out to be the correct answer to the independent question of why (64) cannot converge will combine with the ECP/ *that-trace filter to explain the *que-trace effect, that is, to drive the que/qui alternation.

4.   Summary

This chapter started out from a critique of Rizzi's (1990) account of the French que/qui alternation. Although the analysis proposed here endorses Rizzi's hypothesis that a wh-phrase in Spec-CP may agree with a feature in C (a number feature raised from I, in my analysis), it does not consider qui as a spell-out of [$_C$ Agr]. Nor do we need to assume that Spec-CP is ever an A-position or that functional heads that are containing agreement have a privileged status, alongside (certain) lexical categories, in the licensing of traces.

The analysis of the qui in examples like (2) as the usual complementizer followed by the expletive i, on the model of the Vallader data discussed in section 2, explains the characteristic properties of this qui and draws support from the existence of the expletive (t)i in complex inversion structures in colloquial French. If my characterization of the properties of the latter is correct, my analysis is essentially for free, as promised, and different analyses introduce unwarranted complications above the minimum required to account for the empirical facts. Likewise, the analysis of the que/qui alternation turns out to be significantly similar to the analysis required for the Scandinavian patterns discussed in section 1.

In all these cases, subject extraction applies to a DP in a position lower than the usual preverbal subject position (Spec-IP), and in that sense, French (and Scandinavian) has more cases of subject inversion than is normally assumed.

NOTES

Parts of this chapter have been presented in talks at NELS 27 (McGill University), University of Venice, the Colloquium on the EPP and Expletives at the University of Tromsø (May 1998), and the Amsterdam Conference on Inversion in Romance (May 1998). I am grateful to the respective audiences for questions and comments. I am particularly indebted to Anders Holmberg and Peter Svenonius for their comments on preliminary drafts. I take the blame for all remaining errors.

1. West Germanic agreeing complementizers are also possible when nothing at all has been moved to the corresponding Spec-CP.

2. The separate question of why the object DP, in Spec-AgrO, does not license the number feature of I remains open. Probably, Case considerations play a role.

3. See Linder (1987), which (29) is taken from. The other Vallader examples are constructed on the basis of Linder (1987) and Liver (1991), except when otherwise noted.

4. The *–d* is perhaps a reflex of the fact that *i(d)* is the descendant of Latin *id* 'it'. Example (31) is from Linder (1987).

5. Notice that Vallader (*i)d*, unlike the subject clitics of North Italian dialects, never co-occurs with preverbal "full" subjects; cf. Linder (1987), and Savoia and Manzini (in press). Thus, taking the wh-phrase to extract via a preverbal subject position in (28) would complicate the analysis of the general pattern.

6. I provisionally take the lower subject position to be Spec-VP, but see section 3 for a different analysis.

7. The possibility that the French *qui* of (2) should be analyzed as *que* followed by an expletive (for them, *que il*), on the model of Rheto-Romance, is suggested independently by Savoia and Manzini (in press), who do not, however, discuss the status of French *i* vs. *il*. Rooryck (1997) also analyzes *qui* as *qu-* (= C) plus *il*.

8. In other words, the subject may surface in a position lower than Spec-IP only in sentences with Stylistic Inversion. This will follow from the analysis presented in section 3.

9. In section 3, we consider a different analysis of Stylistic Inversion, which does not make use of null expletives. Rather, the (extended) VP raises to Spec-IP. When this movement is blocked, an (overt) expletive appears in Spec-IP.

10. In view of the analysis in section 2.4., it is important that this *t-* is not identified as the 3sg verbal agreement inflection. Such an interpretation would not be straightforward since *t-* combines with non-3sg verbal inflection in examples like (i):

(i)   Pourquoi nous devrions-ti partir?

The suggestion made by an anonymous reviewer that interrogative *–ti* should be related to the 2sg pronoun *tu* does not seem particularly appealing in spite of the fact that certain dialects of French, for example, Québec French, actually have interrogative *–tu* instead of *–ti*. It is unexpected, in our analysis, that such dialects still have *qui*, rather than [ky], with subject extraction. If the proposal mentioned in note 12 is correct, the expletive combining with t- would be in a Spec-position lower than the one filled by *i* that is combining with *qu(e)* and might conceivably have morphosyntactic features that distinguish it from *i*, a property that could have a morphophonemic reflex in dialects like Québecois.

11. The contrast *il at été ... vs. *ils ont été* ... with pronounced final *t*, may also indicate that not even the *–t* of *a-t-il été* ... ? is a part of the verbal agreement inflection that is escaping phonological deletion in liaison contexts.

12. Kayne (1995) and Sportiche (n.d.) propose that the verb does not move to C in the complex inversion construction and that the preverbal subject is not in Spec-CP (or adjoined to CP). As becomes evident in section 2.4., the choice between their analysis of complex inversion and the one reproduced in (46) has ultimately no bearing on my account of French *i*, the relevant generalization being in either case that *i* only occurs in contexts where some other element can license the number feature of I.

13. In section 2.4., we see that (51) is also excluded for another reason. The number feature on AgrS fails to be licensed since *i* lacks a number feature. Therefore, **Pourquoi est/sont-(t)i arrivé tant de touristes?* is also excluded, even though no violation of the Θ-criterion arises.

14. Since *Pourquoi la copine de Jean part-elle?* is grammatical, although the gender and number of the chain are spelled out both by the postverbal subject clitic and by the determiner *la*, heading the prenominal subject (according to the DP hypothesis), the general principle invoked in the text must be refined. Perhaps it is relevant that the gender and number features of D are checked by those of an N in *la copine de Jean*. The analysis by Kayne (1995) and Sportiche (n.d.) mentioned in note 12, might account for (47)–(48) vs. (43)–(49) by assuming—as suggested by Cardinaletti (1996) or Savoia and Manzini (in press)—that different (preverbal) subject positions are specialized for different types of subject: ["strong" subject X ["weak" subject pronoun Y [i. ... The fact that *i* should be restricted to a position lower than that of the *il* series should still be attributed to a morphological difference between the two—in fact, the one assumed in the text—if, as proposed by Cardinaletti and Savoia & Manzini, the elements that occur in the intermediate subject position must license number/person features of Y.

15. See Kayne (1989) and Taraldsen (1992), who also propose that the number feature of I may raise to C and be licensed by Spec-CP. My analysis is incompatible with a strict version of Chomsky's (1995) idea that all strong features of X must be checked before XP is embedded in a larger structure. Nor is it consistent with Zwart's (1993) claim that features of X raised to Y cannot be checked against Spec-YP.

16. This view of "strong" vs. "weak" is not required for the case of complex inversion with *i*, if complex inversion is analyzed as suggested by Kayne (1995) and Sportiche (n.d.). Then, the number feature is checked in its base position either by a subject clitic in the intermediate subject position or by a "strong" subject that is moving through that position on its way to the highest subject position (in the cases with *i*).

17. The fact that *qui* cannot be split up into *qu(e)* X(P) *i* by an intervening constituent X(P) may follow from the blocking effect of an intervening head on feature raising from I to C.

18. This predicts that Vallader *i(d)* should never occur without an associate, a prediction borne out by the data we have had access to so far.

19. Similarly, *pro* is licensed in certain subjunctive clauses.

20. More accurately, an extended projection of V raises; see the end of this section for discussion. Stylistic Inversion could not easily be analyzed as involving only movement of the finite V since the postverbal subject also follows the past participle in the compound past tenses and certain complements of the V (cf. Kayne 1972). For the same reason, the postverbal subject cannot simply be thought to remain in Spec-VP.

21. This presupposes that "minimal domain" is defined on the basis of dominance rather than inclusion: The minimal domain of X contains just those categories that are not dominated by some other category in the domain of X. According to Kayne (1995), Spec-XP is only dominated by a segment of XP. Overt agreement with the subject's Spec is seen in Aleut (cf. Bergsland & Dirks 1981).

22. Phrases in an A-position do not reconstruct with respect to A-binding, although they may do so with respect to quantifier scope; cf. May (1985) on "quantifier-lowering" effects.

23. Covert raising of the subject to a position c-commanding the raised V-projection must also be countenanced in certain subjunctive clauses (cf. Kayne & Pollock 1978). The required extension would not be more straightforward if we took an alternative approach to Stylistic Inversion that is licensed by wh-movement—that is, taking the subject DP to raise to Spec-IP (licensing number agreement directly) and taking the complement ZP of I to have an initial Spec much like Spec-CP, so that a wh-phrase that is filling Spec-ZP pied-pipes XP when raising to the "external" Spec-CP. In this alternative analysis, the dependence of Stylistic Inversion on wh-movement would reduce to pied-piping under wh-movement, with the proviso that the XP must be stranded in the first external Spec-CP under successive cyclic wh-movement.

24. We agree with Kayne (1991) that clitics adjoin to a functional head, not to V itself. This functional head might be lower than the adverbial positions, however, if subject-initial sentences could be analyzed as having XP that contains the clitic position(s) raised to Spec-IP (above the adverbials), with the subject DP still in Spec-XP rather than previously raised to Spec-FP, as in the Stylistic Inversion cases.

25. If the subject DP remains inside XP that is raising to Spec-IP, the outcome will show the same linear order as if the subject had raised to Spec-IP alone. The ungrammaticality of (i) remains an embarrassment to the text analysis or to any other account of Stylistic Inversion in terms of "remnant" VP raising:

(i)   *Où se sont **tous** cachés les chats?
       where themselves are all hidden the cats

26. Kayne and Pollock (1978) point out that impersonal constructions like (59) without an overt expletive are more marginal in wh-movement contexts than in subjunctive clauses. Yet, the fact that they are much better even in this environment than outside the contexts that license Stylistic Inversion requires an explanation.

27. It is not quite clear, however, how one could make the analysis of (60) that is suggested here compatible with the analysis of subject extraction argued for in this chapter.

REFERENCES

Bergsland, K., & M. Dirks. (1981). *Atkan Aleut School Grammar.* University of Alaska, Anchorage.

Cardinaletti, A. (1996). "Subjects and Clause Structure." *University of Venice Working Papers in Linguistics.*

Chomsky, N. (1995). *The Minimalist Program.* MIT Press, Cambridge, Mass.

———. (1998). "Minimalist Inquiries." Unpublished Ms., MIT, Cambridge, Mass.

Kayne, R. S. (1972). "Subject Inversion in French Interrogatives." In J. Casagrande & B. Saciuk (eds.), *Generative Studies in Romance Languages.* Newbury House, Rowley, Mass., 70–126.

————. (1980). "Extensions of Binding and Case-Marking." *Linguistic Inquiry* 11, 75–96.

————. (1983). "Chains, Categories External to S, and French Complex Inversion." *Natural Language and Linguistic Theory* 1, 107–139.

————. (1989). "Notes on English Agreement." *CIEFL Bulletin* I, 41–67.

————. (1991). "Romance Clitics, Verb Movement and PRO." *Linguistic Inquiry* 22, 647–686.

————. (1995). *The Antisymmetry of Syntax.* MIT Press, Cambridge, Mass.

Kayne, R. S., & J.-Y. Pollock. (1978). "Stylistic Inversion, Successive Cyclicity, and Move NP in French." *Linguistic Inquiry* 9, 595–622.

Linder, K. P. (1987). *Grammatische Untersuchungen zu Charakteristik des Rätoromanischen in Graubünden.* Günter Narr Verlag, Tübingen.

Liver, R. (1991). *Manuel pratique de romanche.* Sursilvan—Vallader, Ediziun Lia Rumantscha, Cuira.

May, R. (1985). *Logical Form: Its Structure and Derivation.* MIT Press, Cambridge, Mass.

Pesetsky, D. (1982). "Paths and Categories." Ph.D. diss., MIT, Cambridge, Mass.

Rizzi, L. (1982). *Issues in Italian Syntax.* Foris Publications, Dordrecht.

————. (1990). *Relativized Minimality.* MIT Press, Cambridge, Mass.

Rizzi, L., & I. Roberts. (1989). "Complex Inversion in French." *Probus* 1, 1–30.

Rooryck, J. (1997). "A Unified Analysis of French Interrogative and Complementizer Qui/Que." Ms., Leiden University.

Savoia, L., & R. M. Manzini. (in press). "Varieta romanze a Verbo Secondo." In Gaetano Chiappini (ed), *Studi per Giorgio Chiarini.* Editore Alinea, Firenze.

Sportiche, D. (n.d.). "Subject Clitics in French and Romance: Complex Inversion and Clitic Doubling." Ms., UCLA.

Taraldsen, K. T. (1992). "Second Thoughts on *der.*" In H. G. Obenauer & A. Zribi-Hertz (eds.), *Structure de la phrase et théorie du liage.* Presses Universitaires de Vincennes, Paris.

————. (1996). "Review of the Minimalist Program by Noam Chomsky." *GLOT International* 2, 3.

Zwart, J.-W. (1993). "Dutch Syntax: A Minimalist Approach." Ph.D. diss., University of Groningen.

7

The Constraint on Preverbal Subjects in Romance Interrogatives

A Minimality Effect

MARIA LUISA ZUBIZARRETA

There is a well-known constraint, pervasive in the Romance languages, that disallows the subject to intervene between a fronted wh-phrase and the verb. I illustrate this constraint with examples from standard Spanish, French, European Portuguese, and Italian:

(1) a. *Qué Pedro compró? (Spanish)
         what Pedro bought
     b. *Que Pierre a acheté (French)
     c. *Que o Pedro comprou? (EPortuguese)
     d. *Che Piero ha comprato (Italian)

The existence of such a constraint can also be appreciated in constructions like French complex inversion (where V-to-C has applied); it minimally contrasts with English, where the constraint does not apply:[1]

(2) a. A qui a-t-il (*Pierre) parlé?
         to whom has-nom.cl. (Pierre) spoken
     b. To whom did Peter speak?

In Zubizarreta (1998), I proposed that the preverbal subject in Spanish is always associated with a discourse-related feature (topic or focus or emphasis). Two further assumptions will then join to account for the constraint on preverbal subjects in interrogatives: (A) The topic feature is always projected above the focus feature at the left edge of the clause, and (B) the wh-phrase is associated with the focus feature. It therefore follows that a topic subject must precede the wh-phrase when they co-occur at the left edge.

There are various problems with such an analysis. One of them is lack of generality. The constraint is also active in French, a language that lacks a focus projection at the left edge of the clause. It is furthermore empirically insufficient. Whereas the constraint on preverbal subjects holds systematically in root clauses in most Romance languages, there is variability in embedded clauses. Whereas it applies in embedded interrogatives in Spanish and Italian, this is not the case in French and European Portuguese; for example, the Spanish and French contrast below:

(3)   a. *Me pregunto a quién Juan busca
          (I) wonder who Juan is looking for
      b. Je me demande qui Jean cherche

Another fact that the above analysis does not readily account for is the contrast between bare and nonbare wh-phrases. Whereas bare wh-phrases activate the constraint on preverbal subjects, nonbare wh-phrases like "which N" and "how many N" do not (cf. Ambar 1988; Pollock, Murano, & Poletto 1998):

(4)   a. (?) Cual libro Pedro compró?
      b. (?) Quel livre Pierre a acheté
      c. Que livro o Pedro comprou?

(5)   a. A cuanta gente María invitó a la fiesta?
          How many people María invited to the party
      b. Combien de gens Marie a invité à la fête?

In this chapter, I articulate a different proposal. I suggest that there are two basic ingredients that interact to account for the unexceptional application of the constraint in most Romance languages and its variability in embedded interrogatives. (A) The so-called clitic left-dislocation construction is pervasive in the Romance languages but nonexistent in English. We assume (in the spirit of Iatridou 1990) that the existence of the clitic left-dislocation (CLLD) construction in the Romance languages indicates that the predicate-argument structure may be syntactically articulated in these languages in a different way than in English. Whereas the verbal arguments in English are systematically projected within the VP, in the Romance languages under discussion they may be merged with an abstract (lambda) operator generated above TP. Such an operator in turn binds an argument variable within the VP. We refer to it as the Cl operator because the argument variable it binds is typically identified by a clitic or "strong" inflectional element (see section 1).[2] (B) The Q-feature in the left edge of the CP field (which expresses the interrogative force of the sentence) must be phonologically lexicalized, but there are more options available for lexicalizing a Q in embedded than in matrix interrogatives (see section 2). When the Q-feature binds a variable, it acquires the status of a syntactic operator and interacts with the Cl operator, giving rise to a minimality effect from which the preverbal subject constraint follows immediately (see section 3).

1. The Cl Projection

What is this Cl projection? It is neither a scope position associated with a +specificity feature (as suggested by Sportiche 1998) nor an Agr position (as suggested by Franco 1993). I suggest instead the following:

(6) Cl is an abstract operator whose function is to "externalize" an argument of a verb v with respect to the tense associated with v.

Externalization of an argument via a Cl operator thus gives rise to the following type of structure:

(7) [DP_i [Cl_i [T [$_{VP}$ ... [V e_i ...

The proposal is thus that there is more than one way in which the predicate-argument relation may be syntactically instantiated:

(8) a. In the familiar way, via projection within VP, in which case the DP argument is merged with V or with a projection of V: [V DP] or [DP [V ...]].
     b. The DP argument is merged with the projection of a Cl operator that binds an argument variable within the VP. The DP is coindexed with Cl via Spec-head agreement and therefore with the argument variable that Cl binds: [DP_i [Cl_i ... [$_{VP}$ ... e_i ...]]].

We may refer to the structure obtained via projection of DP arguments within VP as the lexical or small proposition, and to the structure obtained via merging of DP with the Cl operator as the syntactic or large proposition. Proposal (8b) has as its predecessor the analysis of the CLLD construction put forth by Iatridou (1990). Although the details of the proposal here differ in important respects from those of Iatridou, they share a basic insight, namely, that the predicate-argument relations in the CLLD construction is articulated in a fundamentally different way from other constructions.

The most convincing argument in favor of (8b) are the binding facts first reported in Zubizarreta (1993) for Spanish and reproduced in other languages with a CLLD construction such as Arabic (Aoun & Benmamoun 1998) and Greek (P. Schneider-Zioga, p.c.). See also Cecchetto (1995) and Guasti (1996) on Italian. These data show that there is a preverbal and postverbal subject asymmetry in cases in which the fronted accusative topic (which contains the intended bindee) and the subject (which contains the intended binder) originate in the same clause:[3]

(9) a. A su$_i$ hijo, *cada madre$_i$* deberá acompanarlo$_i$ el primer día de escuela
         acc. his child each mother must accompany-acc.cl. the first day of school

     b. ?*El primer día de escuela, a su$_i$ hijo deberá acompanarlo$_i$ *cada madre$_i$*
         The first day of school acc. his son will accompany-acc.cl. each mother

(10) a. A su$_i$ propio hijo, *ningún padre$_i$* lo$_i$ quiere castigar
         acc. his own child no father acc.cl. wants to punish
         'No father wants to punish his own child.'

     b. ?*A su$_i$ propio hijo no lo$_i$ quiere castigar *ningún padre$_i$*
         acc. his own child not acc. cl. wants to punish no father
         'No father wants to punish his own child.'

No asymmetry is found when the binder is the matrix subject and the bindee is contained within a fronted accusative object that originates in the embedded clause:

(11) a. A su$_i$ hijo, *ninguna madre$_i$* debió aceptar que se lo regañe
         acc. his son, no mother should have accepted that indef. subj.cl.
         acc.cl. scold

     b. A su$_i$ hijo, no debió aceptar *ninguna madre$_i$* que se lo regañe
         acc. his son, not should have accepted any mother that indef.
         subj.cl. acc.cl. scold
         'No mother should have accepted that someone scold his son.'

The above data suggest that there is reconstruction of the fronted object to a position within the clause that it originates but that this position is not within the VP [cf. the ill-formedness of (9b) and (10b)]. The fronted object may be reconstructed to a position above the VP and below the preverbal subject of the clause in which it originates [cf. the well-formedness of (9a) and (10a)]. The fact that there is no reconstruction of the fronted object within the VP of the clause it originates suggests that the fronted object is inserted higher up in the structure, that is, in the Spec of Cl (cf. Zubizarreta 1993, 1998). This means that there is no copy of the fronted object in the canonical object position within the VP; the binding facts then follow immediately.

The proposal we are putting forth here may be summarized as follows:

(12) In languages with a nominal clitic or strong Agr system, a direct argument
     of the verb (nominative or accusative) is externalized by merging the
     argument with Cl (located above T) rather than by merging the argument
     with V (or a projection of V) and then moving it outside the scope of T.

It follows from (12) that the preverbal subject in languages with a CLLD construction of the sort under discussion is also generated in the Spec of Cl.[4] This means that in sentences like (9a) and (10a), there are two Cls: One externalizes the nominative argument, and the other one externalizes the accusative argument. As the binding facts indicate, in these examples the nom-related Cl is generated higher than the acc-related Cl. The dislocated object may there-fore "reconstruct" to a position within the scope of the nominative subject. But it is also possible for the acc-related Cl to be generated higher than the nom-related Cl. As predicted, in such cases the fronted object may bind into the fronted subject:

(13) a. A cada niño, su madre lo acompañará el primer día de escuela.
          Acc. each child(O), his mother(S) acc. cl.+ will+ accompany the first
          day of school
      b. A ninguno de estos niños, su padre lo quiso acompañar.
          Acc. none of this children(O), his father(S) acc. cl.+ wanted to accompany.

Hence, in (9a) and (10a) have the structure of (14a), and the sentences in (13) have the structure of (14b).[5]

(14) a. $[DP_j [Cl_j [DP_i [Cl_i [T [_{VP} [e_j [V [e_i \ldots$
      b. $[DP_i [Cl_i [DP_j [Cl_j [T [_{VP} e_j [V [e_I \ldots$

Let us return to the generalization in 12. Why is there a connection be-tween the existence of Cl and of morphological clitics or strong agreement affixes? The answer is that the abstract category Cl must be morphologically identified in the following manner:

(15) Morphological identification of Cl is achieved by some nominal morpheme
      with a phi-feature contained within the local T. This may be a clitic or a
      "strong" agreement affix.

The clitic or verbal agreement affix is of course related to the DP in the Spec of Cl. In the case of the clitic, this relation is captured by the fact that a nomi-nal clitic is nothing else than a copy of the D and phi-features of the argument variable bound to the DP. In the case of the agreement affix, this relation is captured by the Spec-head relation that the argument variable bound to the DP bears with the verb at some point in the derivation. See below for further details.

    I can now raise the question of the relation between the type of morpho-logical identification required by Cl [as summarized in (15)] and the one im-posed by the *Functional Projection Activation Principle* (*FPAP*) put forth by Koopman (1997), Poletto (1998), Speas (1994), and others:

(16) *Functional Projection Activation Principle*: A feature in the head of a
      functional projection is activated if the appropriate morphological material
      occupies either the head or the Spec of that projection at some point in
      the derivation.

Note that the requirements on the morphological identification of Cl are stricter than the one imposed by the FPAP. In effect, a DP argument in the Spec of Cl is insufficient to identify Cl because Cl does not encode a (semantic) feature like other functional categories. Its role is purely formal, namely, that of establishing a connection between a DP in its Spec and an argument variable of the verb. More precisely, Cl serves the role of externalizing a DP argument with respect to the T associated with V. Some morphological nominal element on such a T is required to identify Cl. In other words, the position of syntactic activity of Cl and the position of its feature content are dissociated; its feature content is not under Cl as one might expect. Rather, it is contained within the T-node immediately below it.

The Acc-related Cl is typically identified by an accusative clitic. There is no other option in the Romance languages because they lack morphological object agreement on the verb. The accusative clitic is a copy of the D and phi-features of the accusative argument variable. It left-adjoins to V prior to the application of V-to-T (I assume with Kayne 1994 that adjunction is always leftward):

(17) $[DP_i [Cl_i [[_{V_j} acc cl_i [v+agr]] T] [_{VP} \dots [V_j e_i \dots$

The identification of the Nom-related Cl is not uniform across the Romance languages. Some languages (like many of the northern Italian dialects) have a nominative clitic that is systematically used to identify the Nom-associated Cl. The nominative clitic is a copy of the D and phi-features of the nominative argument variable. Since the Nom argument variable is located above the verb in the verbal projection, its copy (i.e., the Nom clitic) cannot left-adjoin to the verb. Instead it left-adjoins to the T to which the verb has been adjoined. (As we see in the next section, this difference between nominative and accusative clitics is important because it explains why accusative clitics are always proclitic but nominative clitics are enclitics when V-to-C applies.)

(18) $[DP_i [Cl_i [nom cl_i [[v+agr]_j T]] [_{VP} e_i [V_j \dots$

In languages that lack a nominative clitic (like Spanish and standard Italian), the subject agreement element is used to identify the Nom-associated Cl:

(19) $[DP_i [Cl_i [[[v]agr_i]_j T] [_{VP} e_i [V_j \dots$

In other languages, like standard French, it would seem that either a nominative clitic or the subject verb agreement element may identify the Nom-related Cl [see (20a, b)]. But on closer scrutiny, we see that in French (unlike Spanish and standard Italian), the subject agreement element is not "strong enough" to identify the Cl operator on its own. It can function only as an identifier in conjunction with a coindexed lexical DP that is "close enough" [see (20c)].

(20) a. Pierre il a vendu sa voiture.
          Pierre nom-cl has sold his car

    b. Pierre a vendu sa voiture.

    c. Pierre sa voiture *(il) l'a vendu
       Pierre his car (nom cl) acc cl has sold

We suggest that the notion of "closeness" invoked above should be formalized in the following way:

(21)   DP and Agr are close if they are coindexed and they are contained in the
      Spec of—or in the head of—adjacent projections at the point of spell-out.

To summarize, I propose to dissociate the Cl category from the morphological clitic itself. Rather, Cl is an abstract operator whose function is to "externalize" an argument of a verb V with respect to the T associated with V. This is achieved by merging a DP with a projection of Cl that binds an argument variable of the verb. The function of the clitic contained within T (and, in certain cases, of the verbal agreement affix) is to morphologically identify the abstract Cl category. This Cl category in conjunction with the Q-operator constitutes the linchpin of my analysis of the preverbal subject constraint in Romance interrogatives.

2. The Q-operator and Ph-lexicalization

As mentioned earlier, I assume that an interrogative sentence has a Q-feature, which encodes the force of the sentence located at the rightmost edge of the CP field. As we see in the next section, when the Q-feature is coindexed with a certain type of wh-phrase (such as the bare wh-phrases), the Q-feature acquires the status of a syntactic operator. I furthermore assume that a feature that expresses the force of the sentence (such as the Q-feature) must be phonologically lexicalized. I define *ph(onological) lexicalization* as follows:[6]

(22)   *Ph-lexicalization*: A feature in the head of a functional projection is
      ph-lexicalized if the head or the Spec of that projection is associated with
      appropriate ph-features at the point of spell-out.[7]

The hypothesis that ph-lexicalization applies at the point of spell-out can be formalized within the general architectural framework proposed in Zubizarreta (1998, sect. 1.3.3). It is argued there that the syntactic derivation proper and the PF interpretation accompany each other for a stretch, namely, the stretch that starts with S-structure (a point in the derivation where the structure involved is a single phrase marker) and ends with L-structure (the last phrase marker in the derivation before it branches). As indicated by the left slashes in the diagram below, PF interpretation begins at S-structure and continues after the derivation branches. I refer to the derivation between S-structure and L-structure as the shallow part of the syntactic derivation and to the structures generated at this point as shallow structures.

(23)   (set of phrase markers)

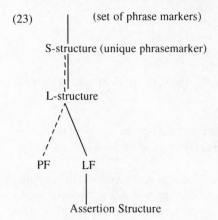

S-structure (unique phrasemarker)

L-structure

PF   LF

Assertion Structure

I argue in Zubizarreta (1998) that the Nuclear Stress Rule, the Focus Promi-nence Rule, and some prosodically motivated movements apply in the shal-low part of the syntactic derivation. Here I suggest that movement operations triggered solely by the need to ph-lexicalize a category apply in the shallow part of the derivation as well.

There are several ways in which a Q-operator may be ph-lexicalized:

(24)   a. By a verbal element:
            (i)   Via movement of V-to-Q (in direct questions)
            (ii) Via merging of Q with matrix V (in indirect questions)
       b. By merging Q with a complementizer
       c. By a wh-phrase in Spec of Q in cases in which the wh-feature is
           syncretized with Q

As we see in section 3, the manner in which the Q-operator is lexicalized is crucial in understanding the cross-linguistic differences for the preverbal sub-ject constraint in embedded interrogatives. I briefly illustrate below the parame-ters in (24) and return to it in section 3.

French and English illustrate the parameter in (24a). In direct questions, V moves to Q (via T), where Q is the head of a functional projection at the rightmost edge of the CP:[8]

(25)   a.   Qui Pierre a-t-il rencontré hier?
       a'. [Qui [Pierre [a_i-t-il [Q]] [$_{IP}$ e_i rencontré hier]]]
       b.   Who did Peter meet yesterday?
       b'. [Who [did$_i$ [Q]] [$_{IP}$ Peter e_i meet yesterday]]

V-to-Q also applies in yes/no questions:

(26)   a.   A-t-il mangé?
       a'. [A_i-t-il [Q]] [$_{IP}$ e_i mangé]
       b.   Did he eat?
       b'. [Did$_i$ [Q]] [$_{IP}$ he e_i eat]

In indirect questions, where there is no V-movement to the CP field, we may assume that Q is lexicalized by merging with matrix V:

(27) a. Je me demande qui Jean a rencontré hier.
      a'. Je me [Q [demande]] qui Jean a rencontré hier
      b. I wonder who John met yesterday.
      b'. I [Q[wonder]] who John met yesterday

In many northern Italian dialects, V-to-Q also applies in matrix questions, but in embedded questions Q merges with a complementizer at the rightmost edge of the CP instead of merging with the matrix V, as in French and English (cf. Poletto 1998). The examples below are from Monnese, discussed in detail in Benincà and Poletto (1997):

(28) a. fe-t majà? (yes/no question)
          do-you eat
      b. ke fe-t majà? (matrix wh-question)
          what do-you eat

(29) i ho domandà kol *ke* l'ha fat (embedded wh-question)
      to-him have asked what that Nom cl.(3rd. pers. sing. masc.) has done

Finally, I suggest that standard Spanish has recourse to the parameter in (24c). The wh-feature syncretizes with the Q-feature, giving rise to a mixed projection of wh/Q. On the one hand, the wh-phrase in the Spec of wh/Q checks the wh-feature, and on the other hand, it ph-lexicalizes the Q-feature:

(30) a. Qué compró Juan ayer?
          What bought Juan yesterday
      a'. [[qué [wh/Q] [$_{TP}$ compró Juan ayer]]]
      b. Me pregunto qué compró Juan ayer?
          (I) wonder what bought Juan yesterday
      b'. Me pregunto [[qué [wh/Q] [$_{TP}$ compró Juan ayer]]]

Another way of rephrasing this proposal is to state that wh-words in Spanish have a dual morphological function: In addition to functioning as a wh-morpheme, they also function morphologically as an interrogative operator. The same analysis can be assumed for standard Italian.[9]

Spanish interrogatives have two salient properties that may support the above analysis. First, there are no matrix/embedded asymmetries, as shown in (30). This is to be expected since there is no reason that the syncretism of the wh- and Q-features should be restricted to either matrix or embedded CPs. Second, in embedded questions, the wh-phrase follows the subordinating complementizer, if they coexist (cf. Suñer 1994).

(31) Me preguntaron **que** a sus padres, **qué** querrían los niños regalarles para Navidad.
      (They) to-me asked that their parents, what would-like the children to-given-them for Christmas

This fact may be taken as evidence that syncretism of the wh- and Q-features takes place in Spanish. In effect, whereas the fact that the subordinating conjunction appears to the right of the wh-phrase in Monnese can be taken as evidence that the complementizer and the Q-feature occupy one and the same position, the fact that the subordinating conjunction appears to the left of the wh-phrase in Spanish can indicate that the wh- and Q-features occupy one and the same position. This correlation is sustained by the assumption that the Q-feature occupies the rightmost edge of the CP field and that this position is fixed. In other words, features that encode the force of a sentence delimit the (rather weak) frontier between the CP and the IP fields. Therefore, if a feature (such as wh) syncretizes with Q or if a complementizer merges with Q the effects will be seen at the locus of the Q-feature (i.e., at the rightmost edge of the CP field). In Spanish indirect interrogatives the effect is that the wh-phrase appears at the rightmost edge of the CP field, and in Monnese indirect interrogatives (as well as in other northern Italian dialects) the effect is that the subordinating complementizer appears at the rightmost edge of the CP field.

There is a clear generalization that emerges: V-to-C never applies in embedded interrogatives. If this were simply a tendency, we could attribute it to the assumption that "movement" is more costly than "merge." But this explanation cannot account for why the root/embedded asymmetry is absolute rather than a trend. The analysis proposed above can readily explain that generalization. On the one hand, V-to-C in interrogatives is triggered by the need to ph-lexicalize Q. On the other hand, a movement triggered by the need to ph-lexicalize a category applies at shallow structure. *Suppose furthermore that ph-lexicalization, like lexical insertion, is strictly cyclical (where the cyclic nodes are CP and DP).* Since the tree is constructed bottom-up and since movement triggered solely by the need to ph-lexicalize a category applies at shallow structure (i.e., at the end of the syntactic derivation), it follows that V-to-Q can only apply on the last cycle (i.e., the root clause).[10]

3. The Preverbal Subject in Romance Interrogatives Reconsidered

3.1. The Interaction of Cl and Q-Operators: A Minimality Effect

I begin by restating the problem:

(32) Unlike in English, in the Romance languages there are restrictions on the position of the preverbal subject in interrogatives:
    a. Matrix interrogatives do not allow a DP subject to be realized within the IP field:
        $*[_{CP}$ wh Aux $[_{IP}$ S V]]; $*[_{CP}$ wh $[_{IP}$ S (Aux) V]]
    b. Embedded interrogatives in which the Q-morpheme is lexicalized in the CP field (more precisely, at the rightmost edge of the CP field) do not allow a DP subject to be realized within the IP field:
        $*\ldots [_{CP}$ wh Q $[_{IP}$ S (Aux) V]]

What is the particularity of the position of the preverbal subject in the IP field in Romance? I suggest in section 1.1 that in Romance the subject is "externalized" from its VP-internal position to a position between CP and TP via merge with Cl; Cl is an operator, which binds a variable within the VP. When the Q-feature is coindexed via Spec-head agreement with a [+wh] DP, Q acquires the status of an operator, and the trace of the wh-phrase with which it is coindexed acquires the status of a variable:

(33)   [[$_{wh}$wh-]$_i$ [wh$_i$ [e$_i$ [Q$_i$ [. . . [$_{VP}$ . . . e$_i$ . . .

The claim in this chapter is that the generalization in (32) is due to the relation between the *Cl-operator and the nominative variable it binds*, which intervenes between the *Q-operator and the variable bound by it*. More specifically, I suggest that the generalization in (32) is to be attributed to a minimality effect. To illustrate, consider the French example in (1b) [repeated in (34a)], which has the structure of (34b). In this structure, the binding relation between the variable e$_i$ and the operator Q is blocked by the presence of the operator Cl, which is closer to *e$_i$* than Q.[11]

(34)   a. *Que Jean a acheté?
            What Jean bought
        b. [[$_{wh}$que]$_i$ [wh$_i$ [e$_i$ [Q$_i$ [Jean$_j$ [Cl$_j$ [T [$_{VP}$ e$_j$ [. . . e$_i$ . . .]]]]]]]]
                                                      |_____|
                                |_____|

In matrix interrogatives, Q is always present as the head of a projection, and therefore the generalization in (32a) holds in all the Romance languages that "externalize" their subject via Cl. On the other hand, as mentioned in section 2, in embedded interrogatives there are cross-linguistic differences. In French the restriction on preverbal subjects is absent because, in embedded interrogatives in this language, Q merges with the matrix verb (see section 1.2). Therefore, the Q-feature never functions as a syntactic operator in such structures; see (35b):

(35)   a. Je me demande que Jean a acheté hier
            I to-myself ask what Jean bought yesterday
        b. Je me [Q [demande]] [que$_i$ [wh [Jean$_j$ [Cl$_j$ [$_{TP}$ a [$_{VP}$ e$_j$ [acheté e$_i$ hier]]]]]]]

In Spanish, Q never merges with V; it always defines a projection (albeit the mixed projection wh-Q; see section 1.2). Therefore, the minimality effect induced by a Nom-associated Cl is present in both matrix and embedded clauses:[12]

(36)   a. *Me pregunto qué Juan compró ayer
            (I) to-myself ask what Juan bought yesterday
        b. Me pregunto [qué$_i$ [wh/Q$_i$ [Juan$_j$ [Cl$_j$ [$_{TP}$ comprò [e$_j$ [V e$_i$]]]]]]]
                                                  |_____|
                                |_____|

We turn next to the exception to the generalization in (32), noted in the first section; see the examples in (4) and (5), which are repeated below:

(37) a. (?) Cuál libro Pedro compró?
      b. (?) Quel livre Pierre a acheté
      c. Que livro o Pedro comprou?

(38) a. A cuanta gente María invitó a la fiesta?
          How many people María invited to the party
      b. Combien de gens Marie a invité à la fête?

It is to be noted that such nonbare wh-phrases are precisely the ones that in Romanian require clitic doubling (cf. Dobrovie-Sorin 1994). Dobrovie-Sorin argues that whereas bare wh-phrases systematically function as syntactic operators, nonbare wh-phrases do not. The intuition behind Dobrovie-Sorin's proposal may be expressed in the following way:[13]

(39) A wh-feature in the Spec of DP may or may not percolate to the DP node. If the wh-feature percolates to the DP and if this DP is in the Spec of Q at some point of the derivation, it will be coindexed with Q; Q will then acquire the status of a syntactic operator, and the variable it binds will acquire the status of a variable.

In the sentences in (37) and (38), the wh-feature in the Spec of DP has not percolated to the DP node. Therefore Q does not function as an operator, and the trace of the wh-phrase does not function as a variable:

(40) $[[_{DPj} [wh] N] [Q [DP_i [Cl [T [_{VP} e_i [V e_j$

Compare (40) with the representation in (41), where the trace of the wh-phrase is bound by Q and therefore has the status of a variable.[14]

(41) $[[_{DPj[+wh]} [wh] N] [Q_j [DP_i [Cl [T [_{VP} e_i [V e_j$

Dobrovie-Sorin (1994) shows that in the case of "how many N," there are actually two different semantics. If it functions as a syntactic operator [cf. the structure in (41)], it ranges over quantities, and if it does not function as a syntactic operator [cf. the structure in (42)], it ranges over objects. Dobrovie-Sorin shows furthermore that *how many N* may have a narrow scope with respect to the subject only in the former case (where the trace of the wh-phrase functions as a variable). The prediction, then, is that in structures in which the preverbal subject constraint does not apply, the narrow scope reading should be unavailable. The prediction is borne out: (42b), but not (42a), allows for a distributive reading. *Cada* ('each') being an obligatory distributor, (42a) is uninterpretable.

(42) a. Cuantos libros María/*cada estudiante leyó ayer?
How many books María/each student read yesterday
b. Cuantos libros leyó María/cada estudiante ayer?
How many books read María/each student yesterday

Now one wonders how the Q-feature is ph-lexicalized in (37) and (38). These sentences have a salient intonational property; that is, there is an intonational hiatus at the right edge of the intonational phrase. More precisely, the pitch falls down to the baseline and then rises again, indicating the presence of a prosodic boundary. I suggest that the prosodic boundary feature is attached to the Q-feature and serves the purpose of ph-lexicalizing it.

Given what I have said above [cf. (39)], I need to readdress the status of the trace of the wh-phrase in the embedded question in (35). Clearly, the trace of the wh-phrase *que* functions as a variable in embedded questions as much as it does in matrix questions [cf. (1)]. I have proposed that the trace of the wh-phrase functions as a variable if the wh-phrase is associated with Q. When Q defines a projection within the CP field, this association is obtained via Spec-head agreement (as a result of overt movement), but when Q is adjoined to the matrix verb, the association must be obtained in some other fashion. I propose that the mechanism that gives rise to that association is the same one that underlies the association between the Negative Polarity Item (NPI) and the matrix negative verb in the following type of example:

(43) Pierre doute que Marie ait vu personne.
Pierre doubts that Marie has seen anybody.

In this example, the NPI *personne* is licensed by the negative verb *doute* (= *not sure*). In other words, *personne* and *douter* are associated in some way. We may assume that this is done by covert Neg-feature movement. Let us assume that the wh-phrase and the interrogative verb Q + *demander* are associated in the same fashion (via covert wh-feature movement). The resulting representation would then be that in (44), rather than that in (35b). In this representation, the lexical interrogative verb functions as the operator that binds the wh-variable (i.e., the trace of *que*):

(44) Je me [Q [demande]]$_i$ [que$_i$ [wh$_i$ [Jean$_j$ [Cl$_j$ [$_{TP}$ a [$_{VP}$ e$_j$ [acheté e$_i$ hier]]]]]]]

The question that arises about such a representation is why it does not give rise to a minimality effect. I suggest the following answer. In (44), the operator Cl does not intervene in the relation between the operator *demander* and e$_j$ because Cl is a functional category and *demander* is a lexical category. In other words, I suggest that minimality should be relativized not only for the distinction between phrases and heads (cf. Rizzi 1990), but also for the types of heads (lexical vs. functional).

3.2.   Getting around Minimality: Projecting Cl within the CP Field

Given the minimality effect created by the projection between CP and TP of a nom-associated Cl in interrogative structures like (34), one wonders whether a nom-associated Cl may ever coexist with a Q-projection. The answer is that they can coexist if the nom-associated Cl is projected higher than the Q-projection. According to Poletto (1998), in French and in many northern Italian dialects, the subject may be realized within the CP field, as in the examples below:

(45)   A qui **Pierre** a-t-**il** parlé? (French)
        to whom Pierre has-he(nom cl) spoken
        'To whom has Pierre spoken?'

(46)   I me ga domandà **Gianni** quando che el vien. (a northern Italian variety)
        nom cl. me have asked John when that nom cl comes
        'They asked me when is Gianni coming.'

(47)   A venta che **Majo** *ch*'a mangia pi' tant. (Piedmontese)
        Cl. need that Majo that nom cl eat more
        'Majo must eat more.'

The possibility of realizing the subject within the CP field might actually be an option more widely available within the Romance family. This option is made available by the fact that the subject is externalized via Cl in these languages. Whereas Cl is generally projected at the left edge of the IP field (i.e., immediately above TP), the grammar allows for the option of projecting Cl within the CP field in order to avoid a minimality violation, that is, above the Q operator and below the wh-projection in French but above it in the northern Italian dialects. Thus, the French example in (45) will be associated with the structure below (before V-to-Q movement applies in shallow structure):

(48)   [A qui$_j$ [wh$_j$ [Pierre$_i$ [Cl$_i$ [e$_j$ [Q$_j$ [il$_i$ a [e$_i$ [parlé e$_j$]]]]]]]]]

In (48), Cl is above Q; therefore Cl does not interfere in the binding relation between Q and e_j. The question that arises is why Q does not interfere in the binding relation between Cl and the variable e_i. I suggest that this is due to the so-called antiagreement effect discussed by Ouhalla (1993) and references cited therein. A variable bound by Cl has the status of a pronominal variable because the clitic or "strong" agreement element that identifies Cl is [+pronominal]. There is a parametric variation among languages:

(49)   Some languages allow a [+pron] to be bound by the interrogative Q-operator
        and others do not.

I refer to pronouns bound by the interrogative Q-operator as Qu-bound pronouns. Spanish allows for Qu-bound pronouns under certain conditions (see

Zubizarreta 1999), but French and most northern Italian dialects do not (see Poletto 1998).[15] Thus, in the French structure in (48), the pronominal variable in Spec of VP (bound by the nom-associated Cl) cannot be bound to Q. In other words, Q is not a possible binder for the pronominal variable (*il, e*). Consequently, Q does not interfere in the relation between Cl and e_i, and no minimality effects are observed.

The fact that French does not allow for Qu-bound pronouns in conjunction with the analysis of nonbare wh-phrases in section 3.1 can readily explain the contrast in (50). In (50a), the bare nominative wh-phrase is coindexed with Q; therefore Q is bound to the nominative pronominal clitic. In contrast, in (50b) the nonbare nominative wh-phrase is not coindexed with Q; therefore Q is not bound to the nominative pronominal clitic (Grevisse, cited in Sportiche 1998):

(50) a. *Qui a-t-il lu un livre?
          who has-he read a book
      b. Quel féroce magicien a-t-il enfermé ton secret?
          What terrible magician has-he locked up your secret

Two issues concerning the structure in (48) must still be addressed. Why is the nominative clitic obligatory, despite the fact that the nominative DP and the subject agreement element are contained in adjacent projections after V-to-C applies? This might be due to the EPP (as suggested in Rizzi & Roberts 1989). Whereas the DP in the Spec of Cl projected within the CP field fulfills the th-requirement of the predicate, it fails to fulfill the EPP requirement:

(51) a. The EPP applies specifically to the IP: The IP must have a subject.
      b. An IP subject is either the DP in Spec of TP or a clitic/strong Agr
          adjoined to T (see Alexiadou & Anagnostopoulou 1998).

The other question is why the nominative clitic is an enclitic in (45). Recall that the nominative clitic originates above V (see section 1) and therefore cannot adjoin to V. Rather, it left-adjoins to T (after V left-adjoins to T), giving rise to the following structure:

(52) $[_T$ nom cl $[_T$ [V] T]]

When V-to-Q applies in shallow structure for the purpose of ph-lexicalization, it moves only the category with ph-content, namely, V (i.e., T has no ph-content):

(53) $[[V_i [Q]] [_T$ nom cl $[_T [_V e_i] T]]]$

The nominative clitic will then attach at PF to the verbal category to its left. My claim that the nominative clitic may attach to a word to its left by a phonological, sandhi-type rule receives some support from the northern Italian dialects, in which the nominative clitic may optionally attach to a complementizer to its left (cf. Poletto 1998):[16]

(54) a. Ara che el vien (Veneto)
          Look that nom cl comes
      b. Ara ch'el vien

3.3. Similarities with Chinese with Respect to Minimality

It is timely to mention the case of the indefinite wh in Mandarin Chinese, discussed by Li (1992). Li shows that wh-words in Chinese can have a noninterrogative indefinite interpretation, as well as an interrogative one, depending on the semantic properties of its binder. The relation between a noninterrogative wh and its licensor is a binder-variable relation, such as the one that exists between an interrogative wh and a question operator. These binder-variable relations are subject to Minimality, as illustrated by the configurations below:

(55) a. +QP ... –QP ... wh1 ... wh2
          |_____|
          |_____|

      b. *+QP ... –QP ... wh1 ... wh2
          |_____|
               |_____|

      c. *+QP ... –QP ... wh1 ... wh2
                    |_____|
          |_____|

The configurations in (55b, c) illustrate minimality effects; –QP is closer to wh2 than is +QP. In (55a), –QP is inactive; therefore, it is not a potential antecedent and does not trigger minimality effects. Li (p. 144) indicates the generalization that emerges from these and other configurations in the following terms:

(56) The linking of a wh-element with an operator is subject to minimality.
      The linking of A with B [... A ... B ...] obeys Minimality iff there is no
      intervening C [... A ... C ... B] such that C is linked to another
      element D, D =/= B =/= A

My claim is that the structure in (34b), repeated below, is formally identical to (55c):

(57) [[$_{wh}$que]$_i$ [wh$_i$ [e$_i$ [Q$_i$ [Jean$_j$ [Cl$_j$ [T [$_{VP}$ e$_j$ [e$_i$]]]]]]]]]

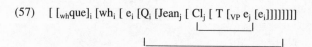

Li (1992) remarks that there are no minimality effects when the two operators involved are of the same type:

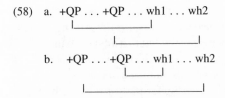

(58) a. +QP . . . +QP . . . wh1 . . . wh2

b. +QP . . . +QP . . . wh1 . . . wh2

This observation is particularly interesting because in the case of the Cl-operator we find the same generalization, as illustrated by the well-formedness of the structures in (14), which is repeated in (59). In these structures there are two Cl-operators with identical function, and no intervention effects are observed.

(59) a. $[DP_j [Cl_j [DP_i [Cl_i [T [_{VP} [e_j [V e_i]]]]]]]]$

b. $[DP_j [Cl_j [DP_i [Cl_i [T [_{VP} e_i [V e_j]]]]]]]]$

4. Conclusion

In this chapter I have reconsidered the constraint on preverbal subjects in Romance interrogatives. My explanation is crucially based on a particular analysis of clitics and strong Agr.

According to this view, clitics and strong Agr are the morphological manifestation of an abstract Cl position, which has the status of an operator. Projected above TP, Cl has the function of "externalizing" an argument of the verb with respect to the T associated with the verb. It achieves this via a combination of binding and merge. More precisely, Cl binds a DP argument of the verb, giving rise to a syntactic predicate; a pronominal or lexical DP merges with Cl and functions as the subject of the predicate. Thus Cl is formally comparable in status to a relative operator and is morphologically identified by a pronominal clitic or strong Agr contained in T. Languages with clitics and strong Agr, like many of the Romance languages, thus have a mechanism other than movement to "externalize" an argument, in particular the subject. The proposal, then, is that preverbal (nonfocused) subjects in Romance are in the Spec of a Cl-operator, and this Cl creates minimality effects when a question is formed by moving a wh-phrase above it. More precisely, a wh-phrase moves to the Spec of a wh-projection through the Spec of a Q-projection (located at the rightmost edge of the CP field). This creates a coindexing relation between the wh-phrase and Q, which then binds the trace of the wh-phrase as well, giving rise to a Q-operator/variable relation. But because the Cl operator is closer to the wh-variable than is the Q-operator, a minimality violation thus arises.[17]

The absence of the preverbal subject constraint in interrogatives with fronted nonbare wh-phrases is attributed (following Dobrovie-Sorin 1994) to the fact that the wh-feature in the specifier of such phrases may fail to percolate to the DP, in which case there is no coindexing of a wh-category with Q. In such structures, Q does not function as a syntactic operator and no minimality ensues.

Whereas Cl is generally mapped in the higher part of the middle field, between the Q-projection and TP, in certain cases Cl may project above the Q-projection, thus avoiding a minimality effect. This is the case of the so-called complex inversion construction in French and a similar construction in the northern Italian dialects.

It was suggested that the differences among the Romance languages with respect to the preverbal subject constraint in embedded interrogatives is to be attributed to parametric differences in the ph-lexicalization of the Q-feature that expresses the force of the sentence.

NOTES

I would like to thank Aafke Hulk for very useful comments and discussion.

1. As Poletto (1998) argues, the restriction on the position of the preverbal subject in interrogatives is independent from the V-to-C parameter. This is shown by examples in northern Italian dialects such as the following, where no V-to-C has occurred but the restriction on the preverbal subject is still present:

(i)   ho domandà kol ke (??Mario) l'ha fat
       to-him have asked what that (Mario) he has done

Suñer (1994) makes the same point for Spanish.

2. Note that in this view the topic nature of the clitic left-dislocated argument is entirely tangential to its grammatical properties. The discourse property of "topic-hood" is extrinsic to the grammatical properties of the construction.

3. It has been brought to my attention by Xavier Villalba (p.c.) that for some speakers the binding relation in (9a) and (10a) is facilitated by the presence of a modal. For such speakers, the availability of a bound reading decreases in the absence of a modal, as in the following example:

(i)   A su$_i$ hijo, cada madre lo acompaño el primer día de escuela
       acc. his child, each mother acc. cl. accompanied the first day of school

This observation, if correct, deserves further investigation.

4. The hypothesis that preverbal subjects in some of the Romance languages do not originate within the VP is not a novel one (e.g., Barbosa 1995). Here, I am generalizing the assumption to all languages with a CLLD construction.

5. A question that arises at this point is why the structures in (14) do not violate minimality. This question is particularly relevant in view of the fact that, as we see in section 2, when Cl interacts with Q, it does give rise to minimality effects. It would seem that two identical operators (i.e., two operators with exactly the same function) do not interfere with each other, but two distinct operators may do so. See section 3.3 for further discussion.

6. It is likely that factive predicates, which presuppose the truth of their propositional complement, contain an Ass(ertion) operator in its CP. This operator is lexicalized by the complementizer, which explains why it must be obligatorily present [cf. *John regrets (*that) Mary is bald*]. Complements of propositional attitude verbs lack an Ass operator; therefore, their complementizer may be absent in some languages [cf. *John thinks (that) Mary is bald*].

7. We see later that not only a morpheme but also a feature may fulfill the function of ph-lexicalization.

8. In the next section, I discuss the position of the subject in sentences like (25a).

9. Rizzi (1991) notes that in standard Italian, but not in Spanish, an embedded interrogative in the subjunctive does not trigger the "preverbal subject constraint." Poletto (1998) notices that this is a more general property of modal contexts:

(i)   Mi chiedo cosa Gianni avrebbe fatto in quel frangente.
       myself ask what Gianni have-cond done on that occasion
       'I wonder what Gianni would have done on that occasion.'

This could be accounted for by assuming that in standard Italian a verb that triggers an irrealis mood can merge with Q.

10. As is well known, V-to-C is blocked in matrix interrogatives when the matrix subject is extracted (cf. *who did leave?* vs. *who left?*). A possible explanation is that in such structures one and the same morpheme (Aux) enters into a Spec-head agreement relation with the subject twice: once as the head adjoined to T and another time as the head adjoined to Q (i.e., the wh-phrase moves through the Spec of Q on its way to the Spec of the wh-feature projection). We may speculate that this one-to-many relation between the verb and the subject is not tolerated by the grammar. Or more generally, one and the same lexical head may not enter into multiple Spec-head relations with one and the same argument. Thus, in languages like English, in which the subject moves to Spec of T, the verb cannot move to T. The correlation seems to be correct: Only the feature V moves to T in English, without pied-piping the verbal constituent. Languages differ in the default mechanism they turn to in such cases. Some of the northern Italian dialects resort to the mechanism that they use in embedded questions; that is, they merge Q with a complementizer, giving rise to such sentences as 'who that left' (see Poletto 1998). It is not clear what strategy French and English use as a default mechanism in the case of 'who left' (*qui est parti*). We might speculate that they resort to a suprasegmental feature that is spelled out as a rising contour. In other words, what I am suggesting here is that the grammar does not generally rely on intonational properties to lexicalize the Q-operator, but it may do so in certain default cases. See also section 3.1.

11. I have ignored here the so-called inversion construction (cf. *Qu'a acheté Jean?* 'What bought Jean?'). But one wonders whether the postverbal subject occupies the Spec of Cl in such a construction (as the analysis put forth by Kayne & Pollock, chapter 5 in this volume, would suggest), in which case this construction is relevant to our present concerns. Their proposal is that the entire TP is moved into the CP field in this case. If TP moves to a position above the Q-operator (perhaps to the Spec of Q), there will be no minimality effects in such structures:

(i)   [que$_i$ [WH$_i$ [[$_{TP}$ a [e$_j$ acheté e$_i$]] [Q Jean$_j$ [Cl$_j$ [TP]]]]]]]

12. I have not discussed long distance wh-movement such as (i) below:

(i)   Que (*Juan) dice (Juan) que (María) compró (María)
        What (Juan) says (Juan) that (María) bought (María)

The restriction on preverbal subjects applies in the matrix but not in the embedded clause. I assume, first, cyclic wh-movement in such cases and, second, the trace that is locally bound by Q functions as a variable, that is, the wh-trace in the embedded Comp (rather than the trace in the embedded VP):

(ii) $[Qué_i [Q_i \dots [_{CP} e_i [DP_j [Cl_j T [e_j V e_i]]]]]$

13. Dobrovie-Sorin (1994) argues that whether or not a wh-specifier percolates its feature to the DP is lexically determined in Romanian (e.g., 'which N' vs. 'what N'). Our prediction is that whereas a question with a fronted 'which N' in Romanian would not be subject to the preverbal subject constraint, 'what N' would be.

14. My proposal here is that the trace of a wh-phrase functions as a variable if the wh-phrase is associated with Q. The trace of the wh-phrase *que* functions unambiguously as a variable, which means that *que* is unambiguously associated with Q. If Q is projected as an independent projection in the CP field, this association is obtained via Spec-head agreement [as in structure (41) in the text]. The question that arises is how the association between the wh-phrase *que* and the Q adjoined to the matrix verb in the French example in (35) is obtained.

15. Although rare, there are northern Italian dialects in which a nominative enclitic coexists with a wh-subject (cf. Bellunese *chi é-lo che vien?* 'Who is it that came?'). Such clitics are generally invariable in that they do not vary in gender and number and also appear with verbs that lack an external argument (cf. *quando te pare-lo che 'l sia rivà?* 'When does it seem to you that he has arrived?'). This suggests that such clitics are not related to Cl at all but have the status of an interrogative marker. In some dialects, such as Torinese, an invariable enclitic may in fact coexist with an inflected nominative proclitic, which, I claim, is related to Cl (cf. *lon ch'a l'a-lo fa?* 'What has he done?'). These examples are from Munaro (1997.) In fact, it might be a total misnomer to refer to such enclitics as "nominative" although they appear only in tensed contexts. The fact that such enclitics surface only in matrix interrogatives might be due to historical reasons if they are indeed nothing else than a historical relic.

16. Sportiche (1998) claims that the nominative enclitic has a tighter morphophonological connection to the verb than does a nominative proclitic, and therefore he proposes that enclitics be lexically generated with the verb. I suggest that this is a more general morphological property of words: Morphemes to the right of a stem are closer to the stem than the morphemes to the left of the stem. This is true not only of clitics but also of affixes. Consider the possibility of coordinating prefixes but not suffixes, for example, 'pre-' and 'postposition'.

17. An exception is Brazilian Portuguese. In effect, the preverbal subject constraint is absent in Brazilian interrogatives. This is as expected: Brazilian Portuguese lacks Cl because it has no way of morphologically identifying it; it has a weak subject agreement system and has lost (or is in the process of loosing) the third-person accusative clitic. See Modesto (1999) and references therein.

REFERENCES

Alexiadou, A., & E. Anagnostopoulou. (1998). "Parametrizing AGR: Word Order, V-Movement, and EPP-Checking." *Natural Language and Linguistic Theory* 16, 491–539.

Ambar, M. ([1992] 1988). *Para uma sintaxe da inversão sujeito-verbo em Português.* Colibri, Lisbon.

Aoun, J., & E. Benmamoun. (1998). "Minimality, Reconstruction, and PF Movement." *Linguistic Inquiry* 20, 141–172.

Barbosa, P. (1995). "Null Subjects." Ph.D. diss., Department of Linguistics and Philosophy, MIT, Cambridge, Mass.

Benincà, P., & C. Poletto. (1997). "A Case of *Do* Support in Romance." Ms., University of Padua.

Cecchetto, C. (1995). "Reconstruction in Clitic-left Dislocation." Ms., Department of Cognitive Science, Intituto Scientifico, San Raffaele, Milan.

Chomsky, N. (1993). "A Minimalist Program for Linguistic Theory." In K. Hale & S. J. Keyser (eds.), *The View from Building 20.* MIT Press, Cambridge, Mass.

———. (1994). "Bare Phrase Structure." *MIT Occasional Papers in Linguistics* 5. Reprinted in Webelhuth, G. (ed.). (1995). *Government and Binding Theory and the Minimalist Program.* Blackwell, Oxford.

Dobrovie-Sorin, C. (1994). *The Syntax of Romanian.* Mouton de Gruyter, Berlin, Germany.

Fernández-Soriano, O. (1989). "Rección y ligamento en español: Aspectos del parámetro de sujeto nulo." Ph.D. diss., Universidad Autónoma de Madrid.

Franco, J. (1993). "On Object Agreement in Spanish." Ph.D. diss, Department of Spanish and Portuguese, University of Southern California, Los Angeles.

Guasti, M. T. (1996). "On the Controversial Status of Romance Interrogatives." *Probus* 8, 161–180.

Iatridou, S. (1990). "Clitics and Island Effects." Ms., MIT, Cambridge, Mass.

Kayne, R. (1991). "Romance Clitics, Verb Movement, and PRO." *Linguistic Inquiry* 22, 647–686.

———. (1994). *The Antisymmetry of Syntax.* MIT Press, Cambridge, Mass.

Koopman, H. (1997). "Unifying Predicate Cleft Constructions." Paper presented at BLS special session, Berkeley, Calif.

Li, A. (1992). "Indefinite Wh in Mandarin Chinese." *Journal of East Asian Linguistics* 1, 125–155.

Modesto, M. (1999). "Null Subjects without Rich Agreement." In M. Kato & E. Negrão (eds.), *Brazilian Portuguese and the Null Subject Parameter.* Vervuet-Iberoamerican, Frankfurt and Madrid.

Munaro, N. (1997). "Propieta strutturali e distribuzionali dei sintagmi interrogativi in alcuni dialetti italiani settentrionali." Ph.D. diss., Dipartimento di Linguistica, University of Padua.

Ouhalla, J. (1993). "Subject-extraction, Negation and the Anti-agreement Effect." *Natural Language And Linguistic Theory* 11, 477–518.

Poletto, C. (1998). *The Higher Functional Field in the Northern Italian Dialects. Oxford Studies in Comparative Syntax,* Oxford University Press, New York.

Pollock, J. Y., N. Munaro, & C. Poletto. (1998). "Eppur si muove! On comparing French, Portuguese, and Bellunese wh-movement." Ms., CNRS and University of Padua.

Rizzi, L. (1990). *Relativized Minimality.* MIT Press, Cambridge, Mass.

———. (1991). "Residual Verb Second and the *Wh*-Criterion." *Technical Reports in Formal and Computational Linguistics* 2. Faculté des Lettres, Université de Genève.

Rizzi, L., & R. Roberts. (1989). "Complex Inversion in French." *Probus* 1, 1–30.

Speas, M. (1994). *Phrase Structure in Natural Language.* Kluwer, Dordrecht.

Sportiche, D. (1998). *Partitions and Atoms of Clause Structure.* Routledge, London.

Suñer, M. (1988). "The Role of Agreement in Clitic-doubled Constructions." *Natural Language and Linguistic Theory* 6, 391–434.

———. (1992). "Subject Clitics in the Northern Italian Vernaculars and the Matching Hypothesis." *Natural Language and Linguistic Theory* 10, 596–640.

———. (1994). "V-movement and the Licensing of Argumental Wh-phrases in Spanish." *Natural Language and Linguistic Theory* 12, 335–372.

Zubizarreta, M. L. (1993). "The Grammatical Representation of Topic and Focus: Implications for the Structure of the Clause." *Cuadernos de Lingüística* 2. Instituto Universitario Ortega & Gasset, Madrid.

———. (1998). *Prosody, Focus, and Word Order*. MIT Press, Cambridge, Mass.

———. (1999). "The Cl Projection in Questions." Paper presented at the IX Colloquium on Generative Grammar, Barcelona.

Index

205